CHASING WATER

—— ELEGY OF AN OLYMPIAN ——

ANTHONY ERVIN
& CONSTANTINE MARKIDES

EDGE
of SPORTS

Chasing Water is the debut title in Dave Zirin's **Edge of Sports** imprint. Addressing issues across many different sports at both the professional and nonprofessional/collegiate level, Zirin brings to the table select stories of athletes' journeys, what they are facing, and how they evolve.

Published by Akashic Books
©2016 Anthony Ervin and Constantine Markides

ISBN: 978-1-61775-444-9
Library of Congress Control Number: 2015954115
Photograph of Anthony Ervin swimming on page 95 by Michael Lewis.
Photograph of the London Aquatics Centre on page 27 by EG Focus.
The wording at the top of page 63 is an excerpt from *Dragons of Winter Night* by Margaret Weis and Tracy Hickman.
The illustrations in Chapter 12, "Serpent Skin," are by Armando Garma-Fernandez.

Second printing

Edge of Sports
c/o Akashic Books
Twitter: @AkashicBooks
Facebook: AkashicBooks
E-mail: info@akashicbooks.com
Website: www.akashicbooks.com

ALSO FROM EDGE OF SPORTS

Fair Play: How LGBT Athletes Are Claiming Their Rightful Place in Sports
by Cyd Zeigler
(forthcoming)

Constantine Markides

ANTHONY ERVIN is an American Olympian who resides in Los Angeles, where he continues to pursue his career as a professional swimmer, speaker, and coach. As the oldest competitor at the 2014 national championships, he won the title in the men's 50-meter freestyle. He is currently training for the 2016 Olympic team.

Claire Barwise

CONSTANTINE MARKIDES is a New York–based swim trainer and former correspondent for the international daily newspaper *Cyprus Mail*. He has worked with CNN's Anderson Cooper and was featured on CBC and NPR's *Marketplace*. His essays and fiction have been published in various magazines and journals, including *Rolling Stone*. A high school state champion swimmer, Markides also swam for Columbia University.

ACKNOWLEDGMENTS

First and foremost I want to acknowledge and thank Constantine Markides, a.k.a., Conz or the Conman, without whom this book would have never happened. I can't imagine anybody else was up to the task of managing the sudden sea changes of my creative, writing, and remembering processes. There were many verbal and written battles—battles of persuasive diplomacy and open hostility. And yet, I cannot deny that we are a great team.

Next, I must thank Emily White, who works tirelessly for my benefit in all areas, but with a certainty drove forward the publishing and writing of this book. Without you, Emily, I do not doubt that this book would still be something Conz and I would be talking about one day doing. Instead, the book is done!

I want to acknowledge Lisa Gallagher, my lit agent, and Johnny Temple of Akashic Books, who took a chance on us.

I want to thank all of our friends—Conz and mine—who gave us places to stay, food, and drink while we did research and interviews.

A special thanks to Rebecca, whose work on our family genealogy led to some of the coolest parts of this book.

And, of course, I have to thank my family for everything ever. Love you.

—*Anthony Ervin*

In August 2012, *Rolling Stone* published "The Rebel Olympian," the embryo of this book; thanks to *RS* and editor Sean Woods for helping pave the way. Once on our way, it was far easier because of the generosity of so many, all of whom can't be listed here: Coleman Barks, Casey Barrett, Mike Bottom, Melpo Charalambides, Natalie Coughlin, Amir Dibaei, Dave Durden, Nick Folker, Rowdy Gaines, Gary Hall Jr., Mamade Kadreebux, Lono and co., Della Lorenzetti,

David Marsh, Teri McKeever, Lars Merseburg, Steve Neale, Milt Nelms, Derek Van Rheenen, Alex Schliefer, Margot Schupf, Gareth Williams, and Joe Jacobs, to whom a promise is hereby fulfilled.

We are indebted to our talented visual artists: the photographer Mike Lewis; Armando Garma-Fernandez for the tattoo illustrations; Frank Zio for the graphic art. A nor'easter shout-out to Alison Hill for offering her home and art studio as our offshore brainstorming retreat; to Mary and Matt Weber for the fortifying keg of Monhegan Brewing beer and bucket of sea bugs; to Star and Moon and Charley the one-legged seagull for their company.

A special thank you to our literary agent, Lisa Gallagher, for skillfully assisting through any vines and tangles, and for believing in me and standing by me for so many years; to Anthony's manager, Emily White, for her unflagging energy and creative outside-the-water thinking; to Dave Zirin, who honors us by launching the Edge of Sports imprint with this book; to the excellent team at Akashic Books— Johanna, Aaron, Susannah, Ibrahim, Katie—and to Akashic's publisher and our attentive editor, Johnny Temple, for his belief in and commitment to this unorthodox hybrid, Hydra heads and all.

I am especially grateful to Anthony's parents, Sherry and Jack, for their hospitality and generosity during the research, and to his brothers Jackie and Derek. My love to my parents, Emily and Kyriacos, and to my sister, Vasia, swimmers all of them: they support me more than they can ever know.

Adequate gratitude cannot be expressed here to Claire Barwise, who devoted incalculable hours at every stage and whose editorial acumen and exceptional feel for language left no sentence unturned. This is a far better book because of her. Last but foremost, my enduring appreciation to Anthony for having the belief and mettle to bring me onboard and put his life at my fingertips. I don't know anyone else who would have dared so mercurial a passage with me.

—*Constantine Markides*

TABLE OF CONTENTS

But Hermes did not find great-hearted Odysseus indoors,
but he was sitting out on the beach, crying, as before now
he had done, breaking his heart in tears, lamentation, and sorrow,
as weeping tears he looked out over the barren water.

—Homer, *The Odyssey*

It's just me and the bartender. Maybe a handful of us are left in the entire hostel. The bartender leans against the bar, looking up at the TV. He glances at my pint glass.

"Another Victoria Bitter?"

I nod. He watches the TV as he pours. The closing ceremony has started. The athletes enter the stadium, the gold medalists leading the procession. Gary is somewhere out there. I think about my medal, buried in dirty laundry in my bag under the bunk bed.

The athletes converge into the center of the track and the stadium darkens. The crowd roars as the show begins. Bands perform, floats roll in and out, strobes swing around. The stadium is now a throbbing sea of revelers leaping and yelling and punching at giant balloons. Midnight Oil comes on. *How do we sleep while our beds are burning?*

"It's going off," the bartender says. "You just know they're all on the piss. Hell of a party to be at."

I think about the man who threw me out of the Olympic Village.

"No doubt," I say. "Hell of a party."

I finish my beer and step outside. A crescent moon hangs over the breaking water, a sliver of violence. The ocean is loud, belligerent. It seethes.

I head back inside. It reeks of stale beer and smoke. On the television Paul Hogan is buffed out as Crocodile Dundee, perched on a float of a giant black safari hat and giving a thumbs-up to the cheering Olympic stadium.

My mouth tastes of ashes. I push my glass toward the bartender. "One more bitter."

PART I

THE DIVE

1   *The Ready Room*

I swear, gentlemen, that to be too conscious is an illness—a real thorough-going illness.
      —Fyodor Dostoyevsky, *Notes from Underground*

Are you ready for a good time? Are you ready ready ready?
      —AC/DC, "Are You Ready"

London Olympics, 50 Free Final, August 2, 2012
The reigning Olympic champion is beating his chest. His hand is cupped, which makes the sound even louder. A few others start doing it too, some sitting, some standing. The chest-slapping echoes through the makeshift room. Does inducing blood flow to these muscle groups really make any difference? Or is this a war cry, a preparatory battle sound? Maybe it's a confidence boost.

    Drop these thoughts. They're distractions. There's no room for error in the 50 and distractions lead to error. *It is a truth universally acknowledged that an athlete in pursuit of victory must be in want of an empty mind*—why is Jane Austen in my head? My thoughts are swinging like monkeys from vine to vine. I try to turn my focus back to my upcoming swim: the start, the breakout, the swim, the finish. It's a constant tug-of-war, rehearsing my game plan without letting other thoughts interrupt it. If the thoughts come along I try to just recognize them and let them go. Same idea behind meditation.

But I can't maintain my focus, can't help but circle back to the chest thumping. César's pecs are mottled red from the blows. Maybe all the hitting is a cry for attention. I look down at all the tats covering my arms. Who's to say these aren't a cry for attention too? Maybe I've also inflicted pain on myself to stand out and be noticed. I've always talked about them as my way of reclaiming my body after I left the sport, but maybe that's just me trying to make something noble out of my peacocking.

Races are won and lost in this room before they even begin. It can get intense: some pray, some smack themselves, some try to intimidate their opponents by staring them down. Right now a few guys are bouncing on the balls of their feet, pummeling and kneading their muscles, shaking their dangling arms. A couple are praying and murmuring to themselves. I'm sitting perfectly still—ironic, because my mind is all over the place. How'd I get here again? It's been twelve years and I'm back in the ready room of the 50 free Olympic final. In a few minutes, I'll once again vie with seven other swimmers for the title of fastest swimmer in the world.

In this room, the ready room, time is compressed, magnifying my isolation. There are almost no familiar faces this time—no Bart Kizierowski, no Gary Hall Jr. But there is Roland Schoeman, who's older even than I and still in the game. I first swam against him freshman year of college and we've been friends since. A knowing look passes between us. A fiber also connects me to the people I care about who are in the stands right now, who've flown across an ocean to watch me. I try to shake off the pressure of their expectations and redirect my attention to my start.

But that only makes things worse. My start in yesterday's semifinal is still a radiating, pulsing memory. It's so raw even my muscles and nerves remember it. When the starting signal went off, I pulled on the block too hard, causing a subluxation of my shoulder. I left the block in a bolt of panic and hyper-awareness.

I've only felt adrenaline like that once before, when I almost died while running from the police. In the adrenaline rush time slows down. It gave me the space to yank my arm while in the air, causing my shoulder to suck back into place as I entered the water. But I recovered and the rest of the race fell into place perfectly. I caught up, placing third and making the finals heat. Fortuna may have shone down on me then, but I can't afford another start like that.

There's a roar from the crowd. We're up. This is no time for self-doubt. We stand in file and prepare to make our entrance. It's far less theatrical here in London than it was at Olympic Trials in Omaha, where the entire stadium was darkened except for spotlights on the lanes. But far from diminishing the occasion's significance, the austere brightness only makes it stand out more starkly.

Do I belong here, at the world's premiere swim contest? I do. I'm not one for false modesty. But do I *deserve* to be here? Probably not. Others have worked harder, sacrificed more. I'm only here because I excel at a stunt, because I'm able to move my body through water for 50 meters faster than others. It's just a little trick, a well-performed acrobatic. For this I get to be paraded around the world and ogled over. I'm not saving a life or writing a magnum opus or masterminding some epic heist. I'm just sprinting down a pool, like a prize racehorse galloping around a track. And yet a lot of value is imposed on this. For some reason, the world finds this meaningful.

Who am I kidding, playing the blasé intellectual? For months now I've been correcting reporters for labeling my return to swimming a "comeback," telling them I'm just here to enjoy the journey, to regain a love of the sport. Which is true. And bullshit. As much as I hate to admit it, I want to win. I know it in my overcharged nerves. I was just trying to trick myself into thinking I didn't want it. It was my way of keeping the pressure off. But here, at the worst possible time, I recognize it, feel overwhelmed by it. I'm trapped by my own ploy.

It's time. The announcer calls us out one by one. Even through my headphones I can hear the crowd. The memory of my shoulder is hovering over me as I step out onto the stage.

I'm not ready.

⁂

On January 14, 2012, a mere seven months before the London Olympics, an unexpected figure stepped up to the blocks at the Austin Grand Prix as the fastest qualifier in the 50-meter freestyle. At 6'3" and 170 pounds, he was the smallest among towering competitors—a cadre of the fastest sprinters in the US—and, with tattoo sleeves, also the most heavily inked. The Universal Sports commentator Paul Sunderland identified him to the viewers at home: "Anthony Ervin. And what an interesting story this is. Tied for the Olympic gold medal at the [2000] Sydney Olympic Games with Gary Hall Jr. and then has had, to put it mil—" he stopped himself, "some difficulties, let's just put it that way, and has come back to swimming."

"You know why I love this story, and this is a tremendous story," interjected the other commentator, three-time Olympic gold medalist Rowdy Gaines. "This guy now can retire from swimming in a good way. He's going to be happy about it. And he wasn't happy when it happened the first time."

It was odd to hear talk about Ervin retiring again. There wasn't really anything to retire from yet. Except for some halfhearted, abortive attempts to work out, he had only returned to serious training the previous year after eight wayward years. During that time he had purged swimming from his life, including his Olympic gold medal, which he auctioned off on eBay in 2005, donating the $17,100 proceeds to the UNICEF tsunami relief fund. His return to the pool was motivated more out of a need for psychic rehab than any desire for a comeback. But by the end of that sunny January day in Austin, the thirty-year-old found himself in the unlikely position of being the second fastest American sprinter.

When I first met Anthony Ervin, he was sitting in the bleachers of a Brooklyn pool, reading *The Professor and the Madman*. He had a gaunt-English-major-turned-tattooed-indie-hipster vibe going. The kind of guy you might find behind the counter in a record store or tattoo parlor on Berkeley's Telegraph Avenue. Not the type you expect to encounter in a swim school, except maybe in New York City.

In short, I thought I had him all figured out. It was early 2009 and I'd just moved to New York from London. A former college swimming teammate had hooked me up as a part-time swim instructor with Imagine Swimming, a thriving swim school that boasted a hip roster of instructors with elite swim pedigrees or—in keeping with the program's ethos—artistic/creative backgrounds. It was my first day on the job, so when I arrived and saw him reading on the pool bleacher, sporting a bushy goatee, I figured he fell under Imagine's creative camp.

I went over to him. "Good book. Have you got to the penis part yet?"

He looked at me askance, as if appraising whether or not he should respond. "There's a penis part?" he said finally.

"You'll know when you get to it. Hard to forget."

He shrugged. I couldn't tell if he was amused or being dismissive. "I'm Constantine, by the way."

He paused. "Tony," he finally said, and returned to the reading.

As I was getting my cap and goggles, the shift supervisor approached me. "So, I see you met Tony," he said. "You'll be coaching with him after lessons." This was unexpected. Not all Imagine instructors have competitive experience, but the coaches do, and often at the sport's highest echelons. With *him*? I scoffed to myself. Perhaps he had the ideal creative spirit for working with three-year-olds, but was he qualified to coach? He probably swam freestyle with the earnest low-elbowed chicken-wing stroke one finds at YMCA lap swims.

"Really?" I said, trying to keep the smugness out of my voice. "Did that dude ever swim?"

There was a pause. "Yeah, you could say that. He was the fastest swimmer on the planet for two years."

Over the next few months, we got to know each other. He had the engaged, nervy presence of someone who's had too many cups of coffee, as well as a caustic wit, sharp tongue, and lack of any self-censoring mechanism, which made him come across as more New Yorker than California native. We rarely talked about swimming, but sharing an aquatic history no doubt buttressed our friendship. Though I had dropped out of competitive swimming much earlier than he (sophomore year in college), and though I had been a big fish only in the smallest of puddles (high school state champ in Maine, a state where, with rare exceptions, the only swimmers famed beyond its borders are crustaceans), we had both left the pool to front life on our own terms, taking divergent paths that led into literary territories. As a writer who, for better or worse, had always felt uncomfortable within writer communities and rebelled against its circles and programs, I could relate, at least inversely, to Ervin's rejection of hypermasculine sports culture. I had spent more time among lobstermen and carpenters than around writers, so it was only natural for Anthony's unconventional merging of physicality with analytic bookishness to resonate with me. He was intrigued by my compulsion to write and I was intrigued by his rebuff of the golden platter. And what a golden platter it was.

The 50-meter freestyle sprint—one length down an Olympic-sized pool—is swimming's glory event, the aquatic equivalent of the 100-meter dash. The world champion can boast, as could the Jamaican runner Usain Bolt after the Beijing Olympics, of being the fastest human on earth. The compound word *freestyle* is meant literally: any technique is permitted, even doggy paddle, corkscrew, or double-armed backstroke. Freestyle is synonymous with front crawl, the default stroke in any freestyle race, only because it's the fastest way to swim across the water's surface.

Though Michael Phelps is heralded as the most dominant swimmer in the history of the sport, he isn't the fastest sprinter in history, or even of his era. If he were, he wouldn't dominate as many events as he does. The 50-meter sprinter is a different species of creature, more cheetah than antelope, built and bred for stupendous but short-lived speed. Genetic marvels of nerves and fast-twitch muscle fibers, few can maintain their top speeds for much more than the twenty-something seconds that the event lasts. The current men's world record, held by Brazilian César Cielo, is 20.91 seconds. He swam this Herculean time in 2009 during the two-year stretch when "tech suits" were foolishly allowed in competition, thus leading to the subsequent shattering of practically every world record.[1] While purebred sprinters also often reign at the 100-meter sprint—the distance where one first starts to cross into the vast estate of Phelps's watery kingdom—their high-RPM engines seize up when revved over longer distances.

Ervin belongs unambiguously to the cheetah camp of swimmers. USA Swimming and FINA announcer Michael Poropat once called him "possibly the most naturally gifted sprinter in swimming history." But when Ervin was nineteen and stepped up to the blocks in the Sydney Olympics, the buzz wasn't about his speed. It was about his race. With a Jewish mother and black father, he found himself branded as "the first African American swimmer to make the Olympic team." It was a confusing label as he'd never viewed himself through the lens of race.

---

1 By reducing drag and increasing buoyancy, tech suits turned humans into hydrofoils, especially in sprints. They were swiftly banned. But by then the damage was done, both to the record books as well as to all the swimmers not around for that two-year tech suit bonanza.

Ervin's gifts, like his heritage, are unconventional: less physical than abstract, less about power than finesse, as much about cognizance as natural ability. After so many years of shunning competition, his return to swimming had reignited his competitive streak. But he was wary of this renewed impulse to win. To even express hesitation over one's competitive drive is a rarity among athletes. Even the most easygoing tend to be fiercely competitive. Some would even say that competition is to athletes what creativity is to artists: without it they're stagnant. Competition, after all, invigorates. Though often viewed with disdain or skepticism by the intelligentsia, athletic fervor is more than a predictable by-product of cutthroat capitalism or team spirit jingoism. The absurd particularity of any sport—whether it involves running around and slapping a hollow yellow rubber ball back and forth over a net, or running around and kicking a bigger ball into a bigger net, or even just running around—is simply the incidental stage upon which the passion and physical artistry play out, a clash of wills that rejuvenates both participants and spectators.

But at the same time, competition also favors antagonism over cooperation and necessarily entails winners and losers. Reconciling his zeal to win with his ambivalence over the nature of competition itself is one of the many ways Ervin resists the stereotype of the one-track-minded athlete. He brings to his swimming the analysis and hyper-self-consciousness of the modern intellectual, a self-awareness that facilitates his speed in water, even if it may undermine him on the starting block. Again and again, Ervin deconstructs the socially defined binaries: thinker vs. jock, black vs. white, rebel vs. role model. If there were such a thing as a postmodern swimmer, he'd be its poster boy.

The established story is that Ervin left swimming because he met his swimming goals and wanted to pursue other interests like music; that he auctioned off his gold medal out of humanitarian impulses. All true enough. But truth is like a matryoshka doll, with dolls nested within dolls: take apart the outer shell and you're left with a severed façade and a deeper truth. His athletic efforts may have transpired under spotlights, but deeper struggles unfolded in isolation. Medals, titles, and records may bestow fame, but a short-lived one; athletes are doomed earlier than most to the fate of time-ravaged Ozymandias. As A.E. Housman wrote in "To An Athlete Dying Young":

And early though the laurel grows
It withers quicker than the rose.

Or as Charles Bukowski more bluntly put it:

being an athlete grown old
is one of the cruelest of fates . . .
now the telephone doesn't ring,
the young girls are gone,
the party is over.

By discarding the laurel, Anthony Ervin preempted destiny, cheating it of its cruel withering hand. As with Andre Agassi, another gifted athlete who resented his sport for most of his career, Ervin stands outside the archetype of the driven, striving champion. His story is interesting not for what he achieved and lost, but for what he rejected and rediscovered.

❖

Waiting behind my block before the race, I'm an automaton, body and mind on cruise control. The entire process is ritualized and rote—walking out in line, sitting down, removing the uniform and headphones, standing up, taking deep breaths—every aspect programmed to keep all distractive thought at bay. The official's whistle calls us up to the blocks. The crowd is loud. I bend down, arms hanging, poised to clutch the block. There are a few final cries and exhortations before it finally goes silent.

"Take your mark" rings out. I hunch down, gripping the block. But I'm unable to obey the simple command of those three words, unable to take my mark, or at least stay on it. Instead I'm off balance, swaying. For whatever reason, I can't keep my energy coiled and find myself falling forward. It's a slight movement, but it's enough. The starter holds the signal for longer than usual. I pull my body weight backward, trying to offset my forward momentum. Just as I lean back, the starting signal goes off. Maybe the official was waiting for me to stop moving. Or maybe someone else took awhile to come down. Who knows.

We all dive off the block, but not at the same time. The seven of them dive and I follow. I'm last off the block, last by a lot, still airborne when the others are already underwater. I was hoping that by some miracle I'd have a great start, one that might put me in favorable position for gold. That miracle doesn't come. But this time I can't blame it on my Achilles shoulder. There's no dislocation, no shockwave of adrenaline in midflight, no need to pop my shoulder back into socket. There's only the awareness that I had a terrible start.

When I surface, over half a body length behind the others, I do the one thing I know how to do. Or rather the one thing that comes naturally to me. It's less something I do than a feeling I search for, one of continuous acceleration, a feeling not of fast but faster. It's the essence of how I train and race. It's something like what opium addicts refer to as chasing the dragon, the desperate quest for that elusive and irreproducible first high. Except in my case, it's not a high I'm chasing but a fluid connection. And the vessel isn't opium but water.

I put my head down and swim.

2

All in the Game

Go then if you must, but remember, no matter how foolish your deeds, those who love you will love you still.

—Sophocles, *Antigone*

All in the game, yo. All in the game.

—Omar from HBO's *The Wire*

The 50-meter freestyle Olympic final was minutes away. It was the first event of the evening session so Ervin and the other seven finalists were either in the ready room or about to head there. From my height in the stands of the London Aquatics Centre, the blue glassy rectangle below all the thousands of spectators looked more like a dinky hotel pool. And I wasn't even among the unfortunate

ones exiled to the uppermost gulag regions of the two temporary seating wings. These inelegant structures, which had been attached exclusively for one-off expanded Olympic seating and which jutted up vulgarly out of the low undulating body, gave the appearance from the outside that a giant pancake had been dropped upon an open book.[2] They had transformed the much hullabalooed

2 Or to quote the architect's (Zaha Hadid) Wikipedia entry: "Her buildings are distinctly neofuturistic, characterized by the 'powerful, curving forms of her elongated structures' with 'multiple perspective points and fragmented geometry to evoke the chaos of modern life.'"

3,000-capacity Olympic Stingray into a 17,500-person albatross.

But forget the exterior. It was from the inside, at least from within the temporary wings, that its form-over-function character was apparent. Below, one could see the fans and, beyond that, the pool; but in front, instead of a panorama of the far side of the stadium, all one could see were white steel girders and the low gray belly of the ceiling—an impressive ceiling, no doubt, one that "swells and ripples with sinuous energy . . . buckles and writhes," to use the words of one inspired reviewer, but nonetheless one whose sinuous swelling blocked my view.

In past centuries, people attended athletic events because it was the only way to watch sports. Today, anyone with a TV, or even just a few bills to buy a beer at the local bar, can not only watch the world's premiere sporting events but also observe them in greater detail and precision than even those with the best tickets. (Think of the mesmerizing and almost voyeuristic pleasure we get in watching vids of Rafael Nadal's facial contortions as he savages a forehand or the slow-mo replay technology used after the Beijing Olympics 100 fly[3] to prove Phelps actually *did* impossibly out-touch Cavic by 1/100th of a second, without which we'd still be hearing allegations of an American conspiracy behind his octuplet gold medal haul.) Competitions were once exclusive to live spectators: now they include, and in reality entirely cater to, the televised and streamed audience. But though the armchair TV and laptop viewers of the world may have a better close-up on the action, they're still only watching on a small two-dimensional screen—and "small" includes all rectangularly framed screens, from 4" mobile phones to 64" high-def LEDs. They still aren't *there*, and it's exactly the *being there* aspect—the immersive sublimation of self into a thousands-strong throng of fellow roaring nationalist barbarians, or in brief the "atmosphere"—that accounts

---

3 By 100 fly, I mean 100-meter butterfly. From this point forward I'll use this form, which leaves out the -meter or -yard suffix and abbreviates the name of the stroke (freestyle=free, butterfly=fly, backstroke=back, breaststroke=breast). In some cases I'll specify whether a race is in yards or meters, but then again, if you're not a swimmer you probably don't care, and if you are, you probably don't need anyone to tell you.

for why we still pay for flights and hotels and $175-per-session tickets for a couple of hours of straining our eyes and hearts while a bunch of kids splash around in a glorified fishbowl.

Though I only had an albatross's-eye view of the action below, I was in stellar company. In the seat to my left was Katie Ledecky's brother, who later that evening would sprint down the stairs yelling hoarsely as his fifteen-year-old sister swam the final lap of the 800 free to Olympic gold.[4] And directly to my right was Missy Franklin's uncle, who had tears running down his face after his niece won gold and broke the world record in the 100 back. Stadiums during Olympic finals sessions are essentially giant conductors for frazzled nerves and raw emotion: a month's worth of heartbreak and exultation is often packed into a minute of competition.

I was grateful just to have a finals ticket, but something did seem fundamentally amiss that the two fans to my left and right, both family members of Olympic finalists (make that gold medalists), were seated so far from the action. One would think they'd have been closer to the pool—down in the illustrious Stingray seating that was nontemporary and unobstructed by sensual low-hanging ceilings—but most of those seats, especially the best and often empty ones, were corporate reserved. The sponsors owned and ran the show and would ensure that the £269 million cost of the London Aquatics Centre (originally projected at £73 million) would fall not on them but on the public, which is its own special corporate way of spreading the love. But what the hell, it makes good TV programming and the advertisers are happy, and granted, there may be a protest here and there, but that sort of collateral fallout can be carefully managed. The main thing is that politics stays out of sports,

---

4 I take some credit for his flight down the stairs. When it became apparent his sister was going to win, he began throwing his arms and jumping around. This offended the disgruntled British fans seated behind him, who'd put all their hopes for a UK swimming gold in their fellow Brit and defending Olympic champion Rebecca Adlington. They began booing and barking that he sit. Flustered and overwhelmed, he tried to tell them that Katie was his sister. "Just run down to the balcony," I urged him. "Security won't stop you. You're her *brother*." When Ledecky touched the wall, I cheered, perhaps overzealously, mostly to rub in the victory on his behalf, but by then the belligerence of the British fans had gone out of them.

or rather a certain kind of politics: outpourings of national support during anthems are acceptable and encouraged. Just don't lower your head and raise a black-gloved fist during the medal ceremony as did US sprinters Tommie Smith and John Carlos at the 1968 Mexico City Olympics as a show of black solidarity, after which International Olympic Committee president Avery Brundage—the same fellow who as an Olympics official at the 1936 Berlin Games deemed the Nazi salute acceptable because it was a "national salute" rather than an individual one—forced their expulsion from the Games. The closest we got to color-coordinated medal ceremony apparel this time around, and just as telling of our times, was Ryan Lochte and Michael Phelps's matching fluorescent lime-green shoes on the podium, a symbol of Nike power. But that didn't ruffle any plumage: the essential thing is that the Games remain pure and unadulterated by ideology or profiteering, at least of the non-national, non-official-sponsors variety.

The audience roared as the announcer called out the 50 free finalists. The moments before the men's 50 free Olympic final is about as loud as a swim meet gets, aside of course from a race's final stretch and the relays, which are seen primarily as contests of national dignity. The crowd's energy contrasted with the very clean, bright, and stark deck area. The scene was nothing like the US Olympic Trials, which involved pyrotechnics and sound and light displays that would rival any rave and fans pumping giant cardboard Ryan Lochte faces. The London Olympics were a more minimalist and dignified affair (think Wimbledon vs. US Open), with swimming and partying confined to their proper places, the pool and pub respectively.

The swimmers took their positions behind the blocks. Even after the official's whistle, even after they'd stepped up, curling their toes into position and hunching over the edge of the block, waiting for the "Take Your Mark" command, people were still yelling and hooting. Ervin's coach at the time, Dave Durden, later told me the announcer should have called down the athletes from the blocks and calmed the audience because of all the noise—or, as he put it, the "tons of energy just kind of swirling around." Not that he was trying to excuse Ervin's start, which Durden conceded was terrible; he just felt the eight finalists weren't given the starting conditions they expected and deserved.

Aside from the usual stresses that come with rooting for a 50 free sprinter, with Ervin you have to contend with the additional anxiety that something gut-sinking might happen on his start. It's not that you're even hoping for a *great* start; you just want him to be in contention when he hits the water. You're basically praying for no imminent disaster. Watching him crouch down for the start feels, on a less consequential scale, something like what the Russian roulette player must go through before pulling the trigger: *Please, God, just no bullet.* The 50 free is always something of a gamble, but with Ervin you feel like the gods also have to be on his side, at least for the first second.

Even from my height I could tell Ervin was unstable on the block. The announcer held the swimmers for a hair loss–inducing length of time after the "Take Your Mark" signal (about 1.8 seconds, actually). Ervin looked to be leaning forward precariously, then shifted his weight back as the buzzer went off. What happened next was pretty much how the broadcaster put it during the slow-motion replay on the Olympic Channel's YouTube video of the race: "Ervin completely missed the start. Look at him come up with the black cap, four across. He was a *mile* behind." He gained on them, but this time he was too far behind to catch the leaders. A longer pool, another ten or fifteen meters, and he would have been in it. But this was the 50 free, not the 65. He touched fifth.

The next day I was at the P&G US Family Home, a vast, many-leveled Procter & Gamble utopia where US athletes and their families could hang out to watch the Games, gorge on free buffet and beer, have American flags painted on their fingernails, launder clothes at the 24-hour Tide booth, change infants into Team USA diapers in the Pampers room, freshen up at a private sink in the Crest & Oral-B zone, get a makeover in the CoverGirl area, and score a shave from a hot, overly made-up hairdresser in a Gillette lounge unironically called the "man-cave." Even their press release was a nugget of heartfelt commercialese: "P&G Family Home is 'Home away from Home,' Featuring Services from Leading Brands including Pampers®, Tide®, Pantene®, Crest®, Duracell®, and Gillette®." The metal detectors and X-ray machines you first had to get through and the security guards stationed around the perimeter only added to the weirdly dystopian corporate Shangri-La feel of the place.

Inside the lavish embrace of the P&G womb, Ervin and I were huddled around a screen in one of the lounges along with other Team USA swimmers, watching the track-and-field 100-meter-dash final. As Usain Bolt pulled away from the pack, I turned to Ervin: "You and Usain look alike when you race. Except that he starts on par with the others and pulls away. You start from behind and catch up." I meant it as a compliment. He just winced and nodded.

◆

I climb out of the pool and walk, dripping, across the tiled floor. NBC and the other television media ignore me as I pass them. Just yesterday they were holding up microphones to me, starry-eyed to talk. But now they avert their eyes. They're waiting for Florent Manaudou, the gold medalist, the one who matters now. Or one of the other two, who won the "lesser" medals. Those of us who didn't medal move unseen, as if in a cloak of invisibility. Like some shame to be avoided.

The coffee I drank before my race, in combination with the lactic acid, has dried out my mouth and left me parched. My suit constricts me even more now that my body is swollen from all the blood pumping through it. I walk down the hallway under the stands where I pick up my clothes and belongings from a basket.

I pass a logistics manager, who awkwardly murmurs, "Good job," and looks away.

I soon get to the team prep area, where athletes mill about, getting ready for their races. I sense pity from all sides. Most of them gingerly keep their distance from me, either unsure of how to interact with me in my disappointment or lacking confidence that they're close enough to me to approach me. A few offer a tentative congratulations but nothing sounds authentic. I deck change in a towel and sit by myself on a plastic chair. I don't feel pitiful, but I'm conscious of the pity that others are projecting upon me.

I'm not alone for long. Natalie Coughlin comes over and sits next to me. Aside from greeting me, she says nothing. But she understands, she's been in this position before. I don't need words. What matters is that she's here, fully here, not acting or tiptoeing around me as if I need to be avoided. It's all I need.

Tomorrow the press won't even mention my name. And to think that yesterday the *Guardian* referred to me online as "possibly the most interesting athlete in the entire Games."

I don't know how interesting I am. But it sure has been a strange ride.

PART II

GOLD

The Iron Fence

Man does not control his own fate. The women in his life do that for him.

—Groucho Marx

And if you wanna find hell with me
I can show you what it's like.

—Danzig, "Mother"

Anthony Lee Ervin's first sprint was out of the womb. The orderlies at California's Northridge Hospital didn't even have time to wheel his mother, Sherry, into the delivery room. They were running her down the corridor, urging her to hold on and paging the midwife, when he slid out onto the gurney. The only thing the doctor delivered was the afterbirth. Within fifteen minutes Sherry was up on her feet again. "The easiest part about me and Anthony was his birth," she says. "After that it all went downhill."

For the first six or so weeks of his life, Anthony had gastroesophageal reflux, a condition where the valve connecting the esophagus to the stomach opens at the wrong times, causing regurgitation. Sherry had to hold him at an angle and feed him slowly so the milk would stay down. Breastfeeding sessions could take two hours. Even after the nursing, Anthony was a slow, fussy eater. Sherry sometimes prechewed the food because he found it more palatable. He rarely ate meat, although his mother once walked in on him sitting on the kitchen floor, surrounded by grizzle and smeared in what looked like Crisco: he had eaten half a package of raw bacon.

Graduating from diaper to toilet was initially a source of anxiety for Anthony. The prospect of discharging directly into the toilet bowl terrified him, possibly out of a fear that he was losing part of himself. He'd stand in the corner of the bathroom, arms tightly crossed, refusing to participate in this monstrous violation of his anatomical integrity. Sherry found creative ways around such biological and existential obstacles. To first get him to pee standing up, she poured glitter into the toilet water and told him to shoot for the stars.

He was restless from infancy. Sherry doesn't even remember him crawling. Athletic and wiry, he went "straight from the crib to running." Even the crib phase was brief: he soon began clambering out of it. She once found him standing on the rails, his back against the wall and arms outspread. That night his mother transferred him from the crib to a bed, but he wouldn't stay put. He was back on his feet every time she left the room: "I must have put him to bed forty times that first night." This pattern would play out metaphorically for many more years: her trying to put him to bed, him trying to get out. Even when asleep, he wouldn't stay in bed. An intrepid somnambulist, Anthony once sleepwalked right out of the house. His elder brother Jackie recalls waking to his mother's cries that Anthony was gone. The front door was wide open. His parents found him around the corner, standing on the sidewalk, still fast asleep. After that Anthony's father, Jack, installed a chain on the door.

For the first four years of Anthony's life, the Ervins lived in a house with a pool in Canoga Park, an ethnically diverse, predominantly Latino neighborhood in the San Fernando Valley, north of Los Angeles. His mother occasionally took him into the pool with Jackie, who was six years older. But it wasn't until Anthony was two, shortly after his brother Derek was born, that he had his first unmediated encounter with the water. It was an especially hot afternoon.

Exhausted from nursing, his mother unintentionally dozed off on the living room couch with Derek, who was also asleep in her arms. Outside, beyond the glass patio doors, the pool sparkled, the sun flashing and vanishing on the surface like flaring matches. Moments after she fell asleep, Anthony awoke from a nap in his bedroom.

Wakie wake. Stretch ssttrreettcchh
Uppie.
Up.
Up.

Carpet sssssssoft. Door. Turn. Push.

Walk walk walk.
Momma and Deerek on couch.
Sleepytime for Momma and Deerek.
Walk   walk   walk.
Glass. Closed. CLOSED.
Push glass. Push. Puuuuuuush.
Ope-ope-opening door. Oooooopen.
O   P   E   N
Hot. Feet hothothot.
Walkwalkwalkwalkwalk.
Pool Sun Sparkly

po
ol
st
ai
rs

Step.
　　Stop.

feet wet

Step.
　　Stop.

knees wet
Sit.

Pool Cool. Pooool. Cooool.
Foot splishie foot splashie.
Tick-tock, Tick-tock, I'm a little cuckoo clock.
Like Jackie swimming. Swimming like Jackie.

S　　h　　S　　h
　p　s　　p　s
　　l i　　l a

　　　　r
　　a　　i
　　i　　n
　　n　　g

i'm swimming.
i'm Swimming.

Sherry awakened to find the glass patio door open. Little Anthony was sitting on the pool stairs, splashing his legs. She rushed outside, her stomach in knots. As she reached down to scoop him up, Anthony looked up and said, "Look at me, Momma. I'm swimming."

Within a week, contractors were erecting a black wrought-iron fence around the pool. The imposing barrier, with its skyward spears tipped by black spades, transformed the pool into an object of fascination and fear for little Anthony. "Not necessarily *my* fear but others' fear," he recalls. "The pool came to represent freedom. A freedom that could lead to annihilation." In retrospect the fence was as ironic as it was iron: by high school Anthony would feel fenced into a pool, not out of one.

Though Anthony actually *wanted* to join the swim team from the age of four or five, his parents insisted he wait because they felt he was too young. His older brother Jackie was on the team and Anthony would watch him compete at meets; it was only natural he'd want to follow in his wake. Jackie in turn assumed the role of protective big brother. Years later, when Anthony was on the swim team, an older kid once grabbed him by the ankles and tried to dunk him headfirst into the toilet bowl. Anthony fended off the submersion while dangling upside down by grabbing onto the bowl. When Jackie found out, he tracked down the kid and warned him that next time he'd answer to him; nothing like that ever happened again.

If Jackie was Anthony's idol, his younger brother Derek was his doppelgänger. In photos you can barely distinguish between them, grinning side by side under similar shocks of chestnut locks. They were inseparable. When the Ervins later moved to Castaic in 1985, Sherry put a bunk bed in Anthony's room because he and Derek wanted to sleep in the same room, often even in the same top bunk. Twice Derek fell out, once fracturing his arm.

While they still lived in Canoga Park, Anthony also spent time with a boy down the street with whom he'd sing and dance to Michael Jackson in his bedroom. It wasn't his first time listening to the king of pop. Back when he was an infant, his brother Jackie, who was seven at the time, used to run through the neighborhood while pushing Anthony in a stroller and blasting the *Thriller* album at top volume from a portable Fisher-Price cassette deck. The combination of speed and music delighted Anthony: "I'd be blasting 'Beat It' and 'Thriller' and 'Billie Jean,'" Jackie recalls, "and he'd be giggling in the front."

One of Anthony's most vivid memories is from when he was six or seven. One day he climbed up onto the kitchen counter to explore the top of the cupboards. While reaching up and groping blindly, he knocked down a thermometer, which shattered on the tiled countertop. At the time he had no idea what it was. He quickly lowered himself and began trying to scoop together the mercury beads that spilled over the tiles. Every time he attempted to collect them, the silver beads vanished mysteriously under his hands. "I tried to clean up the mess," he recalls, "but the mess just got absorbed into me."

Far less toxic was his earliest memory: his mother reading to him. The first book she read to him without pictures was Jules Verne's *20,000 Leagues Under the Sea*. He was wowed by the grand adventure, by the renegade outlaw antics of Captain Nemo. These readings and his mother's instruction in basic math put him ahead of the curve by the time he entered kindergarten. He was taller than the other kids, who didn't know how to read and write like him. Easily bored, he grew disobedient, and his teachers would often send him to the counselor.

When Anthony turned seven his parents relented to his requests to join a swim team, hoping he'd channel his impulses and energies into the pool. He took to the water with relish and right away showed signs of being a natural. Initially he was most comfortable as a backstroker.[5] In retrospect there was something allegorical about the way he'd wildly windmill his arms while staring into an uncooperative sky, often swerving and colliding into landlines. Unlike indoor swimmers, who can chart a straight path by the geometries of the ceiling, backstrokers in outdoor pools are either blinded by the

---

5 Michael Phelps also started swimming at age seven as a backstroker, although in his case it was because he was afraid to put his face in the water.

sun or like sailors without navigation, forsaken and unaided under the blank canvas of a blue sky.

Backstroke would be Anthony's primary stroke until high school. "There was something to not seeing where I was going, to just spinning my wheels," he reflects. "I was good at that." At his first competition that same year, he won his backstroke race despite being unable to maintain a straight course. He reveled in the flush of victory.

His speed caught the eye of the older age group coach and Anthony was transferred to the more advanced team. This was no longer swim school; he was now in the blood, toil, tears, and sweat domain of competitive training. Anthony rebelled against the demands for obedience. The coach, Dave, regularly singled him out, punishing him with push-ups, often in excess of fifty per practice. This disciplinary form of strength training served him well, and he continued to prevail over his opponents.

Calculating distances and time intervals in practice also honed Anthony's aptitude for mathematics. He exceled in his subjects—scoring in the 99th percentile in math and reading on standardized tests throughout elementary school—but his behavior only worsened. He openly disobeyed his teachers, who started writing misconduct notes and calling his parents.

Though Castaic was no ghetto, it was also no gated community, and there was occasional spillover from the nearby prison. For a period, a flasher in a raincoat and pants with the crotch cut out started frequenting the neighborhood. Sherry used to let the boys walk alone to and from the bus stop but now began escorting them. One day when Anthony got in trouble in second grade, he decided not to return home, fearing the rebuke. When he didn't disembark from the bus, his mother called the police.

I see a police car in the distance. Maybe Mom called the police because I didn't go home. I turn and walk down the side street. The police car also turns down the street and starts driving toward me. *Don't run*, I tell myself. But I start to run anyway. I may be able to run faster than my friends but not faster than a car. I hear the engine. A voice says, "Stop running," but I don't stop. And then louder I hear, "STOP," and the car makes a loud sound like a giant chicken and the lights flash. And I stop.

The policeman isn't mean but he has a gun and his uniform is scary. He asks what my name is and I don't say anything and he asks again and I tell him, "Anthony," and he asks for my last name and I say, "Ervin," and he tells me that my mother is upset and frightened and it's dangerous to be out by myself. Then he asks me why I didn't go home on the bus. I don't say anything because I'm not supposed to talk to strangers and I already told him my name. I don't tell him that Miss S. called Mom because I was a disruption in class and that she moved my desk far away from the others. Like I have a disease or something. I don't tell him that I don't want to go home because I don't want to be spanked. He asks me again. I just say, "Sorry."

He tells me to get in the car. I tell him Mom told me not to talk to strangers or get into cars with them. He say he's not a stranger, he's a police officer. I know police aren't the same as strangers but Mom always told me not to trust ANYBODY. So I just stand there. He shakes his head and says I should get in unless I want him to call more police. So I get in.

He doesn't do anything bad to me. He's not even mean. He just drives me home. Mom is going to yell and yell. And Dad will tell her to take it easy and let it go, but she'll still use the wooden spoon or the belt or something. The worst part about getting spanked on your bum is you can't see it coming. And then I'll be grounded and stuck in my room for days and days without video games and I won't be able to see my friends except at the pool, and even there Dave will shout and say, "Give me ten push-ups," whenever I try to have fun. That's why I don't want to go home. But then I only get more punishment. And then I don't want to go home even more.

Mom is standing outside on the road when we arrive. She looks mad.

⚜

Parents often fall into one of two camps: those who want to recreate their own childhood for their children and those who want to rectify it. Anthony's mother is among the latter. She won't talk about her childhood. Even her three sons know little about it. When I broached the matter, she retorted that she saw "no valid reason for opening that door." Only later, after a few more attempts and after I added that it might give context to her protective mode of child-rearing, did she toss me a valuable scrap from her past: "The most I'll tell you is I was on my own at a very young age. When you don't have parents, you have to protect yourself. That's hard work for a young person. So I was going to protect my children."

The foster-care past she alludes to may explain why Sherry prickles at the mention of a more hands-off parenting approach. It's hard to know if one's survival odds are better getting between a grizzly and her cubs or between Sherry and hers. "I would kill to protect them," she tells me matter-of-factly. Not the soft-spoken, mousy, blend-into-the-wallpaper type, Sherry runs her domestic affairs with the monomaniacal zeal of an Ahab, except her White Whale is a far more practical beast: order in the house and order in the family. Referring to herself as half-Jewish, half-Italian (she was called *half-breed* as a child), Sherry exudes a matriarchal charisma and maintains a maternal dictatorship, aligning in this sense more with her Mediterranean ancestry than her American upbringing. It's from her that Anthony inherited his long limbs and cutting quips, which both mother and son can deliver with an infuriating and amusing nonchalance.

Though nearing seventy, she looks a decade younger and has the energy of someone half her age. The blood pressure and sleeping pills she takes are probably more due to hyperactivity and stress than ailing health, which she maintains with daily treadmill runs and neighborhood walks. One might be tempted to say that her intrinsic vigor and bullish tenacity played a role in helping her defeat cancer in 2000 despite the doctors giving her a 60 percent chance of dying within five years. Sherry considers it her duty to protect her children against the perils and treacheries of a poor, nasty, and brutish world. Whatever unspoken demons lie buried in her past, they inform her outlook: "I don't let anyone walk on me. There was a time when I was more submissive, but not anymore. Shit on me once, shame on you. Shit on me twice, shame on me. I taught my kids that. *Protect yourself.*"

Though the family celebrates Christmas, not Hanukkah, and though there's bacon in her fridge, Sherry feels connected to her Jewish heritage, especially to what she refers to as the Jewishness of valuing education. "I *demanded* good grades," she tells me. Although the good marks came, they were often qualified by remarks about behavior misconduct, which never sat well with Sherry. As disciplinarian and keeper of order in the home (her husband was the good cop), Sherry had the most trouble with her middle son: "Anthony always had me frustrated. I never found my footing with what to do. I spanked, I yelled, I confined him to his room. Took away this, took away that. It was his personality. When I say, *I want it now,* I mean now. You say *now* to Anthony, and he says, *I'm going to make you wait twenty minutes because you said 'now.'* He stymied me all the time."

The eldest sibling, Jackie, didn't give his mother as much as grief as Anthony, but mostly because he was better at not getting caught. "There was crazy stuff that Mom had no idea about," Jackie recounts. "Like riding bicycles over makeshift bridges across the roofs of houses, playing with nail guns on construction sites . . . I look back now and say, *Thank God I lived.*"

Anthony, on the other hand, didn't try to hide anything: he'd openly flaunt his waywardness. Even so, the criteria for good behavior were stricter for the oldest brother. Whereas his younger siblings might be punished with a "time-out" that required them to stand in the corner, Jackie would be grounded for a month or longer for minor infractions like not doing homework, getting a bad grade, or lying. And though the others were also spanked, Jackie recalls receiving the lion's share, usually delivered on his backside by spatula, spoon, shoe, or belt. Sometimes he was compliant, but other times he'd sprint away, running circuits around the house while "being chased and swung at." Jackie admits he often exacerbated matters: "Part of me was just rebelling because I grew up in such a strict environment. You try to take the win from the loss. Lose on your own terms."

It was a tug-of-war mother-son dynamic of bizarre, fiendish proportions: one evening Jackie took off sprinting on his usual circuit of the house with his mother chasing him, spoon in hand, only to encounter a wall where a door had been just that morning. "She sealed it up," he says with a wry laugh. "And then I was trapped." The purpose of the renovation was less diabolical: to raise the home value by forming an extra bedroom. But Jackie is convinced his mother instigated a skirmish that same day to lure him—or have him lure himself—into her dead-end snare.

In retrospect, Sherry has misgivings about the corporal punishment she doled out: "It was wrong, and now they're always throwing up to me that I spanked with the wooden spoon." But especially for Anthony, Sherry has always felt a guiding hand was essential, not only in elementary school but also throughout junior high, high school, and even beyond.

In contrast to Anthony's mother, his father Jack took a more live-and-let-live, hands-off approach. Jack's own father, a West

Virginia coal miner, had been a tough man whose exchanges with his children included belts, stakes, and whatever else he could get his hands on. Jack didn't want to raise his sons that way: "I'd had enough of that with my father. I'm not a yeller. I'm the level-headed guy, the peacekeeper." Or as Sherry puts it, "Jack was always the diplomat, whereas I don't give a shit."[6] Having experienced plenty of hooliganism and police run-ins in his youth (he enlisted in the military as a way to keep out of trouble), Jack never felt Anthony was a problem child or troublemaker; he saw him rather as a "mischievous instigator" who merely required a calm talking-to now and then. Perhaps because the dominating presence of their mother eclipsed Jack's more laid-back approach, the boys at times felt their father could be a detached, even absent figure. But they would also later come to realize that the trauma from his thirteen months in Vietnam had led to depression, anger, and anxiety that unraveled his first marriage and caused him difficulties within the family structure for years to come.

Whatever tunnels Jack had to work through, he seems to have emerged to a place of peace and acceptance. His Southern roots come through in his easygoing manner and lilting speech, whose musical cadence, deep timbre, and lullabyish geniality would, one assumes, be equally effective in coaxing both infants and women to bed. He's a man of few but well-chosen words, delivering them in a way that makes even a mundane remark sound wise and meaningful. When I first visited the Ervin household, Jack motioned me into the kitchen, where he set before me a tumbler and a bottle of twelve-year-old Scotch that he saved for rare occasions. Then he motioned to the bottle. "Pour your own trouble, son."

Before tribal societies went the way of the dodo, initiatory rites of

---

6   Sherry and Jack also diverge ideologically in other areas. To take one exchange:
   Jack: Nothing wrong with having a relationship with that spiritual entity up there.
   Sherry: There is no spiritual entity up there.
   Jack: There is a universal knowledge out there you have to plug into time to time.
   Sherry: I don't believe in that nonsense.

passage under male guidance existed for young men as a ritualized way of severing their dependence on their mothers: the combination of, say, peyote and desert, was a method of forcing the teens to cope with physical and psychological hardship so that they might return to the tribe no longer as children but men. Such ventures into the wilderness would probably not jibe with Sherry's pedagogical philosophy. She once told one of Anthony's college girlfriends that she needed to be more involved in managing him because he required controls and parameters.

At one point during my visit, Sherry asked Anthony if he'd taken a nap. When he said it was none of her business, she retorted: "Always my business, because I'm your mother." He was thiry-two at the time. Their exchanges often resemble those of a curmudgeonly couple, where each one anticipates the other's responses and then mulishly digs in and refuses to budge, all the while maintaining the resigned calm that comes from the recognition that life cannot be otherwise. For example:

—*Nap, Anthony. Listen to your mother.*
—*Don't tell me what to do.*
—*I'll always tell you what to do*
—*Don't tell me what to do.*
—*I'll always tell you what to do.*
—*Don't tell me what to do.*

For Sherry, the duties of motherhood are eternal, beyond the ken of time's passage. When I asked if she felt that her Big Mother–style monitoring and the draconian reins she maintained over Anthony through his childhood and teen years were necessary, she scoffed: "For Anthony? Absolutely! Good grief, are you kidding? If he had parents that didn't give a shit and fed him McDonald's and KFC and left him on his own devices, he would have been the kid in jail. Absolutely."

Sherry equates discipline with care: her involvement in her son's life is not control but a fundamental and necessary expression of love, as essential as feeding him real food (she repeatedly points out that she never fed her sons fast food or pseudo-food like bologna). Cracking down on misbehavior is as much an expression of proper child-rearing as is preparing nutritious food. And a ferocious protectiveness accompanied that discipline. Woe befall those who criticize her sons. She refers to Anthony's elementary school principal as a "hardnose" who presided under the delusion that Anthony was a juvenile delinquent. When his club coach at Canyons Aquatic Club prefaced Anthony's "Swimmer of the Year" award at the banquet by saying that at best it should have been shared with another swimmer, Sherry bristled: "Jack had to hold me back in the chair. I thought I was going to run up on the stage and pop him one." To this day, she hasn't forgotten the two words *at best*: "I hold a grudge. I don't forgive and I don't forget."

Yet Sherry's brusque and guarded exterior belies a generous, doting, and self-sacrificing spirit. She's always worked unceasingly in service of her children, at times holding multiple part-time jobs, while also cooking, cleaning, and ferrying her sons to and from swim practices. When turtles stray up to her house from the nearby pond, she picks them up and returns them to their watering hole. When her neighbors moved and abandoned their cat like undesirable furniture left curbside, she took the feline in. The pain of the disadvantaged and vulnerable distress and activate her at a primal level.

"I'm not very trusting from being burned too many times," she once told me, and something in her tone made me realize that whatever her childhood details may be, my youth was a swaddled pampering in comparison. Her Cerberean posturings and iron grip over her sons, like that iron fence she once built around the pool, seem to stem more from her fear of being a neglectful parent than from the actual dangers of the world.

On my last visit, shortly before I left, Sherry leaned in toward me: "Not to threaten you, but if you harm my son through this book, either consciously or indirectly, I will hurt you."(It wasn't the first warning. On my previous visit, as I left, she said, "Be nice, or I'll come after you. Even if I'm dead, I will hunt you down.")

"Can I quote you on that?"

"Absolutely."

She then invited me to join them for Thanksgiving and sent me off with a hug and a sandwich for the plane. When I later declined her invite, explaining by e-mail that my mother would have my head if I didn't spend the holiday with my parents, she simply replied, "I approve."

❈

The others are so much bigger than me. This is Junior Olympics. Like Olympics for kids. Maybe one day I'll go to the real Olympics.

I'm so nervous. If my time is in the top eight of all the backstrokers then I make finals. And then, no matter what, I get a medal. I've never won a medal before. But maybe not this year because I'm swimming now with the big kids, the nine- and ten-year-olds. I'm the only eight-year-old racing them.

It's bright and loud with cheering. I'm nervous. I hear Mom yelling, "Go, Anthony!"

Phweeee: the whistle.

I jump into the water. I'm so nervous. I turn and face the wall and grab the handles.

Phweeee. "Take your marks."

Don't let the feet slip.

Beep! My feet stick to the wall and I shoot backward.

I kick hard and swing my arms as fast as I can. They made a new rule that you don't have to touch the wall with your hand when you turn. Now you can roll to your stomach after the flags and then do a flip turn. It's faster that way. But you have to time it right. I've practiced and practiced so that I don't mess it up here.

I see other arms swinging behind me, so I'm somewhere near the front. But there are at least two others ahead of me. I need to be first or second in this heat to make the top eight. I can't hear any cheering, only water splashing. There are no clouds today. I swim into the lane line a few times, but I don't pull on it.

When I finish, two swimmers are already at the wall, so I won't make the top eight. But then I find out that the top seed disqualified. He rolled over for his flip turn too early, right at the flags, and he missed the wall. This means I'm in eighth place overall, not ninth.

I've made finals!

And all because I practiced and practiced my flip turns. That's why it's important to learn everything, even the littlest thing, and practice until it's perfect. You never know when that little thing will make all the difference.

Later in finals I get seventh place and it's my best time. AND I get a medal. My first ever medal, not just another ribbon. Everyone is congratulating me. I am so happy. Mom says, "I am so proud of you, Anthony." And Pops says, "Well done, son." And Jackie and Derek look pleased too.

I won a medal against the big kids. I am so happy.

❖

It was evident Anthony was going places with swimming, even if he couldn't quite see where. At the age of nine he was selected to his first all-star team, the youngest member. On one away meet he shaved his entire body of its pale fuzz and rubbed baby oil all over himself, except on his hands and feet, which his coach warned him required friction. At the starting signal, he shot backward off the wall and like an oily mink raced to victory, defeating all the ten-year-olds in the Los Angeles region. The next year he set a Southern California age group record in both the 50- and 100-meter backstroke. After one record-breaking race, a few kids approached him for an autograph. This confused him and he turned to his mother for guidance. "I said, *Sign it!*" Sherry recalls. "He was embarrassed. He was so cute. He really was sweet."

As the seasons passed, Anthony continued breaking California records. In junior high, he made new friends, many of which, as Anthony put it, "were just as good, if not better, at troublemaking." As much as he loved the thrill of the race and the praise that followed, his resentment of the sport and its demands only grew. He regularly had to miss sleepovers, birthday parties, and, most devastatingly, a Megadeth and Iron Maiden concert. He pleaded to go to the show with his friends but wasn't allowed because of a weekend swim meet, despite it being a minor one. Angry though he was, he had no choice but to put it behind him.

In junior high band, he came to idolize an eighth-grade bandmate who once tattooed himself with a safety pin during practice and told a wide-eyed Anthony that he "did the sister" of another bandmate. "He had long hair and a Danzig T-shirt with a chick in a skull helmet holding a bloody knife over a dead dude," Anthony remembers. "And I was like, *Wow, this is awesome! This is what music is all about!*" The badboy unrestraint seemed far more enticing than the monotonies of swim training.

When he turned eleven he faced a stronger, older pool of competitors. Though he no longer dominated, he nonetheless qualified for regional championships in Seattle. It was his first time flying across state boundaries for a swim meet. It was a high-tier competition but racing had become routine. Comfortable and confident, he also felt bored. So he decided to pass the time by playing with fire.

❖

I'm not racing this morning so I get to stay at the hotel while the others are at the pool. Nothing to do in the room so I wander through the hallways. It's boring though. Every hallway looks the same. Mundania. I pass a maid's cart. She's not there so I snatch a matchbook and run back to my room.

I sit on the bed and light a match with just one hand, using my thumb the way Tim showed me. That's the cool way to do it. I watch it burn down. The edge of the flame is blue and the match glows red at the place where it burns. When the match goes out, a thin line of smoke shoots up. Like a soul shooting up from a fresh corpse. So cool. I light a match and then put the tip of another unlit one inside the flame. *Sssshhphwweeee!* Awesomeness. The flame is better when you combine two matches.

There's a box of tissues by the bed. I hold one up and place a match under it and *FWOOF,* it bursts into flame and floats up like a spinning fireball! Dope! Not like paper, which burns slow and boring. With tissue it's fast. The fire leaps to life when I feed it tissue. I can't stop. I keep burning tissues. I'm like a magician but even cooler because I throw up fireballs from my palm instead of doves. Like I'm now in Xanth and this is my magical power. Burn, Mundania, burn.

One tissue lands on the bed and the sheet catches on fire. I put it out but not before it's burned a hole into the bedsheet.

Back in Mundania. And in deep, deep shit.

The maid reported the damage, and Sherry soon learned that Anthony was being sent back on the next flight. She and Jack would have to foot the bill. When they met him, he was hiding behind the air hostess, who'd served as his steward in transit. Anthony, who'd been in tears on the flight back to LA, feared the physical punishment that awaited. But there was only disappointment from his mother. It was his first memory of shame. Her anger was instead directed toward the swim league for leaving Anthony unattended. (Due to her subsequent pressure, the rules were changed to mandate that swimmers had to be on deck for all races and could never be left unsupervised.) Around Thanksgiving he had to appear at a tribunal, where he was given community service and barred from all-star trips for a year.

There were other sources of tension at home. Jack had been working in production control for an aerospace firm but was laid off when the industry shrunk after Reagan left office. For supplemental income, Sherry returned to waitressing at an upscale restaurant. The swim club made an exception on their swim fees, offering them a reduced rate. Between chores, homework, swim practice, meets, and the frequent punishments, where he'd be sequestered to his room without video games, Anthony felt like he was missing out on life. He begged to quit swimming, but to no avail. Now that he was competing less and practicing halfheartedly, his performances suffered and he no longer dominated in his events. He harbored anger toward his parents—not just about the swimming, but also about what he saw as his mother's disciplinary excess and his father's lack of intervention. The decades since then have given him a new perspective: "As I've gotten older I feel like they were just trying to do what they thought was best. My mother tried to let us live the lives we wanted within reason. Yeah, we had to help out around the house, but somebody had to. She had enough responsibility. On the one hand was the iron fist and on the other was a boy who needed control and structure because he was wildfire."

That winter, not yet a teenager, Anthony started running off for short periods, often absconding through his bedroom window. It was nothing dramatic—he usually went to his friend's house or wandered through an undeveloped scrubland area nearby called "The Wash." He sometimes found sanctuary in a treehouse that he and his friends had built. On the day before Christmas Eve one year, he took his winter jacket, a blanket, and a flashlight, and headed out. He didn't return until the next day.

The sky looks like the lox we used to have for breakfast before Dad got laid off. Against it, the tree looks haunted. The birds are still chirping but not as much as before. I hurry and am soon climbing up the tree. One of the footholds is shaky. We have to fix that. I climb onto the platform. The scrap chain-link fence around the perimeter of the platform comforts me. I feel safer behind it.

I make a bed with the various blankets scattered around and lie on it with my back propped up against the fence. The rollout carpets provide some softness and warmth against the wood. I zip my jacket up all the way. Outside it's silent and dark except for the hum of the highway. It's ominous. I learned *ominous* from *Man from Mundania*. Or was it *Heaven Cent?*

I don't have those two books anymore. Mom made me return them. That was bad. *Anthony, where did you get these?* And me not knowing what to say. *Tell me, Anthony, where?* And me telling her I stole them. And then all the yelling and screaming. I couldn't take it. So to avoid Mom's advance I ran outside to the backyard, circling the pool. And she was red and shaking. *Jack, do something about this, would you? Just do something!* But Dad had never gotten involved before that, so I didn't expect him to actually reach for me as I circled by. He didn't cuff me that hard but my nose opened up because I get nose bleeds so easily and blood sprayed all over my shirt and splattered and dripped all over the concrete patio. And I looked up at Dad with eyes as shocked as his as I cupped my hand under my nose, the blood blossoming and pooling in my palm. And Dad stood there stunned, his mouth hanging open, not knowing what to say. He had never once spanked me before that, and I knew by his eyes that this would be the last time. But even after that Mom still made me take the books back to the store. And my ears were so hot and I just wanted to run away. And the manager looked so serious while writing my name and address on a little card, saying if I ever did anything like that again she would report me to the police.

I tried to explain to Mom that I'd read all the other Xanth books so many times and none of the libraries had those two. And I couldn't buy them because I didn't even have pocket money anymore. I just wanted to read them. She said that was no excuse. And after that Mom even took away my books because that was the ultimate punishment. But that didn't last long because she felt bad and she likes to see me read.

The stars come out. I try to imagine which ones exist and which don't because some stars can be gone but you still see them because the speed of light is super slow compared to how far away they are. So some of the stars I see aren't even there anymore. It's like somebody filmed the sky thousands or millions of years ago and now I'm watching it. Like looking into a crystal ball except into the past, not the future.

I get nervous thinking about what will happen tomorrow so I take out my flashlight and *The Source of Magic*. I've read it before. But I know it will make me feel better. And it does. Because soon I'm no longer Anthony in Mundania. I'm Bink in Xanth.

I read half the book. It's getting cold. I put the book down and throw the rest of the blankets over me and lie flat on my back. I stare up at the sky through the tree. The branches look scary without their leaves. Ominous. But at least there's no yelling here. No arguments. No punishments. Just me and the tree and the stars. The stars from now and the stars from before.

A Nervous Condition

Oh the nerves, the nerves; the mysteries of this machine called Man!
Oh the little that unhinges it: poor creatures that we are!
—Charles Dickens

F-f-f-feel like-a l-l-l-lightnin' hit my b-b-brains . . .
—Willie Dixon, "Nervous"

One morning after Anthony had entered junior high, he and his brother Derek were on the couch watching Saturday cartoons. His mother walked into the den and right away noticed something out of the ordinary. Anthony's eyes were rapidly blinking. It wasn't the first time she'd seen this. On occasion it had happened before, but only for a few seconds. Since he'd recently been prescribed glasses, she'd always assumed it was an ophthalmological issue related to his nearsightedness. This time, however, it seemed more pronounced and longer lasting. "What's wrong with your eyes?" she asked. He knew something was off but didn't know what. Not wanting to interrupt the cartoon, he shrugged it off. The blinking soon passed, and they both forgot the incident.

A few weeks later, Sherry received a call from the pool. They told her to come immediately.

It happens toward the end of swim practice. That itchy feeling around my eye. It's never happened before during practice. And this time, the tense feeling spreads downward. I can't help but move my jaw as I wait on the wall. When I push off it stops. But when we get to the other wall it starts up again. Moving my jaw relieves the pressure. Like scratching an itch.

But this itch doesn't go away. The guys in my lane are looking at me funny. They can't see the blinking because of my mirrored goggles, but they can see my jaw moving side to side. The itch gets stronger. Now it's happening when I'm swimming. Just before the turn in the shallow side, my head jerks down during my side breath. Instead of gulping air, I swallow water.

I stop at the wall, coughing, and scoot toward the lane line to make space for their flip turns. When I look up I see the coach walking toward me. She's about to yell at me for stopping during a set. Then I see her expression change from mad to confused to worried. It's hard to keep my eyes focused on her because they keep blinking and my head is twitching.

When Mom shows up fifteen minutes later, I'm still standing in the shallow end. I didn't get out of the pool. I would have had to take my goggles off and they would see my blinking. The others have already finished the workout. Some are staring at me from the pool deck and saying things to each other. Only me and three older girls are still in the water. One is hugging me and I'm crying and I don't want to cry and it's embarrassing but I can't help it. And I can't help my head from jerking. What's wrong with me? I don't know what's happening.

And then Mom rushes over and lifts me up out of the pool and she's saying, "What's wrong, Anthony? What's wrong, Anthony?" and she looks scared, really scared.

Tourette's syndrome is a neurological disorder typically first noticed in childhood, characterized by repeated involuntary or semivoluntary body movements and vocalizations. In 1972 it was believed that only one hundred people in all of the US had Tourette's. Now it's believed that one in *every* hundred Americans have Tourette's, with two hundred thousand having the most severe symptoms. In milder forms, Tourette's involves rapid blinking, throat clearing, and twitching. More rare symptoms include automatically repeating the words and gestures of others (echolalia and echopraxia), repeating one's own words (palilalia), and involuntarily swearing and uttering obscenities, often related to feces (coprolalia). This last word translates in Greek literally to *shit talker*. Though only about one in ten people with Tourette's exhibit coprolalia, there's a widespread misconception that everyone with Tourette's is subject to uncontrollable outbursts of profanity. This is also the de facto misimpression one gets from TV and other media (e.g., the *South Park* Tourette's episode and the ranting "Tourette Guy" on YouTube).[7]

Little is known about what causes Tourette's. In the fifteenth-century book *Malleus Maleficarum*, considered the first written account of what's now called Tourette's, a priest's tics were believed to be "related to possession by the devil." When it first entered the medical lexicon in the late nineteenth century, it was considered a "moral" social infirmity resulting from roguishness and a debilitated will. From the early- to midtwentieth century, it was characterized as a psychiatric illness requiring psychotherapy. Now that neuroscience has taken epistemological center stage, it's seen as involving abnormalities in the brain and its circuitry, which affect the production and/or reception of dopamine,[8] the neurotransmitter involved in initiating movement.

Although the exact cause of Tourette's isn't known, recent find-

---

7 Fucking pop culture.

8 The *and/or* reflects scientific uncertainty. Research now suggests that individuals with Tourette's don't have an excess of dopamine production, as previously believed, but rather a supersensitivity of the postsynaptic dopamine receptor sites. Specifics aside, the gist is that the nervous system is jacked up and there's some serious neural firing going down.

ings suggest the condition can confer advantages as well as imped-
iments. Tourette's can result in increased attention to detail and
heightened awareness. Neurologist Oliver Sacks has noted that,
while Tourette's is often destructive in its effects, it "can also be con-
structive, add speed and spontaneity, and a capacity for unusual and
sometimes startling performance." In timed neurological tests for
motor coordination, children with Tourette's were faster than their
peers. In other neuropsychological studies, they showed higher cognitive control: all those childhood hours spent trying to suppress tics
served as a form of mental training. One can only guess at how this
cognitive advantage and nervy sensitivity might play out when applied to a complex and sensory-rich environment like water, where
feel and proprioception—the awareness of one's body movement
and position—are so crucial.

A 2014 *20/20* piece exploring the possible relationship between
Tourette's and athletic excellence referenced two athletes. The first
was the US soccer goalkeeper Tim Howard, whose performance
in the 2014 World Cup was so impressive that Americans actually
started watching soccer. The second athlete was Anthony Ervin.

The day after the pool incident, Anthony's mother took him to the
pediatrician, who suspected Tourette's and referred him to a neurologist. After several visits that included sleep-pattern tests and a CAT
scan to rule out a brain tumor, the neurologist diagnosed Anthony
with Tourette's. By now his blinking fits had escalated and would
commence as soon as he woke up. Concerned about the stigma surrounding Tourette's, Sherry asked that Anthony's condition be listed
in his school records as a "nonspecific neurological disorder." As the
family learned more about the condition, some of Anthony's elementary school behaviors made more sense. Tourette's is a complex
struggle between the self and what feels like an outside force besieg-
ing it with physical and mental compulsions. This accounts for the
variety of neurobehavioral conditions that can accompany Tourette's

like OCD and ADHD. Anthony exhibited tendencies of the former: washing his hands repeatedly; spending minutes on end before a mirror to make sure his hair's part and curl were exact; lining up books in ascending order; grouping colors.

His mother suspects that much of the waywardness during his early years could be attributed to "Anthony dealing with things neurologically that nobody realized." And though vocal and physical tics tend to subside with age, the depression, anxiety, panic attacks, and mood swings that can accompany Tourette's often persist through one's adult life. Anthony's cognitive ability in later years to train and race with the undistracted tunnel-like focus of a racehorse with blinders also had a destructive counterpart: a tendency to obsess single-mindedly over disaster scenarios and then paralyze with anxiety over a sense of impending calamity.

A chronic but nondegenerative disease, Tourette's has no cure, though it can be treated. Anthony was prescribed clonidine, a hypertension medication also effective in suppressing tics. They started him on a quarter of a pill. Five days later they increased the dosage to half a pill, but he was still subject to frequent blinking fits. Only when they increased the dose to a full pill did he wake up without blinking or twitching.

Not until later in high school, at higher doses of medication, did the tics fully come under control. In junior high, he was still subject to convulsive episodes. But aside from excessive swearing during emotional moments (which he admits he often indulged in simply because he had the medical excuse), his tics were more physical than verbal. Ervin likens the experience of a Tourette's fit to watching an online video with slow connectivity where the clip keeps pausing to buffer.

Jackie recalls Anthony in junior high sitting on his bed, struggling to read: "It would take him forever to get through one page. His eyes would close, and he would lose track over and over again. It was heartbreaking."

Lorac insane, dying . . .

"Raist!" he moaned, clutching his brother tightly.

Raistlin's head moved feebly. His eyelids fluttered, and he opened his mouth.

What?" Caramon bent low, his brother's breath ■■■■ Caramon bent low, his brother's breath ■■■■■■ head moved fee ■■■ fluttered, and he ■■■■ eyelids fluttered, and he ■■ he opened ■■■■ fluttered ■■■■ opened his mouth ■■■ his mou ■■ mo ■■ mouth ■■■■■■■

I can't. I put down the book and wait for it to pass.

Here in my room, at least I don't have to control it. I can just let it happen. At least here no one is staring at me and avoiding me like at school or like my old neighborhood friends. Everybody avoids me now. Only at swim practice do they act the same around me, probably because swimming is hard and we all do it and what we go through together and have in common is more important than what we don't.

Yesterday I watched a nature show about animals living high up in the tall mountains. In one part there was a crazy snowstorm and nothing but snow and ice and darkness and freezing wind. It was the last place in the world you'd want to be. Most of the show was about nature and animals, but for one part during the snowstorm it showed the people who filmed it inside their tent, with a little light hanging over them. It was cramped inside and they could barely sit up in the tents and they were laughing and joking about having not showered for ages and didn't seem to care at all about being crammed into that tiny space because they were warm and had each other. I remember that.

I remember the one bird stuck in the storm. It didn't have a tent. It didn't even have a tree. Just the ledge on the mountain. It ruffled its feathers and shut its little eyes and shrunk down into itself. It looked like a tiny statue someone had left on the mountain. It went quiet and deep inside its own body, so deep that it was safe and warm even if its feathers were covered in snow.

They showed lots of other stuff too, like mountain goats charging each other and slamming heads together and a wild cat with her baby. But mostly I remember those men with smelly socks laughing in their tents. And the bird all alone out there with its eyes shut in the storm, not moving because there was no other place to go.

<hr />

If April is the cruelest month, then adolescence is one long April. For many of us, it's the hardest period of our life and, like all trying periods, the most formative. It's the time when we most want to conform and blend in with our peers, yet it's also the one when we're most acutely self-conscious of our apartness. It's when we're most prey to an excess of sensitivity—our individuality appearing to us not as uniqueness but as grotesque Otherness.[9] That's why Tourette's is a double whammy: it not only augments that sense of being an

---

9 That, at least, was my experience growing up in a rural Maine blue-collar mill town as a shy, bookish, gangly kid with heavily accented immigrant parents and a long foreign name that allowed for all sorts of mocking back-of-the-school-bus adaptations (the worst two being Constantine Stringbean, which played on my insecurity over my daddy longlegs physique, and Constanteenie-Weenie, which I found grossly unwarranted since the girl who coined it had never even seen my weenie). Junior high felt like a three-year trek through a minefield. But if I now try to pinpoint how I was actually victimized, I come up short, which makes me think I was just hypersensitive and insecure and 90 percent of my angst and fear and persecution complex was self-inflicted. It's representative of what most kids go through, though I probably bottomed out lower on the insecurity spectrum than most. I even told my YMCA swim club coach to call me Chris instead of Constantine, which explains why the bulk of my Y meet ribbons are awarded to *Chris Markides*. My mother and father, who were the inverse of the überinvolved stopwatch-in-hand swim parents, had no clue about my alter ego until a run-in with the pool director, in which he shook their hands and congratulated them on Chris's performance.

outsider, but peaks precisely during that period when it takes so little to feel estranged. That feeling, while less overpowering, has stayed with Anthony. "I've always felt the story of my life has been about being normal but on the fringes of abnormality, and it's the fringes that separate my history from the rest."

Once Tourette's came on full force in junior high, Anthony began isolating himself, spending his free time engrossed in books and video games. His heart no longer in competing, his performances dropped off. His mother eventually let him take a break from competitions so long as he kept attending practices. It would prove to be a three-year burnout, prefiguring the exodus that followed his Olympic success. His tendency to withdraw when upset would remain with him, also manifesting on a micro level: to this day, distress can cause him to shut down even in the presence of others into a kind of human sleep mode, a cocoon-like refuge against interaction with the outside world.

Junior high was coming to an end. The most prominent high school in the area in athletics and academics, Hart High, wasn't in their locale, so Sherry appealed to his academic prowess to get him in. Unlike his regional high school, Hart offered AP courses. His club team was in the same district, so for the first time he'd be attending school with his swim team peers. Even so, Anthony initially resisted this because he'd be going to a different high school than his neighborhood friends. But he changed his mind after an incident that took place in a housing subdivision near their neighborhood. One of the houses there had been empty for years, a blight of a structure overrun by weeds, its back window shot out by a BB gun. One afternoon while Anthony was out with a small group of friends, they decided to climb into the house through the broken window.

❖

Tommy climbs in first, then the others. I follow.

We tiptoe. Nothing in the house. Just a few chairs.

"Check it out, an answering machine." Travis's voice echoes through the house. He holds the phone up. "Hello, helloooooooo." He slams it back down. "I guess no one's home." The laughter echoes.

We wander through the house, then return to the living room. In the corner is a box of fluorescent lights. Tommy pulls one out and tosses it to Mikey. Then he pulls another for himself and raises it up with two hands like a Jedi Master. *"Luke, I am your father."*

Mikey also goes into dueling stance. "I see your Schwartz is as big as mine." Then he swings. The long bulbs shatter on impact, exploding in a puff of white smoke. Tommy and Mikey jump back. We all go silent, exchanging uncertain glances. Then, out of nowhere, Mikey breaks the silence. With a cry, he grabs a chair and smashes it into the ground repeatedly until it's in pieces. And then *everybody* goes apeshit. Tommy charges at the wall with his arms raised, yelling, "Ahhhhhh!" and at the last second slams his leg into it. His foot goes through the plaster all the way to his knee. They're all yelling and running around, smashing things up and ripping tiles off the kitchen counter. It's crazy—all this crunching and shattering and breaking and war cries and whooping and bits of plaster and wood and tiles flying all over the place . . . I don't break anything myself, I just hang back, watching them. But I still egg them on.

"Dude, what about those!" I say, pointing up at the long fluorescent lights in the kitchen.

Travis looks up, eyes gleaming, and then he starts hurling tiles at them. The first misses but the second makes contact and the light explodes, the shards flying through the kitchen in a cloud of white smoke. We huddle for a moment, shielding our faces in our elbows.

"There's more in the box!" I cry, and we run back to the living room where I watch him smash those.

When one of the boys, Tommy, later learned that the owner was sobbing in front of the house, he turned himself in. The families of each boy involved had to pay thousands in repairs. Anthony was let off because he hadn't actively participated in the destruction. He talked himself out of getting in trouble ("lying to save my skin was second nature") but he knew he was guilty through association. The incident became a forewarning of what might come if he didn't make a change. From then on he resigned himself to moving to the new high school. His older brother Jackie, who'd already left for college, convinced him that swimming could be fun again since he'd be on the same high school team as his club teammates. He also began to think of the new school as an opportunity to start over without the stigma of a neurological disorder, since the medication he was taking suppressed his Tourette's symptoms. In late 1995, soon after starting at Hart High, his parents sold their Castaic home and moved to a smaller house in the more upscale Valencia, which was closer to the high school.

At Hart, Anthony's swimming burnout ended. He continued to train at the Canyons Aquatic Club team with Bruce Patmos, a demanding performance-oriented coach whom Ervin acknowledges was a good trainer who got results from his swimmers. But it was his high school coach, Steve Neale, who rekindled his enjoyment of the sport. "If it wasn't for him I probably wouldn't have made it to college swimming at all," Ervin says. "Steve was all about the family of it. He loved the kids." Beyond that personal, even paternal relationship with his swimmers, Neale also cultivated the sense, even if Anthony didn't realize it then, that swimming was about more than just performance.

"Not that it was all fun and cookies," Neale told me. "But swimming has to have a value and purpose. It has to be meaningful." Anthony and his three teammates—Ryan Parmenter, John Terwilliger, and Eric Reifman—became known as the "Fearsome Freshmen." The two standouts of the group, Anthony and Ryan, could, between the two of them, win every individual swimming event at high school competitions. Local newspaper clippings from that period with titles like "Hart Pair Making Splash" include photos of Ryan and Anthony posing in the pool with crossed arms (knuckles pressing out on biceps to make them bulge) and the kind of dour don't-mess-with-me expressions that still seem cool and badass when you're a teen.

Upon beginning high school, Ryan, John, and Anthony made a vow: *All right, boys, we'll be men soon. Our goal should be to each have a threesome[10] before we leave high school.* It was not to be, however, for the young idealists. "We were so far off," Anthony recalls. "Not one of us even lost our virginity in high school." Despite his swimming fame, Anthony remained introverted and shy, especially around girls. His freshman year he was particularly tongue-tied around the older girls on his swim team, who by then had come to recognize the power of their sexuality and had no qualms about exercising it over the young star swimmer.

❖

I still have at least a half hour before the 100. Lauren and Danielle sit on each side of me on a beach blanket laid out on a grassy area right outside the pool. Their towels are tied around their waists and over their bathing suits.

"Hey, Anthony . . . " Lauren says.

"Hi, Anthony, what're you doing?" Danielle says. She's sitting really close to me and smiling. Just last night she was making faces with spaghetti hanging from each nostril and an orange wedge stuffed between her lips, but now all I notice are how her boobs are squished under the bathing suit.

---

10   Not with each other.

"Uh, nothing," I say.

"Oh yeah, nothing?" Lauren says. She scoots over closer to me and puts her hand on my knee. "Nothing at all?" Then Danielle puts her hand on my other knee.

My thighs tense up. "Uhhh, what are you doing?"

"You know what we're doing," Danielle says.

"Or more like, you know what *you're* going to do," Lauren says, smirking.

Their fingers are moving along my knee. "Wha—what are you doing?"

Lauren tosses her hair so that her auburn curls fall down over part of her face. "You're going to *rise* to the occasion for us." Her hand starts moving up my leg.

I'm frozen. I shake my head. "No . . . no, I won't."

Danielle leans into my ear and whispers, "Oh yes, you will."

I look down at their hands and gulp, then look straight ahead. From the pool, I hear the whistle blow for the start of a race. The starting signal goes off to a roar of cheers. I don't look down but I feel their fingers slide along my thigh, slipping under the hem of my board shorts.

"No," I whisper. My mouth has dried out. But it's too late, it's happening. I can feel it happening.

Lauren's eyes widen as she notices the movement in my lap and she looks over at Danielle. They both start giggling and then run off.

⚜

In high school Ervin shifted from backstroke to freestyle—mostly, he claims, because he tired of colliding into lane lines. Though he was the fastest sprint freestyler on the team, his friend Ryan led every practice. Anthony would push off five seconds after Ryan, sprint to catch up, and then hang back and draft off him the rest of the way.[11]

---

11 Drafting is when one swimmer tailgates the swimmer in front—fingertips entering the water just inches behind the toes of the lead swimmer—and thus gets pulled forward in the current, or

This isn't something lead swimmers usually tolerate, since it's like having a parasite dangling off your toes, but Ryan endured it without complaint for years.

Bruce Patmos's workouts often consisted of high-intensity sets with plenty of rest, unlike the default high yardage/minimal rest grind that characterizes most club-level practices. This training was ideally suited for Anthony, who improved dramatically with each successive year. As Ryan, who'd been training with Anthony since the age of eight, recalls, "It was junior year when he really started separating himself from the pack and going crazy fast."

At the biggest regional meet of the year, Anthony qualified for US Nationals in the 200 free, as it was easier to qualify in longer events than in sprints. Though he died in the last 100 yards,[12] he went out so fast that he still qualified: he claims he went out in forty-four seconds for the first hundred yards and fifty-three for the second. At the end of the race, he was, as he puts it, "pretty much vertical." It's a tactic he'd employ in the future for his 100 sprints: go out like spitfire and then, when the polar bear jumps on his back near the end, hang on in hopes that the others can't catch him. But this turn-and-burn, fly-and-die tactic does have a downside: it hurts.

Stroke analyst Milton Nelms remembers watching Ervin light it up off the blocks at a college meet only to perish in the final meters: "It was like he was struck by a headhunter's curare blow dart. But that's why I love to watch the guy. He doesn't care. The dude races. We lose that in the sport because everything is so patterned and planned. You rarely get outliers that way, who break free."

Among the college coaches scoping out potential recruits in the junior class that year was the Cal–Berkeley co–head coach Mike Bot-

---

slipstream, created by the lead swimmer. Basically it lets the person in front do the work for you. For a *Look, Ma, no hands!* illustration of this principle, stand in waist- or chest-high water a few inches behind the head of someone who's doing a backfloat. Then start walking backward through the water and, presto, the person floating will get sucked into your wake and travel along with you.
12 To "die" in swimming is standard lingo for describing the state of All Systems Fail at the back end of a race. Unlike the pleasurable *la petite mort* of an orgasm, this little death brings only the fireworks of pain.

tom. When he first saw Anthony race, he knew he was witnessing a pure sprinter's instinct in action. Even though Anthony didn't win that particular race, and even though his stroke wasn't all that great at the time, there was something about how he moved through the water, something about, as Bottom put it, "how he put his hand on the water," that caught his eye. Other coaches would recruit him, but it was Bottom who pushed the hardest and ensured he was offered a full scholarship. (After meeting Sherry Ervin, he knew it would take a full ride to get him.) Anthony, meanwhile, had no plans to swim in college beyond his first year. He saw swimming as means to an end, as evinced by his quote at the time from a local newspaper article: "I wouldn't say I really enjoy [swimming], but I know it's something I need to do. It's like work to me. I'm out there to get into college." This sunless and calculated mindset is something he now warns against: "It's a cliché, but it really is about the journey, not the destination. Using swimming to get to college or a scholarship is a destination. That's not the right way to think about it."

As Ervin grew taller and larger, his medication requirements also increased. He was soon up to three pills daily. His Tourette's symptoms were now somewhat controlled, but at the cost of sedation. He was constantly napping during the day, which then led to nocturnality. His mother would hear him getting online to play video games in the middle of the night (this was back in the laborious and noisy dial-up era when logging on sounded like R2-D2 getting into a car crash). So she would lift and set down the phone receiver, repeatedly. "I wasn't doing it to be mean," she says. "I was doing it to force him to fall asleep. Eventually I would wear him down."

Ervin has never been a conventional sleeper. To this day, perhaps out of some neurological quirk, he can't sleep in complete darkness. He requires light and sound, preferably the preternatural glow and buzz of a screen. "It's almost like when you eliminate the stimuli, it becomes a heightened sensation," he says. "Nothing wakes me up faster than total darkness and silence."

In high school he started swimming twice a day year-round (previously he only swam doubles over summers), which also contributed to his fatigue. Unable or unwilling to get up on days he had morning practice, Anthony would be dragged out of bed by his mother. After swim practice and before school, he'd take his medication. By the second or third class, when the pill kicked in, he'd often fall asleep. By lunch the medication would wear off and he'd take another pill, leading to lethargy during his afternoon classes. Sleeping in class wasn't as alienating as the tics, but the regularity with which he drifted off still left him feeling like he was on the periphery of the "normal" high school experience. "The meds almost caused me to become less myself," he recalls. "Not much of anything, really."

My eyelids are so heavy. I lift my left foot up and hold it off the ground. That works but I can only do it for so long. I let it drop. I try to just close one eye at a time, but it's a struggle keeping the other eye open. Mr. Mansfield is writing a formula on the chalkboard. I try to focus on it, but my eye starts fluttering. The scraping of the chalk sounds so far away. So far away . . . I let both eyes close. Just for a little while. Just a little.

Just . . .

          . . .

          . . .

I raise my head and look around. There's laughter. Where am I? I don't recognize anybody. This isn't my class. Kids I don't know are grinning at me. Mr. Mansfield is standing over his desk, chuckling. It's the next class. I slept through the end of my class and he didn't wake me.

"Don't worry, Anthony," Mr. Mansfield says. "Your study hall teacher was notified that you were . . . otherwise preoccupied and would be on your way shortly."

Everybody starts laughing again. My face is hot.

"Sorry," I say, and grab my backpack. I try to laugh but a weird sound comes out of my mouth. He smiles and opens the door for me. I walk out, the laughter following me out the door.

I stop and just stand there for a while until my face cools off. Then I walk down the empty hallway toward study hall, trying not to step on any lines.

His first two years in high school, his friends were exclusively swimmers. But as an upperclassman he needed some separation and escape from that world, which incidentally was mostly white. His junior year he met Quincy, a Filipina, who became his best friend. Through her, he made a new posse of friends, among whom he was the only non-Asian. "A couple of them fulfilled a warped form of the 'model minority,' acing tests while regularly ditching or sleeping through class," Ervin recalls. "Otherwise, they probably cared more about break dancing than school. And more about cars and girls than anything." Something about their laid-back indolence as protest against demanding parents, their outsider status as Asian Americans, and even just their plain friendliness and acceptance of him, Tourette's and all, appealed to and comforted Anthony. They also may have helped him get in touch with a minority root he didn't know he needed at the time. But mostly they offered him an alternate community outside of his routine of swimming and family—something he would continue to look for through college and after. One of them, Vouy, cut everyone's hair, including Anthony's, in a high tight fade. "J.R., Peter, Ray, George, Jabez, Sandro . . . it was like the black barbershop thing except it was a crew of Asians," he says.

One day they bought black T-shirts with red *nWo* logos (a pro wrestling team) from the mall, posed in them for a group photo as a wrestling troupe, then returned the shirts for the refund. Another time they took off in a three-car day-trip caravan for San Diego to challenge a master gamer at the video game *Marvel vs. Capcom* in a drop-in tournament, "just like karate masters in old Japan might travel to challenge somebody to a fight." It's the only trip he recalls from high school that didn't involve swimming or family.

Throughout high school he associated swimming with straight-laced restraint. Swimmer gatherings consisted of "eight people sitting quietly in a room, drinking punch and eating cake." It wouldn't be until his recruiting trip to University of Southern California that he got his first sip of college swimming life.

⚜

"Chug it, chug it, chug it, chug it . . . " Others get in on it. "CHUG IT, CHUG IT!"

I raise the wine cooler to my lips. It's half full but I don't lower the bottle until it's empty. It's sugary sweet and goes down easy. I slam the empty bottle onto the table. They all start laughing.

My third bottle. Most I've ever had. Snoop Dogg is bow-wowing from the speakers. Two guys are holding one dude by the legs upside down over the keg and a crowd is around him chanting out the seconds: "One, two, three, four, five . . . " He makes it to twelve and then foam starts spilling out of his mouth and over his face until he gags and sputters, spraying beer everywhere. They put him back on his feet, his face red and dripping. He throws his arms up and beats his chest. The next guy goes up and lasts seven seconds and everyone boos. Another guy is slinging his arm around any girl he stumbles upon, pulling her face into his pecs and whispering into her ear. They don't even seem to care. One girl, after he says something in her ear, even turns to him and squeezes her boobs between her biceps, shaking them back and forth. Her friends start hooting and shouting, "You go, girl, shake those titties!"

What the hell is going on here?

The guy who did the kegstand dry heaves during a game of beer-pong and charges to the balcony. We all watch him through the window as he doubles over the balcony banister and barfs. People throw their arms up, cheering and high-fiving.

Soon people are laughing too loud and too hard over things that aren't even funny, and the place starts spinning, so I head into one of the bedrooms where there are fewer people. I sit on the bed and start talking to a girl. She keeps leaning in close and her T-shirt falls open, displaying the bright orange of her bra. After a while the others in the room leave and it's just the two of us. I don't even know how it happens but we start kissing. I can't believe it. I've only made out with a girl twice before and she was my friend so that was weird and didn't really count.

I don't know what to do so we just keep kissing while sitting on the bed. And then she gets up and turns the light off and comes back to me. I can't believe this is happening . . . *Now what? What if she wants to—*

And then the door opens and this guy comes in and turns the light on.

"Hey! What the hell? That's my bed," he says. He's got the broad jaw and face of an action figure.

"Don't worry, it's cool," I say.

"What do you mean, *Don't worry, it's cool?* Get off my bed!"

And then, next thing, I'm back out in the noise and harsh fluorescence of the living room and the girl leaves with her friend and my chance is gone.

But the following morning, even though I have a killer headache, I don't even care because I know I was at a real college party where I made out with a real college chick.

For real.

Experiments

What in water did Bloom, waterlover, drawer of water, water-carrier returning to the range, admire?

—James Joyce, *Ulysses*

There was something very queer about the water, she thought . . .

—Lewis Carroll, *Alice in Wonderland*

Anthony had no problem getting into college: he was one of the fastest sprinters in the country who also, thanks to AP and honors classes, had a 4.2 GPA. He wanted to attend Stanford, as he thought it would be the best place for him to pursue a degree in computer science or electrical engineering (which was mostly related to his love of video games). As much as he liked Berkeley and the coaches there, he planned to quit swimming after his first year, so Berkeley wasn't his top choice. But though Anthony was admitted everywhere he applied, Mike Bottom was the only one who secured him a full ride. A full scholarship at a top-tier school was, for his mother, the clincher: he was going to Berkeley. The decision may well have sealed his future as a swimmer. At another school like Stanford, where the coach wouldn't have accommodated him or supported him as much as Bottom did, Ervin would have probably, in his own words, "had a mediocre season and washed out," or, more likely, been tossed off the team.

Upon accepting Berkeley's offer, senioritis set in. Anthony's grades slipped, his GPA for the first time dropping below 4.0. After passing one of his AP tests in the spring, he ditched the class in the final weeks to play *StarCraft* in the computer lab with his friends, which led to a brief suspension. Another teacher threatened to try to revoke his college scholarship because he kept sleeping in class. His high school coach remembers receiving calls from other teachers about Anthony's lack of effort and, according to one teacher, insolence.

His senior year, Anthony had a car, as handy for skipping practice as for getting to it. Recognizing her son's propensity for evasion, Sherry would drive by the pool on her way to work to make sure his car was parked there. It always was. What she didn't know was that sometimes he'd be sprawled out in the backseat, asleep. But even slacking off, he still got best times in the 50 and 100. By the end of his senior year, he was the fastest high school freestyle sprinter in the country.

After spending the summer in a suit and tie selling sportswear at Robinsons-May to yachting types, Anthony showed up at Berkeley as out of shape as he'd ever been. It was his first extended period away from home without supervision. During Welcome Week he drank continuously, smoked marijuana for the first time, and, more momentously, lost his virginity.

⚬⚬⚬⚬⚬

I can't believe I just met A the other day and now we're lying here in my bed. *Naked* in my bed. The light from my alarm clock makes her hair shine blue. She's running her fingertips along my head, playing with my hair on the sides where it's been buzzed short. I remember at that party how she was looking at me from across the room, tapping her blue flats to the music. And then how she glanced away when I made eye contact, hiding behind her black hair. She's not glancing away now.

"Have you done this before?" she asks.

I'm about to make a dumb joke, like, *What, talked to a girl?* But she interrupts me.

"Sex, I mean."

Is she hoping I have or haven't? I can't read her. If I say no, I'll look pathetic. Everyone has had sex by now.

"Sure, I've done it."

"Oh," she says, and looks down. "I haven't."

It's too late now to tell her the truth. Now I have to keep up the lie.

She smiles, a little forced. "I still want to do it."

"That's cool," I say. "We should. It's no big deal. It'll be fun."

Fun? I actually like this girl and here I am sounding like a frat guy who just wants to get laid.

But she doesn't seem to mind. Or not enough for us *not* to do it.

A few nights later we come back to my room, but this time my roommate is there. He looks asleep. A and I get in bed and start kissing. After a while, he rolls over in his bed and adjusts his pillow.

"We can't do it here," she whispers. "He'll hear us."

"He won't. We'll be quiet."

And that's two more lies to pile onto my first one.

❖

Even if the relationship lacked elegance in its origins, it was more than a Welcome Week fling: they dated exclusively for the rest of the year. They would often stay up late, fooling around and laughing in bed, much to the chagrin of Ervin's roommate, a quiet and reserved engineering student, who would be trying to sleep a few feet away. And when A wasn't over, Anthony would be up late playing video games. He'd set three alarms for morning practice, often sleeping through all of them. "I'd steal my roommate's protein shakes too," he recalls, shaking his head. "I was the worst roommate ever." He regularly stole food from the dining court that first year. He'd order a sandwich or burrito in one part of the food court, and then stroll past the cashiers by the exit, pretending he'd already paid.

His teammates didn't think too highly of him initially. Even on the recruiting trip, he'd left the impression of being a slightly cocky kid only interested in video games. Still in the virginal wine-cooler phase of his drinking career, he bowed out of all the beery proceedings at freshmen hazing: no Century Club (a shot of beer every minute for one hundred minutes) or Beer Mile (run a lap on the track, pound a beer, repeat three times). The only event he participated in was the one where he had to wear women's underwear for the day: he borrowed a G-string from a classmate ("It's like having a wedgie all the time, I don't know how girls do it."). Even at a liberal bastion like Berkeley, the fact that he went for the thong-a-thon and opted out of the beer guzzling probably only led to more eyebrow-raising over the new kid from Valencia.

At the first team meeting he didn't show up. The coach had to send scouts to track him down. Without his mother there to drag him out of bed, he rarely made morning practice. His former teammate Richard Hall was one of the guys who, along with Anthony, was suspended at one point for not making enough practices. Most of those swimmers had around 70 percent attendance. Richard remembers Anthony's because it set a new record low: 37 percent. Despite the full athletic scholarship, he was making roughly one out of three practices. This didn't sit well with his teammates.

Four-time Polish Olympian Bartosz Kizierowski, Berkeley's upperclassman lodestar swimmer who was known for his dynamism and training intensity, remembers Ervin as "one of the laziest people I ever trained with." At a December team trip to Vegas, they were doing sprint sets from a dive, which involved standing around on deck in the cold air. Bartosz, or Bart as he's known, remembers standing poolside, shivering, waiting for Anthony: "Then he runs out of the shower all nice and cozy with red skin from a hot shower. I'm just freezing there. And we dive in, for a 50 or a 100, and I get my ass kicked. So you can imagine my frustration." Another time, during the first round of an acidosis set meant to train athletes in pain tolerance, Ervin curled up in the pool gutter, groaning, until he vomited. He lay there for a while in a fetal position before slinking off to the showers.

But Bart's initial disdain began to change when he realized that, despite often bailing on training, Anthony swam in a unique way. It was Coach Bottom who insisted that he closely watch Anthony's stroke. Soon Bart began to realize that this kid was doing something completely different. "It was all very technical and connected," Bart recalls. "Eventually we all tried to swim more like Tony."

Ervin's idiosyncrasy paradoxically was not so unexpected in the swimming world. Eccentrics are found in every sport, but swimming seems to attract, or create, them in abundance. Maybe it's a product of the medium—complex, dynamic, unpredictable—or all that chlorine seeping into one's pores, or the countless hours spent suspended in strenuous exertion, staring in virtual isolation at the pool bottom, lap after lap, like a suburban variation on Chinese water torture. Whatever the reason, swimming has an abundance of characters among both competitors and coaches, and not just among its plebeian ranks: it's wacky all the way up to the elite crème. In fact, it can even be more idiosyncratic up top since iconoclasm and outside-of-the-box thinking is often what it takes to stand out from the overwashed masses. On the other hand, the regimentation of workouts also generates a culture of intolerance in the swimming world toward those who disrupt that structure. Free spirits are tolerated, but only so long as they're disciplined and compliant free spirits.

Even traditionalist and by-the-book coaches can sound occult on deck in their use of esoteric terms like *threshold speed*, *VO$_2$ max,* *negative splitting,* and let's not forget *lactate profiles,* which to the uninitiated might sound like a pregnancy fetish or something out of *Mother, Baby & Child* magazine. Of course, there are those coaches and trainers who expand the lingo: there's USC's swim coach Dave Salo,[13] who published the book *SprintSalo: A Cerebral Approach to Training for Peak Swimming Performance,* which includes a "SaloSlang Glossary" with drills like PeekSwim, where one swims with closed eyes, taking occasional "peeks" for orientation (this comes with advice to "tell those around you what you are doing and have them watch and protect you"); there's Milton Nelms whom the Australian press dubbed the "horse whisperer of swimming," also the creator behind the "Nelmsing Code," which according to a *SwimNews* article is a "book of incantation from the holistic school of Brainswimming"; and then there's Mike Bottom.

Bottom is known as one of the world's finest sprint coaches—in the 2004 Athens Olympics, for example, two out of the three 50 free medalists were swimmers he'd coached—with an uncanny motivational ability to enter the minds of his athletes and inspire them to believe they can do things they didn't dare consider before. One way he does this is by first articulating their fears. For example, after a narrow relay defeat at the 2012 NCAA Championships, he reviewed the race with his swimmers: "What happens in the last lap or in the third turn when the field is right there and the splash is big and there's maybe one guy that's way ahead, is you get fear in your heart. You get fear in your heart . . . " And while saying this he's leaning in and stabbing at his own heart with his fingertips, and you can tell by the way the guys are gnawing at their fingernails and staring off with haunted looks that it's sinking in, that he's found a way into their private emotional space, that they're listening. It's not that these athletes have never before heard a you-can-do-great-things voice urging them from within: it's just that, as with most people, that inner voice gets sidelined due to fear or insecurity or laziness or sheer dis-

---

13 Not to be confused with the linguist and "Tolkien language scholar" Dave Salo, who can be found on YouTube reciting the Ring Verse in his Elvish-language Quenya translation.

traction. Bottom excels at getting athletes to find that voice again. Swim journalists call him a "mind guru" and "ultimate mind coach," and no doubt his master's degree in counseling helps with that. But it's more than education. There's something about his manner of speaking—his deep, measured voice, his way of finishing sentences with "right?" as if gently luring you into affirmation, his pensive pauses, his penetrating gaze through thick black-rimmed glasses that seems to be figuring out something about you at the same time that he's telling you something—something that gives a charge to his words, as if they're more than just accurate, they're somehow *essential*. You get the sense that, had his life taken a different turn, he could have easily been a hypnotist—not the stage entertainer sort, but one who uses hypnosis for a therapeutic and transformational reprogramming of the mind.

It didn't take long for Bottom to see that if he pushed Ervin too hard, he'd lose him. Anthony required persuasion: "It was just a matter of talking to him every day, seeing where he was, giving him reasons to be there." Mike Bottom understood the fickle intricacies of Ervin's character and knew that if too many demands were made of him, he'd drop out. So he adapted, appealing instead to Ervin's desire to learn: if Anthony arrived too late to workout, as he often did, Bottom would usher him into his office to watch race videos of swimming greats instead of sending him off in anger.

Before Berkeley, Ervin's swim training had been fairly conventional: the usual back-and-forth slog focusing on yards and intervals that is the de facto foundation of precollegiate competitive swimmers. But with Bottom he was discussing technique, breaking down and analyzing his stroke, and exploring ways of "connecting" with and "catching" the water, [14] concepts Anthony had never even considered or heard of before. It was all new and stimulating and kept him engaged. It allowed him to apply his understanding of calculus to swim-

---

14 "Catch" is the moment when the hand enters the water and applies pressure. It's basically the grip you get on the water. To nonswimmers it may sound esoteric, as it was for swimmers back in the nineties, but it's now as universal and frequently invoked as "kick" or "pull."

ming, analyzing it as a problem set with lines and coordinates, limits and changing variables. Before, swimming was about yards, effort, and times. But now it was research, study, and exploration.

$$F = ma \rightarrow a = F/m$$

so less mass means more acceleration

* increase strength not mass

- diet
- weightroom

draft
off backfll

shave palms?
pros: sensitivity
cons: too smooth
lose grip

Buoyancy   Gravity   Friction
* to reduce F
get over the water
stay narrow
think about lines/vortices

TURBULENCE

resistance

speed

* * *

Even missing as many practices as he did, Ervin was learning more about swimming than ever before. When he did make practice, he was methodical, experimenting with different ways of catching water, reducing turbulence, increasing efficiency. Bottom remembers one of Ervin's eureka moments, when he abruptly stopped during a set to tell him he'd found a new way of connecting with the water. "I don't want to call it joy," Bottom recalls, "but it was excitement. Like a hunter that just shot the deer."

Berkeley was ideal for Ervin: competitive but fun, a place where you could miss practices and screw up on occasion so long

as you kept the course. Only when it came to taking supplements did Berkeley run a tight ship. Most people assume that
cheating in athletics is a clear-cut act (the Hollywood trope of a
baggy-eyed trainer grimly injecting steroids into his athlete behind closed doors comes to mind), but often athletes get busted
simply from taking rogue supplements that claim to be legit but
aren't. To prevent that, Bottom obtained all supplements from a
single, trusted supplier. But when it came to training approaches,
Bottom experimented with the gamut of them, no matter how
outlandish.

"Mike used to come up with so much weird stuff," Bart Kizierowski recalls. "I remember walking on the bottom of the pool [car-
rying] twenty-kilo iron blocks. Just walking fifty meters, no-breath
work." And it got weirder. One of the volunteer coaches, Karl Mohr,
had been researching alternative wellness and recovery practices and
would forward the articles to the head coaches. Bottom's philosophy
was, "As long as it's legal and can't hurt you, we may as well try it."
Co—head coach Nort Thornton, Cal Swimming's venerated veteran
and technical wizard, was also open to it. Few established coaches
would have been.

So Mohr started bringing stuff in, stuff you'd expect to find at a
Berkeley Holism conference but not on deck at a top college sports
team. Stuff like liquid oxygen drops and colloidal silver water and
altered "clustered water." Stuff like a conductive electric glass orb in
front of which the swimmers would sit for five minutes on an insu-
lated chair with their feet on a grounded pad and palms on the orb
as its electric tendrils danced about, in effect charging themselves
with electric currents to stimulate recovery. They once set it up at
one of the meets, which must have been quite a sight for the opposing team. Another time they had twelve guys hold hands, with the
last guy standing on a grounded pad, while the first one dipped his
finger into a canister of electrically charged water, causing a jolting
electrical current to course through all twelve of them—sort of like

a more intricate and communal version of the farmhand stunt of pissing on an electric fence. But probably the most Out There thing they did, albeit the simplest, was writing positive words on their water bottles—words like *Love, Team, Attraction*—based on the premise that water organizes itself around feelings. It's easy to shake your head and snort at that sort of thing and you wouldn't be the first. In his Restoration comedy *The Virtuoso*, the seventeenth-century writer Thomas Shadwell satirized the sports science of his day in describing a young man's effort to learn the breaststroke: *He has a frog in a bowl of water, tied with a packthread by the loins, which packthread Sir Nicholas holds in his teeth, lying upon his belly on a table; as the frog strikes, he strikes, and his swimming master stands by to tell him whether he does well or ill.* But even something as spectacularly eccentric as writing positive words on water bottles reflects the spirit of unabashed exploration and tolerance that pervaded the team, the conviction that one should try things, no matter how bizarre or kooky, because it's the only way to find out what sticks.

It was in this experimental culture that Ervin found himself that first year. It was also the first year that was truly his own. Untethered, no longer under his mother's panopticon, he was alone and ungoverned, free to do what he wanted, as he wanted.

So he experimented.

HYPOTHESIS 1.0

Situating a digital alarm clock at least two meters from subject's bed will, upon initiation of electronic sound, compel the newly and begrudgingly awakened subject to move from a sheltered recumbent state to an exposed ambulatory bipedal one in order to disable, either indefinitely or for an eight-minute increment, the plangent object of his discontent, thereby enabling him to realize his goal of standing poolside, seminaked in the crisp dawn air, ready for wet vigorous activity, at 0600 hours.

CONCLUSION

Negative. Subject awakens, confused, at four minutes before 1200 hours.

HYPOTHESIS 1.1

Identical to previous experiment except for a changed variable. The rectangular digital alarm clock is replaced by a round manual wind-up alarm clock, advertised in stores as "retro" to increase profit margin, with an inverted brass-colored hemispheric bell on both the left and right side of its apex, designed and duplicated for maximum acoustic resonance and reverberation, all of which when viewed from a haze of somnolent languor sometimes takes on the visage of the anthropomorphic rodent mascot of the Walt Disney Company.

CONCLUSION

Again, negative. Subject's eyes don't open until 1121 hours. They close at 1122 hours, then open again at 1123 hours. At 1152 hours subject sits up. At 1153 hours subject's roommate asks if subject could abstain from using wind-up alarm bells in the future, his request both preceded and followed by the word *please*, its second iteration articulated with greater emphasis. Subject responds by pressing the distal phalanxes of his right hand's thumb and forefinger against his temples and emitting a groan.

HYPOTHESIS 2.0

Inviting subject's teammates to watch favorite movie, *Army of Darkness*, may prove beneficial for building consensual nonsexual relationships, thereby having the effect for the subject of relieving, in ascending order of magnitude of distress induced, his sense of disconnectedness, loneliness, friendlessness, purposelessness, and for the teammates of mitigating, again in ascending potency as reflecting the subject's anxieties, their sense of misgiving, annoyance, resentment, rejection.

CONCLUSION

Find new favorite movie.

HYPOTHESIS 3.0

Since a dropped elbow results in an ineffective pull, swimming with a locked elbow and straight arm prevents dropping of the elbow.

CONCLUSION

Affirmative but inadvisable. Subject mashes the water, dispersing it instead of holding it. Furthermore, the potential for shoulder injury is high. Appreciating that deltoid mass and density may be the limiting factor, further assessment and analysis on bulkier, hulkier swimmers is recommended.

HYPOTHESIS 3.1

If a collapsed elbow pull is the problem, the focus should not be on the pull but on the entry and catch. By arriving at the pull in a different way, the problem is preempted.

CONCLUSION
Affirmative.

HYPOTHESIS 4.0
Smoking cannabis confers beneficial attributes for aquatic training and proprioceptive feel for water. (The subject's motive for undertaking this experiment stems from an unsubstantiated and potentially defamatory rumor that celebrated, decorated, and chlorinated former University of California, Berkeley natator Matthew Nicholas Biondi occasionally refined his freestyle technique after inhaling cannabinoid because he found that it heightened sensation, perception, and technical proficiency.)

CONCLUSION
Negative for training; inconclusive for feel. While subject reported a sense of being "more tuned into his body," he resisted all physical action with two exceptions: first, blowing concentric bubble rings from the pool bottom, which he performed by pinching his nostrils from a supine position and expelling brief bursts of air upward; and second, roiling the water with air by pushing and pulling his open palms through the water, and then floating facedown and immobile in spread-eagle position over the cavitation zone as the myriad tiny, newly generated air bubbles rose up and expired upon his torso and appendages in a reportedly pleasurable sensation of kismesis. The tetrahydrocannabinol isomer appeared to cause a significant debilitation and enervation of the subject's will, as he found himself stationary on the wall for long periods of time, too distracted and, to use his col-

loquialism, "stoned" to undertake the rigors of a training regime. He did, however, report enjoyment.

PROPOSED EXPERIMENT

In the days prior to a big taper meet, the subject weans himself off clonidine, a Tourette's medication.

ANTICIPATED OUTCOMES

1. Tourette's symptoms will increase and nervous system will go into overdrive, thereby aiding his race performance.
2. Tourette's symptoms will increase and nervous system will go into overdrive, thereby hindering his race performance.

Experiment postponed for National Collegiate Championships in March of 2000.

The experimentation kept Ervin interested in swimming, but he was falling behind in school. His days of 4.0+ GPAs were over. Toward the end of the semester, his friend asked to see the syllabus for one of his classes. "Syllabus," he said, "what's that?" He didn't buy the course books until two weeks before the final. He failed a class his second semester, though he was able to stay afloat thanks to his Get Out of Jail Free AP credits from high school. The only A he got, also during his second semester, was in the biology class "Brain, Mind, and Behavior."

The intersection between mind and substance became Ervin's main interest that first year. His experience with marijuana during Welcome Week left him feeling like everything he'd been told about recreational drugs was a lie, or at best a naïve and incomplete demonization that lumped all substances—from anodyne cannabis to ruinous meth—under the umbrella of "bad drugs." It was like pulling the curtain on Oz. He wanted to learn more from a reliable source. How were these various substances different? How did they interact with the brain? What were the consequences? Risks? He became a dedicated reader of Erowid, an online library that offers expansive and comprehensive information about legal and illegal psychoactive plants and substances, as well as about techniques for inducing altered states of consciousness like meditation, fasting, prayer, deep breathing, and lucid dreaming. By his estimation, for every hour he spent studying for class, he spent three hours reading up on the Erowid website about ayahuasca, peyote, DMT, LSD, salvia, psilocybin, and so on. It wasn't the party drugs that interested him, nor the uppers or downers, nor the street junk, but rather the hallucinogens, which offered a portal to a new dimension of experience, or as he put it, another way of "trying to get to Xanth." At the time, however, he was purely a researcher, not a "psychonaut." It was consistent with his desire to understand, to be conscious and self-aware about his behavior and actions, in the same way he sought in the pool to understand the subtle details of his body's interaction with the water.

Dealing with Tourette's had given Ervin a foundation in trying to understand the mind and its biochemistry, so exploring the interplay between drugs and mind was a natural next step for him. After years of being at the mercy of his Tourette's, he found something empowering in the knowledge that the mind could be shaped, altered, and molded. He never ingested anything without researching it extensively beforehand and understanding the risks and adverse effects. Though the plants and substances were consciousness-altering, not performance-enhancing, he was intrigued over any insights they might offer regarding his feel for the water.

During this experimental period Ervin came to a conviction,

mostly based on Erowid readings and occasional experiences with marijuana, that consciousness and even "reality" were far more malleable and unstable than he'd assumed. The world wasn't what he thought it was. As a child he'd sought escape from reality through fantasy books; and there had always been an unambiguous delineation between reality and fantasy. But now that line was blurring.*

* See Appendix A

6

Over the Water

When I meet God, I am going to ask him two questions: Why relativity? And why turbulence? I really believe he will have an answer for the first.

—German physicist Werner Heisenberg on his deathbed

I seen the best of men go past
I don't want to be the last
Gimme something fast

—The Sisters of Mercy, "Something Fast"

At the turn of the year, a few months before national championships, Ervin began to lay off the partying to focus on training. Winter training camp had brought him closer to his teammates, and for the first time he felt he was part of a team. On nights before morning practice he no longer drank. He spent hours working on his weak areas, mostly his start. (According to Bottom, he had the worst start in the country at the time.) The discipline paid off, and he delivered faster and faster times in the duel meet season.

A few days before NCAAs, Ervin starting reducing his Tourette's medication. It was his final experiment of the swim season. One of his opponents in the 50 and 100 was Nick Folker, who would become his strength coach at Cal eleven years later. At the time Ervin weighed 160 pounds. "I remember looking at this guy and thinking, *Pfff, done*," Folker recalls. "And then next thing I was like, *What just happened?*"

What happened was that the eighteen-year-old Anthony Ervin won both the 50- and the 100-meter freestyle. What also happened is that in the same 50-meter freestyle short course final, with a time of 21.21, he broke the world record.

And what finally happened is that others started asking a question: *What makes this skinny Berkeley kid swim so damn fast?*

<hr />

The monkeys in the zoo mesmerize me. They're so graceful and easy, chattering as they swing from branch to branch. Though thirty feet up, they have no concern as they leap from tree to tree, only playfulness. They don't even look at the branches and vines that they reach for. They're not operating on a conscious level. But their hands know where to go, they know when to grasp. Every movement is flawless, in perfect synch and connection with their environment. Their bodies just know. All this nerve-wracking acrobatic dexterity is to them as natural and automatic as breathing or walking is for me.

Their coordination and finesse on land awes me because I lack it. Give me a basic and simple land-based athletic task to complete and I'll fail, especially if it involves distance. Hand me a crumpled sheet of paper, and I'll miss the trash can. Give me a soccer ball and it will fly wide of the net; a basketball, and it will clank off the rim or miss it completely. But in the pool, I have a direct and continuous connection with the water. I need that feeling. There's a sense of weightlessness. Maybe that's what it's like in the vacuum of space. Nothing to see or smell or taste. Only feel. It's in that disassociative but connected state that I'm able to manipulate the forces around me to move in a way I can never do on land. It's completely alien to being on two feet.

A few minutes later I'm watching the otters. Some are floating on their backs, others are gliding and twisting below the surface, barely disturbing the water as they slice through it. One of them climbs out on a rocky ledge. As it emerges and the water pours off its sleek body, all of its silky finesse vanishes. It lumbers awkwardly along the shore. Then it slips back into the water and, with a slight but swift undulation of its body, hurtles off.

⊷⊶

The first time I ever saw Ervin sprint was in 2009 at a lower-Manhattan pool where we both taught swimming. Before that I'd never seen Ervin do anything in the water but float around during his lessons. He never arrived early or stayed late to swim, as some of us did. One day before lessons, after I'd gone for a short swim, he asked me how many yards I'd swum. When I told him a thousand (forty lengths in a twenty-five-yard pool, which is warm-up for a competitive swimmer) he simply shook his head and muttered that he could never do that. So when another instructor one day challenged him to race after lessons, I just assumed he would say no. I was wrong. Competitors may abandon competition but competitiveness rarely abandons them.

I was at the far end of the pool, in the next lane over from Ervin. At the start command his opponent made the mistake of dropping underwater to push off instead of exploding immediately off the wall. It cost him: it was over from the start. Little did I know then that seeing Ervin win right off the start was its own rare sighting, like encountering a snow leopard in the wild or witnessing the Northern Lights from the Lower 48. After the race, Ervin gave Richard hell over his start, which was probably as much his way of downplaying the win as it was banter. But even without the advantage off the wall, it wouldn't have mattered. It wasn't even close. And his opponent, Richard Hall, was no pushover. Richard was Ervin's teammate at Berkeley, not to mention the brother of ten-time Olympic medalist Gary Hall Jr., so he had plenty of genetic mojo going for him too.

It was strange to reconcile the unhurried, cerebral Ervin I knew with the swift aquatic creature slicing toward me. But it wasn't even his speed that astonished me so much as the way in which he traveled through the water—although "through" isn't even exactly right. There was something in his swimming I'd never seen before: he seemed to swim not through the water but *over* it. His head reared up from the surface like a speedboat's prow does when the throttle is revved or like a movie rendition of an attacking great white; his arms, meanwhile, drove down rhythmically on each side in a long, loping rhythm. He also seemed *big*, far larger in water than on land, as if the water upon push-off had an *Alice in Wonderland*-esque DRINK ME effect on him, except in enlargement rather than shrinkage. As he approached the wall (the whole thing took under ten seconds) the damnedest thing happened. Since I was in the neighboring lane, I had a head-on view from the water. As he neared me, it seemed—probably due to his elevated body position, high elbows and towering arms, as well as to my water-level perspective—like he was swimming *downward*. It was as if his body had generated a wave in the pool and he was now hydroplaning down the face of it. His movement was smooth and powerful, like one of those waves surfers dream of that barrel up out of a glassy sea.

Some athletes have—or, if you fall more on the environment side of the nature vs. nurture spectrum, *seem* to have—an innate preternatural disposition for their sport that distinguishes them from the rest of the playing field. They look and move differently from other athletes, as if they've figured out a way to slow down time (Muhammad Ali, footwork) or abrogate laws of nature (Jackie Joyner-Kersee and Michael Jordan, gravity). There's also frequently a litheness, even laziness, about their movements: Lionel Messi seemed to spend more time ambling than running through the 2014 World Cup and Jordan's tongue would hang out before his most explosive drives. It's what we mean when we say someone "makes it look effortless," except it's an order of magnitude even beyond the effortless-looking athletes. To the rest of us all-too-human mortals, especially those who appreciate kinetic beauty and excellence, such an otherworldly combination of power and grace (Tiger on the green, Federer on the court) can seem downright deific. It invokes the same kind of ineffable awe that leads to the canonization of humans into saints in religious communities.[15]

Like golf or the luge, competitive swimming is such a foreign activity to most people that it's difficult for them to distinguish good technique from great. (Usually what draws the most *oohs* and *aahs* is merely a proficient display of butterfly: it never fails to impress, even if you suck at it.) But even when Ervin is racing the world's most talented sprinters, with the entire field only a few tenths apart, a nonswimmer with a discriminatory eye will right away see something different about how he swims. Every coach and trainer I've talked to about Ervin has referred to the exceptionality of his stroke:

Mike Bottom (University of Michigan head swim coach/former UCal, Berkeley co–head coach): "The fastest insect in the world is a beetle that runs at an incredible speed because it's got a muscle that stretches as it throws its leg out and then snaps back, causing the leg to spring back quickly. It's the stretch reflex. Anthony has it too

15 If all of this sounds like hyperbole, see David Foster Wallace's 2006 *New York Times* feature "Federer As Religious Experience."

on both arms. His shoulders rotate a lot, which allows the stretch reflex to work. He hits the water with kind of a flat hand and then his shoulder continues to travel downward while his hand stays high and then it pops into place. He also stays narrow and has a long skinny body, like long skis going down a slope. His high kick in the back acts as a barrier, causing the backfill [water] to come in behind his body quickly and shoot him forward. So he's drafting off himself. There's nobody like him in swimming."

Nick Folker (strength trainer and cofounder of BridgeAthletic): "He has an understanding even of what his pinky is doing. What happens underwater from his catch to where his hand exits is phenomenal. There's not as much drag created. He swims like a knife through butter. When it comes to swimming stroke, he's an artist, not a swimmer."

Dave Durden (Cal, Berkeley head swim coach): "He floats and positions himself really well in the water. Not many swimmers value that skill. He stays narrow. It's very classic, just swimming through a narrow hallway. It looks so clean and pure at speed. And he gets depth in his pull. He gets so deep so quick that he's grabbing a ton of water and then can release that quickly and get to the front again. People get caught up in numbers and rates but it's how he grabs water and releases it, then grabs again and releases it. That's his absolute strength. Grab, pull, release. Get back to that position again. Grab, pull, release."

Russell Mark (USA Swimming National Team sports performance consultant): "When he's moving through the water, he's rolling through it. It's a beautiful thing to watch. Just an awesome picture in motion of everything connected and moving in unison."

David Marsh (SwimMAC Carolina head coach): "He's probably the most skilled technical swimmer in the race. His stroke is so fine-tuned. I remember recruiting in high school and he was a gorgeous swimmer back then. He had this ability to cut the water like a barracuda. He's maintained that and added strength. And a lot of life lessons [*laughter*]. He has an aquatic skill. If you watch him walk it's like he wasn't meant for the land. He reminds me a lot of Ryan [Lochte]. They're both much more skilled in water than on land."

Milton Nelms (stroke analyst and training consultant): "An extraordinary thing about Anthony is that when he gets into the water to train, everything sort of shifts into a different gear, as if he's shifting from a land animal into a water animal. It's like he's absorbing everything about the water and recalibrating and reorganizing his nervous system. It's an exquisite thing. I used to crack up watching him train because he was like a seal. You could tell he would randomly make up a movement because he wanted to experiment. People like Anthony and Natalie [Coughlin] have a very unusual ability to interact with the water, even among talented people. He's an outlier among outliers."

Teri McKeever (2012 US Olympic Women's Swim Team head coach): "He looks one with the water. The way the water moves around his body is different. There's an effortless relationship with it. Natalie [Coughlin] has that same look. I equate it to when you see a ballerina or a beautiful diver."

It's not uncommon for others to draw comparisons in Ervin's feel for the water with Natalie Coughlin, the legendary twelve-time Olympic medalist who also trains at Cal, also suffered a derailing physical injury, and who also often stands smallest on the blocks. In Cynthia Gorney's 2004 *New Yorker* piece called "A Feel for the Water," she describes how coaches would invoke "dolphins, cheetahs, gummy worms, screwdrivers, knives, javelins, bows, and the hockey player Gordie Howe" to describe Coughlin's remarkable stroke.

That's why, of all the people I spoke to about Ervin's swimming, the person whose comments most stood out for me wasn't a coach or trainer but Natalie Coughlin herself, his fellow Cal training partner who has been practicing with the men's team since early 2013: "He is the most talented swimmer I've ever seen. If any of us missed as many workouts as he misses, we wouldn't even make Nationals. He knows what he needs, and doesn't need a lot of traditional training. He just has amazing feel for the water. He doesn't power through; he has finesse. It's like he skims the water. If I did what he just did I would be overweight [*laughter*]."

In Coughlin's biography, *Golden Girl*, one coach describes the limber 5'8" swimmer as "flat-out genius" in terms of her physical intelligence. And that's no minority opinion. Yet there was Coughlin, not only matter-of-factly praising Ervin for exactly what *she* is known for, but also saying she would have been on the sidelines had she been in his position. It's like having Mozart tell you he lacks the musical ear of another composer and therefore has to compensate through hard work.

<hr>

Distance freestylers use a hip-driven stroke, arms gliding long in front and legs acting like an engine in the rear. You can swim far like that. But a shoulder-driven stroke is better suited in the 50, the shoulders driving down and the legs almost rising up behind you. I still use my legs for propulsion but additionally employ them as a leveraging tool to rotate my body. Instead of just trying to move the water as fast as I can, I try to anchor it with my leg to slip around and over it. That way, I don't need to generate and expend as much power to get into my catch.

The center for all of my strength is an X axis that crisscrosses my core, from opposite shoulders to opposite hips. A line of tension runs through me from my fingertip to my opposite toe. The hardest part in training is to maintain the flexibility and strength through that X axis, through the core from the shoulder to the opposite hip. If I don't have that deep interconnection and unity, gears start flying and my swim breaks down. In sprinting, the entirety of the body needs to be solid and connected, from fingertip to toe. It's almost like reverting to the state before you learn how to swim, when you're tense in the water. In learning to swim you must relax, let your limbs and ankles be loose and limber so your feet can whip like fins. But when you're sprinting you almost want to regress to the habits you eliminated in learning to swim—to return to stiffness and tension. But not a disconnected stiffness with bent legs and bent arms; you want the tension running through straight limbs, where everything is integrated and working in unison.

In the kick, there's a sense of eliminating your knees. You want to keep your legs stiff so that you're hooking and grabbing the water rather than kicking from the knees down. Same with the upper body and elbows. Aside from the breakout, you want to eliminate the elbows as you pull the water, so that the power flows through you without disruption, like a turbine or an avalanche. It's all about maintaining stability and rhythm as your upper body rotates through the water.

Everything that happens takes place within a larger context. That's why it's so difficult to describe any part of the stroke in isolation. Take the catch, the moment the hand first grabs the water. The momentum and flow of your body is what allows the catch to happen when you're not bending your elbow. It's almost like throwing a weight and also throwing your own body along with it.

To throw your weight, however, you need the right pitch—the angle of your body. If I'm trying to follow my weight through, then I need my legs to be slightly above me so I can follow downward. Even though it's not literal, I want to feel like I'm swimming downhill throughout the race. That's the body position where my sweet spot is, where velocity is maximum. I always know I'm fatiguing because I feel my pitch change, shifting from the downward angle of an airplane about to land to one in takeoff.

There's technical complexity in sprinting, at least for me—the hip flip, the switch kick, the catch, the roll, the recovery—and it's all happening together. It's one motion. If the timing on any of those parts slips, there's an immediate loss of velocity. If I fight to get it back, it only corrupts my rhythm even more. Then I lose momentum and pitch and I'm really struggling and not going fast. It's all about how much you can set up that initial velocity and then ride out that force. Fortunately, it's just one lap.

⁕

Athletes in team sports must contend with changing variables. A quarterback faces any number of unfolding scenarios after the football is snapped to him. In seconds he must read a moving field, calculate, and react accordingly. Even individual sports involve variability: a Brazilian jujitsu fighter responds to his opponent's moves with an intricate series of offensive and defensive measures much like playing chess with one's body; a pro tennis player must return a served ball traveling up to 130 mph and then assess changing factors throughout the rally like spin, placement, trajectory, speed, wind, etc. In higher level competitions, the mental computations and muscular responses are automatic and subconscious. Elite athletes don't necessarily have better reaction times than the rest of us (we're all pretty much in the one-fifth-of-a-second vicinity due to physiological constraints imposed by our neuron gaps and by all the instant messaging required between the retina, visual cortex, spinal cord, and muscles); in that sense we all share the same hardware. The difference lies in the software. Elite athletes can *perceive* better than the rest of us: the tennis player, for example, reads subtle signals in the serving player's hip rotation and in the angle and position of the unfurling arm to predict where the ball will go; this allows her to clairvoyantly begin her return of serve even before the opponent's racket hits the ball, essential since a served ball can take less than half a second to travel from one racket to the other.

Indoor competitive swimming differs in its lack of external variability. Sure, some pools may be slightly "faster" than others because they're deeper or have wider lanes with better turbulence-absorbing lane lines and gutters and so on. But for the most part, a pool is a pool is a pool. A swimmer's result depends not so much on how she responds to the changing variables of the environment or opponents but on how well she performs within the private and isolated domain of her lane. This is even more the case in a 50-meter sprint, where the swimmers are traversing an undisturbed body of water (although if you're Ervin and find yourself too far behind on the start, the turbulence and white water generated by the Goliaths to your left and right can have an invasive effect upon your water). In this sense, a sprint is less a skilled dance with the environment than a solo stage performance.

The primacy of the performance is even more acute when it comes to Ervin. If you're ever around him after one of his races, you may hear him talking about how well he executed his swim and what mistakes he made or didn't make. It's the kind of language a classical pianist might use after bowing off stage. His finest swims require the same combination of technical dexterity and connected feeling that's required for a virtuoso to perform a speedy and technical piano composition with finesse and sensitivity.

Although Ervin may not require the same preemptive perceptual facility of a quarterback or tennis player, the immersive and encompassing nature of water brings other sensory, noncognitive demands. There is, first of all, the unpredictable nature of turbulence, the chaotic and irregular movements inherent to moving liquid that envelop all swimmers. So complex is the phenomenon of turbulent flow that the theoretical physicist Richard Feynman once called turbulence "the most important unsolved problem of classical physics."

Milton Nelms, whom swim stars like Ian Thorpe and Dana Vollmer have credited for helping them with swimming breakthroughs, described to me how prevailing training methods are inappropriate because they don't factor in the unique complexity of water: "The water is the most sensory-dense environment there is. You're immersed in this element that's feeding a massive tonnage of information into your nervous system. And yet all of our references [in training] are from out of the water." In the sport of swimming, where everything is measured out to the millimeter and millisecond, Nelms feels not enough attention is paid to the rhythms of the water, its surges and accelerations, the tiny lags and delays intrinsic to moving liquid: "I think at a gross level everybody is capable of acquiring the ability to interact with that different timing. With Anthony it goes to a much deeper and vibratory level, just a deep brain and nervous system thing. It's certainly a subliminal process, so he himself may not be aware of what is happening."

That's not to say Ervin would dominate as an open-water sprinter, if there even were such a thing. In choppy or even sloppy water he loses one of his advantages—the ability to move sleekly with minimal disturbance of the surrounding water. His clean stroke may also explain why he doesn't hold the upper hand over his rivals in the streamlined underwater dolphin kick, where there's inherently less resistance and fewer opportunities to overcome turbulence. His former strength and conditioning coach Nick Folker elaborated on the efficiency of his pull with a helpful visual that would make a fun but messy science experiment: "If you look at high-def film, when a swimmer's hand goes in, you get all these bubbles. There's not a lot of that with Tony. He's efficient and that's why the water isn't moving around him, or at least is moving in a leaner, sharper line. He has maximum hold from front to end of his stroke. If you put a dye in that water, the dye wouldn't go far. Others would disperse it far because they're not very efficient."

As a former top ten world-class swimmer who once raced Ervin, Folker brings a nuanced aquatic sensibility to the weight room. Before Folker, the dryland standard was that swimmers underwent the same weight regimens as football players, even though the two sports have as much in common as beefcake and celery. Folker not only helped overthrow that practice but also went further by setting a new dryland precedent: instead of promoting a one-size-fits-all workout, he began crafting personalized strength training programs based on each swimmer's needs, body type, stroke, event, and even personality.

Some of the Cal swimmers bench 160-pound barbells in each hand—close to double what Ervin puts up—but Folker puts little import on the power discrepancy. "That's like a Mustang, a muscle car, compared to a Ferrari, finesse," he tells me. "Tony is finesse. He's so connected from his fingertip to his feet. His understanding of what's going on in the water is an art form."

Though Ervin is a physical outlier from the other sprinters in that he lacks the beastly I-must-break-you proportions of Ivan Drago in *Rocky IV*, his body is nonetheless uniquely built for top-end speed. He has long dangling arms for maximum reach and depth, as well as narrow hips, legs, and ankles, over which the water can easily shoot by, making him, in one trainer's words, "like PVC piping going through the pool." One place where Ervin breaks from the traditional ideal swimmer's body type is his long legs, [16] which biomechanics suggest are better suited for running than swimming. Much ado was made during the 2008 Olympics over Michael Phelps's perfect Vitruvian Swimmer body, which unlike Da Vinci's evenly proportioned man, consists of an unnaturally long torso and comparatively short legs. As David Epstein notes in *The Sports Gene*, the long trunk is advantageous for horizontal speed through water because the torso serves like the hull of a canoe: a longer hull means more surface contact and more speed. Despite a 7" height difference, the 6'4" Phelps wears the same pants as the 5'9" world record–holding mile runner Hicham El Guerrouj, whose leg-to-torso ratio may well correspond to Jack Skellington from *The Nightmare Before Christmas*. Phelps and El Guerrouj could highlight the discrepancy by doing a press

---

16 Another place is his size-eleven foot—modest by the flipper-sized standards of most elite swimmers—although he does have a slight pigeon-toed gait that's characteristic of freestylers (in contrast to duck-footed breaststrokers, whose frog-kicking feet turn out).

event where they briefly exchanged and changed into each other's jeans and T-shirts. From the hips down nothing would be out of the ordinary. But above the jeans, El Guerrouj would be in a nightgown and Phelps in a tube top.

In his essay "How Tracy Austin Broke My Heart," David Foster Wallace confessed to a weakness for reading memoirs of champion athletes even though he was repeatedly disappointed by the writing due to its dull PR-speak falseness and absence of insight and genuine feeling. He concluded that "the real secret behind top athletes' genius . . . may be as esoteric and obvious and dull and profound as silence itself." In other words, it's precisely the inability of top athletes to articulate their genius, their lack of debilitating self-reflection, that makes them excel.[17] No doubt, heady self-consciousness can lead to paralysis, breakdown, and failure in competition. When you apply the cumbersome process of mental deliberation to movement and physical action, you override the deep, automated muscle-memory that athletes tap into when they're in the zone. When athletes speak humbly of some great performance, or claim God was working through them, it's not necessarily false modesty (or false religiosity): it's just that they were operating instinctually from their primitive deep-brain so they don't feel they deserve any credit for it. The better your performance, the less you remember. Indeed, Ervin remembers nothing of his gold medal Olympic swim except touching the wall.

But though it's best to power down the prefrontal cortex during races, analytical intellect plays a crucial role for Ervin in training and in prepping for competition. At Cal he applied the knowledge from his physics and biomechanics courses to his swimming. He analyzed videos from the sprint free events in the previous three Olympics to discover just what made the greatest swimmers fast: the catch of Gary Hall Jr.; the torque and extension of Alexander

---

17 DFW was a former amateur tennis player and you can't help but suspect there was something unconsciously self-serving about his argument. If the greats don't choke under all that pressure because of a vapid mind, it follows that a fertile churning mind (like DFW's) is a biological setback that a priori bars him from breaking into the top ranks.

Popov; the confident ease of Matt Biondi. Then he assimilated those pieces, adapting them to his stroke and feel, tweaking them based on scientific principles he'd studied, making them his own.

Almost every discussion about Ervin's swim technique involves the word *talent*, often in exceptionalist terms (i.e., Folker: "He's the most talented athlete I've ever worked with."). But is talent, vague as that word may be, enough to account for his speed? In an article on Phelps, "The Myth of Michael's Talent," the writer Casey Barrett argues that though Phelps's talent and genetic gift (size fourteen feet, an arm span more orangutan than human) are essential to his success, they aren't principal. Instead he makes the case for his hard work and the primacy of his swimming foundation, the endless hours Phelps spent chlorinated in his youth. "The playing field," he writes, "may be much more level than you think."

A slew of books like Malcolm Gladwell's *Outliers,* Matthew Syed's *Bounce,* and Geoff Colvin's *Talent Is Overrated* have delved deeper into this line of thought, pressing for the importance of "deliberate training" and privileging sociological conditions and even random geographical factors over innate genetic advantages. They all seem motivated by an egalitarian impulse that balks at the romanticized nineteenth-century idea of natural genius, which seems reasonable enough, except you often get the feeling that there's an underlying ideological campaign against the G-word (genetics, not genocide), as if any discussion of the role of genes and natural advantage implies support for eugenics or Aryan supremacy.

With Ervin it seems difficult, if not downright ridiculous, to dismiss the genetic and talent factor. Though he started swimming year-round from the age of seven, thousands of swimmers in the US alone can claim the same, as well as a stronger work ethic and commitment to the sport. Endowed with a high-percentage of fast-twitch muscle fibers,[18] a unique nervous system particularly recep-

---

18 Though Ervin has never been tested for fast-twitch fiber percentages, it can be induced that he has a high percentage because all world-class sprinters do. Unfortunately for slow-twitch people who aspire to an Olympic sprint pedestal, slow-twitch muscle fibers won't convert to high-twitch

tive to an aquatic environment, and a PVC-pipe-shaped lower half, there's no question Ervin has "talent." But it seems to be an unconventional aptitude: as much abstract as physical, as much about cognizance as instinct, a merging and integration of the intellectual with the visceral. He may not have put in as many hours or yards as other swimmers, but the focus and analysis he brings to his training is its own kind of discipline and work spirit. Had David Foster Wallace lived to know Anthony Ervin, he might have reconsidered his conclusion that the greatest athletes by necessity have empty, uncomplicated minds. Ervin's speed may well lie in his ability and desire to harness his analytical temperament to his exceptional proprioceptive sense and aquatic sensitivity. The thinking, feeling swimmer. *Cogito ergo s(w)um.*

❖

Many athletes are awesome trainers. They work out like demons but then at meets they replicate what they do in practice. They get locked into racing the same way they trained when their bodies were atrophied and broken down—swimming mechanically instead of by feeling. It's almost an active, athletic rigor mortis. Everybody will be in good shape at the big meets; it comes down to how much you understand about what you're doing and how much you don't.

For me, swimming is thinking about the lines. Proprioception. Feeling where the resistance is and trying to place it in the right direction. I don't think about my hands when I pull. Just my body position, just keeping my thought directed in my line of travel. To focus on the pull is to place my awareness elsewhere than the line I want to travel in. Of course, I'm not a thin line; I'm a mass that rotates around that line. But the farther I pull away from that

---

through training or electrical stimulus (unless you're a mouse). They'll always contract at the same speed. The one exception is when the spinal cord severs: then all muscle fibers become fast-twitch. So there's always hope, I guess.

line, the more energy is expelled outward rather than in the line I want to travel in. It's like riding a motorcycle. If there's a pothole, you should recognize it but not look at it, because you'll start to head for it.

I'm always searching for a feeling of going faster. Again, it's like the sensation on the motorcycle. When you let off the throttle while it's still in gear, you feel the pull backward of slowing down. The opposite is when you're throttling. You feel that tug and acceleration forward. It's the same when you're moving from 10 mph to 20, or from 60 to 70. That's always the plan—doing the things I know will help me achieve that feeling of going faster. I don't try to hold on to any specific technique. My only technique is "Fast," trying to achieve Fast. That's all I've got. It's more abstract than measurable.

There's a point when I'm at full throttle and I'm just trying to maintain the speed. But even then I try not to let myself get tricked into complacency that I'm at top speed. Only for the 100 will I try to limit myself so that I'm not desperately clawing for that feeling and failing and finding myself slogging through molasses. And there's always a sense of desperation to achieve that feeling of Fast. Chase the dragon long enough and the dragon starts chasing you.

7 *The Heat*

*Do not ask who I am and do not ask me to remain the same:
leave it to our bureaucrats and our police to see that our papers
are in order.*

—Foucault

*Tonight when I chase the dragon
The water will change to cherry wine
And the silver will turn to gold*
—Steely Dan, "Time Out of Mind"

Berkeley Hills, April 2000

The bark looks like animal hide. I run my fingers along its surface, press my palm against the leathery wood. The leaves shiver
as the tree breathes under me. It's more than alive, it's conscious.
It senses me. I shut my eyes, press my palm into the tree to see if
I can draw power from it. Nothing happens. Blue and gold fractals bloom against my eyelids but that's all. How conceited, to
think I can draw its power! As if this great elder oak is just some
docile refueling station here to serve me.

I open my eyes. My hand, previously something I'd never
even considered on its own terms, now commands my attention.
It looks fleshy and foreign, almost grotesque. Like a troll's hand
that somehow attached itself to my wrist. What an obscene, cumbersome thing flesh is! To think, we have to lug it around with us

all day, this mass of meat and bone and blood. And do so under the delusion that this pork chop of a body that we trudge around in is who we are. I laugh aloud. What a ridiculous vehicle to be stuck in! And for life!

Joe has disappeared around the bend farther up the trail so I continue onward. The flora glows with an inner incandescence: there are no reds or blues or yellows or greens; there is vermilion and sapphire and topaz and emerald. The crimson-tipped shrubs to my left look like they've been wrenched from the earth, dipped upside down into a vat of angel blood, and then replanted. I step into a patch of sunlight and almost stumble. I now see the sun for what it is—a terrible and awesome fireball. Its light slants through the woods, bathing the sides of the trees in its fiery touch, illuminating them like some enormous all-seeing primordial searchlight from heaven.

The trees sway and rustle and groan under a wind that seems to come from all directions, even from within me. And I feel myself swaying too. The creaking trunks, the shuddering leaves, the heaving wind . . . so many sounds everywhere imposing themselves, charged with significance, vying for my attention. The clouds both press down on me and expand out into a pregnant vastness. I feel overwhelmed by the naked existence of everything. How have I not felt this before, this vividness, this terrible profoundness? All this time I've been walking around half-dead in my default zombie state, locked off like Plato's cave man from the raw power of life. I need to remember this feeling. *This* is how I should be conscious, or at least a milder version of this. This would be too much to sustain on a regular basis. Too intense, too close to where both ecstasy and madness reside.

I need to lie down. Joe is off doing his own thing. There's a grassy glade just off the trail and I stretch out flat under a canopy of trees. The earth feels alive beneath me in a way I've never conceived of before. I feel connected to it, a part of it. Like I'm just another fiber in a greater being. But I'm also Me and I have to do Me things like go to school and train and not just stare off at trees and clouds. I have to live and function. I start thinking about my year and school and swimming. Who am I? What do I want? What should I do? I feel overwhelmed again and alone and nervous. And I realize I've never really believed I can make the Olympic team this year. Even after winning NCAAs and getting that world record. Even then I didn't believe it. It was a fluke event, short course meters, not the long course standard of Olympic Trials and the Olympics.

The grassy area is shaded because of the trees, but as the sun passes through the sky, a ray of sunlight penetrates the leafy canopy. A single beam travels down and lands on my forehead. It's like an angel's touch. I'm suddenly overcome with bliss. An overpowering sense of joy and gratitude. I realize there is no reason to be afraid, anything is possible. As I stare up into that golden pillar, tears dripping off my cheeks, I realize I can do it.

For the first time, I believe.

⊱⋅──⋅⊰

Ervin followed his NCAA victories and newfound swim status with a two-month partying binge (not drinking but *drunking*, as he put it). What was formerly neglect of schoolwork was now abandonment. He failed his first class. His swimming, however, didn't suffer. His April revelation while lying in the grass in the Berkeley Hills—the conviction that he could make the Olympics—ignited a desire in him. So when Mike Bottom invited him that summer before Olympic Trials to train in Phoenix, Arizona, alongside nine international world-class sprinters, he didn't pause to deliberate.

Dubbed the "World Sprint Team 2000," the exclusive invite-only coterie was truly Olympic in spirit; the ten athletes hailed from five

countries: the US, Poland, Ecuador, Croatia, and Venezuela.[19] Cal's
Bart Kizierowski remembers it as "probably the most memorable
three months of my swimming career." The 3.5-hour morning and
late-afternoon sessions consisted of pool workouts, dryland, sports
psychology, cross fitness, stretching, and nutrition. In the middle
of the day they'd power down into a vegetative mode, depleted by
the double whammy of hard training and Phoenix heat. It regularly
climbed above 110 degrees, the kind of heat that blurs vision and
reflects pools of sky on the asphalt, but at least it was a dry heat.
Alongside the weight training, plyometrics, and medicine ball work,
Bottom incorporated obstacle running, basketball layups, jump
pull-ups, martial arts, and boxing. No other swimmers were doing
anything like it. Despite the media attention on his unusual methods, Bottom didn't take on airs. When asked why he incorporated
martial arts and boxing, Bottom replied: "These guys have testosterone [and] we've found that men with a lot of testosterone like to
beat on bags."

Their sports psychologist, Dr. Rayma Ditson-Sommer, ran sessions of light and sound therapy through a device she developed
called the SportsLink Focus Trainer, which claimed to "improve
focus and concentration, overcome preperformance anxiety, [and]
enhance visualization," among other things: the athletes would wear
blackout goggles containing blinking lights and simultaneously listen through headphones to pulsing rhythms or calming Enya-like
music, all the while lying on a bed that moved around under them
like a reclining dentist's chair gone haywire. Another of her methods
involved playing a Pong-like video game while electrodes clipped
upon one's fingertips transmitted how the right brain and left brain
shifted between various states like Stressed, Activated, Relaxed, Very
Relaxed, Aroused, and Very Aroused.

---

19 Here's the group, as categorized into a troika:
The Veterans: Gary Hall Jr., Bart Kizierowski, Gordan Kožulj, and Jon Olsen
The Three Amigos: Felipe Delgado, Francisco Sanchez, and Julio Santos
The Guppies: Anthony Ervin, Scott Greenwood, and Matt Macedo

Aside from such unique exercises, Ervin credits Ditson-Sommer for teaching him that it was unnecessary, even detrimental, to psyche himself up before races. "It was my first introduction to my later meditation," he recalls. "To stay quiet and in control. With taper and the pressure, I'm electric going into races. Canned lightning. You don't want to open that can before the race."

But of all the World Sprint Team 2000's quirks, their nutrition bars got the most press. Bottom had been studying the training regimes and diets of thoroughbred horses, and he found that the supplements given to the horses contained the same branch chain amino acids and Omega-3 and -6 fatty acids that aided human growth and recovery. (This was before fatty acids were even part of mainstream nutrition discourse.) He partnered with an equine provider, Platinum Performance, to develop a "bar" version of its horse supplement powder for human consumption. The bars, which the team nicknamed Horse Bars, became a regular part of their training routine. Ervin, who often substituted the free bars for his snacks and meals since he was short on money, was "shitting bricks" because the bars were "something like 85 percent ground flaxseed, shells included— pure roughage." It was a good period for Platinum: earlier that year the racehorse Fusaichi Pegasus, fueled by its supplements, won the Kentucky Derby. And now their bipedal counterparts were also raking in victories.[20] The swimmers were so devoted to the bars they even embroidered the horse logo on their black World Sprint Team 2000 terry cloth swim robes.

The racehorse was a fitting logo. With their pawing hooves and rolling eyes and whipping tails and poet-temperament caprice, horses bred and trained for the frenzy of the track aren't all that unlike elite sprint swimmers, who are, to quote Bottom, "often rebellious and angry." Of course, it's exactly that rebellion that drives them to find new ways of doing things—"productive rebellion," as Bottom called

20 The company didn't fail to see the marketing promise in this interspecies success; their September 1, 2000 press release was titled "California Company Platinum Performance Fuels Olympians: Two- and Four-Legged."

it—resulting in the technical breakthroughs that later get assimilated by the mainstream.

Not to say rebelliousness is exclusive to sprinters. It can also be found in the opposite end of the swimming spectrum—in the open-water swimmers, those indefatigable St. Bernards of swimming who strike out for hours on end, sometimes days, in foreign and hostile bodies of water, contending with rogue currents, oil tankers, aggressive bull sharks, jellyfish, hypothermia, hallucinations, etc. Lynne Cox comes to mind, gagging her way through a toxic Nile, swimming past bloated dead rats, getting mouthfuls of foam scum, and at one point thrusting her entire arm right through the spongy carcass of a rotting dog. Of course, long-distance open-water swimmers are rebels in a more hard-core, psychospiritual, Zen master kind of way, defying and striking out against primal opponents like Pain and Fear and Suffering, which explains why so many of them are women, and why you always get the feeling after talking to these swimmers or after reading about them that while out in that salty womb they're grappling with something elemental and intense and vision-questy. The open-water swimmer Hank Wise told me he finds it helpful to channel animal spirits on his crossings, in particular the red-tailed hawk, which "soars and then comes screaming down," and the dolphin, which "has to do with life or death situations, because when it's dolphin versus shark, the dolphin wins every time."

In mid-July, a month before Trials, the Janet Evans Invitational took place. Many of the fastest swimmers in the world were competing. Ervin, who'd been sporting a bleached-blond eraserhead, shaved it before the meet into a mohawk. In the 50 free, he set a meet record with a time of 22.30. But more noteworthy than his victory was his company on the blocks.

Janet Evans Invitational
50 Free Award Ceremony, July 15, 2000

I walk to the podium as the announcer introduces me: *"Anthony Ervin, the 2000 Champion in the 50 free—"* I step up to the podium and face the crowd, *"with his college teammate Bart Kizierowski and his club teammate Gary Hall."*

I shake Bart's hand, then Gary's. Mike is grinning below us. He shakes all of our hands, giving us our prizes. Gary's grinning too. Hell, we're all grinning. Who wouldn't be? All three of us standing up here in our black robes. It's badass. We're like a Jedi band, although maybe from the Dark Side.

It's great to stand here on the center podium. I can't pretend I don't love it. But it's so much better to have your teammates on each side, to be flanked here by Bart and Gary. I know I can irritate them and piss them off in practice sometimes, but now it's all good. This is what it's all about.

Jedi band of brothers. Fuck yeah.

⊶⊷⊶⊷⊶⊷⊶

Every discipline requires intensive training when practiced at the world-class level, but competitive swimming places unique and inordinate disciplinary demands upon its victims. Swimming may be the only sport combining insane puke-in-the-gutter-between-sets workouts with an anal obsession with numbers. A standard swim workout is like having to do the SAT math section while bleeding and being pursued by a hungry shark. There's no point in trying to convey how hard swim workouts are because, like torture, they require first-hand knowledge to be truly understood. But at least the regimentation can be described. Since swimming is a sport where 1/100th of a second can determine the difference between ecstasy and disappointment,[21]

---

21 Most lucidly manifested in the London Olympics Men's 100 free finals result:
Gold: USA's Nathan Adrian—47.52 (celebrated as hero and hunk).
Silver: Australia's James Magnussen—47.53 (soon-to-be-forgotten runner-up).

coaches organize workouts with a surgical eye toward shaving off hundredths. For swimmers, this means that while their bodies burn in water for 120+ minutes, they must at the same time coolly calculate yardage, intervals, splits, beats per kick, descending stroke counts, alternate breathing patterns, dolphin kicks off the wall, and so on. That's why a swim workout on a whiteboard looks like an algebra formula. Consider that all this takes place within a rigidly geometric environment with year-round practices often scheduled twice a day, not to mention weightlifting sessions with their own regimes of sets and repetitions and weight loads, and you get an idea of the sort of Apollonian gauntlet that swimmers must traverse to compete at the highest levels.

This is why swimmers need to cut loose now and then. Swim training at the elite level may be idealized as a sanitized, 24/7, no-nonsense operation, but it's always had a culture of Swim Hard, Party Hard. And in Phoenix it was all about swimming fast and having fun. Since there was no practice Sunday mornings, the designated night in Phoenix to get your inward wet[22] on (a.k.a., drink) was Saturday. It rarely got sloppy, although there were a few times, like the night when Ervin, after some earnest and semi-intelligible philosophizing between drags on his pipe Shamu, reeled over to the apartment balcony, overcome by crossfade, and violently vomited over the second-story rail into the communal courtyard.

That episode aside, Ervin laid low in Phoenix. He was too young to go to bars with the older guys. For once he was making practices, in great part thanks to his roommate, Scott Greenwood, who took it upon himself to be Ervin's unsnoozable alarm clock. Even so, many of the veterans had an ambivalent view toward Ervin. He displayed none of the deference expected from young guys and had a propensity for talking smack, which at one point went so far that he wor-

---

22 'Inward wet' is not my wordsmithery. This stand-in for "drinking" is a translation from Latin from a sixteenth-century book of swimming called *Colymbetes*, the first book ever published on swimming, according to the translator. In it, the swim instructor, Pampirus, invites his student home after the swim lesson in order to get on an "inward wet." (The student was male, so no double entendre.)

ried he was going to get his ass kicked by one of his teammates. As Gary Hall Jr. told *Sports Illustrated* months later: "A lot of guys didn't like him at first. I didn't like him at first. He's very confident . . . The more I knew him, the more I liked him, but I still wanted to wring his neck about every other day." But though Ervin might have been oblivious to the unspoken hierarchies of seniority and respect—like giving up the front seat of the van to your elders—he wasn't oblivious to the fact that he was in extraordinary company. He'd never met an Olympian growing up, let alone swam with one, and now they were his training partners, including the American Jon Olsen, one of the nation's great Olympic relay swimmers, and Hall, the 1996 silver medalist in both the 50 and 100.

While Olsen served as mentor for Ervin, the role Hall played was more complex. Though Ervin had a rebellious streak, the veteran Hall (he was twenty-five) was the Obi-Wan Kenobi of rebellion, the "bad boy of swimming before USA Swimming wanted a bad boy," as fellow World Sprint Team 2000 swimmer Matt Macedo put it. You'd be hard-pressed to find a more colorful figure in the history of the sport than Hall, who was always getting into outrageous situations—like when he discovered as he was removing his shorts behind the blocks at the 1995 Pan Ams in Argentina that he'd forgotten to put on his bathing suit; or when he wrestled and punched a shark that attacked his sister while spearfishing; or when he defied orders to not wear his satin stars-and-stripes boxing robe at the 2004 Olympics, prompting a furious US national director to lunge at him in the ready room a few minutes before the 50 free final[23]; or unsettling Donald Trump, with whom he was presenting the male MVP award at the 2012 Golden Goggles ceremony, by wearing fluorescent-orange, zebra-print rockabilly shoes and a playful and incendiary *Al Sharpton for President* pin.

---

23 Events that followed:
1. Security carts off national director, who is practically foaming at the mouth.
2. Hall wins gold.
3. Director fines Hall more than USA Swimming had paid him in the last three years.
4. Hall says fine was worth every penny.

Ervin and Hall had much in common: neither had much patience or interest in high-yardage workouts, both liked learning through play and experimentation, both liked doing things their own way, and neither liked being told what they couldn't do. This last characteristic was dramatically exhibited the previous year, when Hall started experiencing shaking fits, fatigue, and blurred vision before collapsing. He was diagnosed with Type 1 diabetes. Two endocrinologists told him his swimming career was effectively over. But Hall wasn't willing to accept that. With the assistance of another doctor, he found a way to continue training through a careful dietary regime, frequent monitoring of his blood sugar levels during workouts, and injections of insulin up to eight times a day.

Even Hall's public persona was a kind of defiance. To the public, he was an extrovert who shadowboxed before his races, but those close to him also knew he was private and reticent; a lot of that clowning and showboating was evasion, a way of dealing with the limelight by cloaking himself in an outrageous and extravagant guise. I remember watching him on TV flexing behind the blocks in Uncle Sam boxing shorts, and thinking, *What a self-righteous jingoist*, only to meet him many years later and be struck by his affability, intelligence, and eccentric, almost nerdy, Napoleon Dynamite aesthetic. All of this made Hall at once a role model for Ervin as well as a target. Bottom noticed the dynamic: "Anthony's desire to be a champion was always there. But a champion is too respectful—his mother would be proud of that. That's the rebellion. So for him to be the champion there had to be some tension that he had to overcome . . . Gary was kind of the master rebellion guy, so [Anthony] had to beat him. There was always some creative tension. Mostly orchestrated by him. Very rarely would I orchestrate tension."

Hall, in turn, was surely aware that there was something unique and unprecedented in this slender upstart who, as Bottom described, "would intentionally, like a puppy dog, bite on the [older] guys," and whose competitiveness was also pushing Hall to improve.[24] It was precisely what Bottom was trying to accomplish in assembling an elite group. He knew that many of them would be racing in the finals of Olympic Trials and the Olympics, in some cases for different countries. But because their competitiveness would be without malice or antagonism, their presences would support one another. It may sound like something out of a "We Are the World" music video, but all team athletes know how powerful and true it is, and the results from the Janet Evans Invitational testified to it.

A couple of weeks before the end of training camp, Bottom set up mock interview sessions to prepare the athletes for media at Olympic Trials. The questions were catered to each athlete. When Anthony Ervin sat down, the first question was about his African American heritage. He'd never given the question any thought, so he didn't know how to answer it. He responded blithely: "Well, my father is African American and I've always been proud of my heritage and my family."

A few days later, he had a nightmare.

❖

I'm in a cemetery. The tombstones jut up from the earth at crazy angles. The grass is yellow, overgrown, in a few isolated patches blackened, as if scorched by fire. Even through my shoes I can feel the ground, hard, stubbly, baked by the sun. In the distance a hooded figure is sobbing against a tree. As she wails, the tree sheds its leaves. I look away for a moment, embarrassed. When I glance back, she is scurrying away. The tree is leafless. Panic overtakes me. I try to read the tombstone in front of me but the letters are illegible under a layer of dirt. I drop to my knees and scrub it with my forearm, but that only smears the filth. Frantic, I rip out some grass and try to scrub the dirt away but the blades

---

24 Excerpt from an September 2000 newspaper clipping: "'There were several occasions when I wanted to kill him or at least strangle him to the point of passing out,' Hall said, smiling."

stick like glue to the headstone. I try to cry out but no sound comes. I can't stand up. I start to crawl over to the next tombstone. I must read it. The ground is suddenly soaked through, squishing down under my palms. My hands and knees feel so heavy. They sink into the earth. I strain and pull one hand out with a slow sucking sound. It's black with mud. But then I lose my balance and fall forward. My hand gets mired in the mud again. I feel weak. It's impossible.

And then I'm still on all fours except I'm at home in the living room. Mom is there. And Derek and Jackie. All three are motionless on the couch, heads bowed.

"Where's Dad?" I say. "Where's Dad? Where's Dad!"

Mom raises her head up, slowly, slowly, considering me with a flat, lightless face. She looks through me, past me. I try to stand up, to walk over to her, but I can't move. I just stay there, on all fours. I'm helpless. I try to speak but only an infant's garble comes out. She draws a long, rattling breath, then lowers her head again.

And I know what has happened. Dad is dead. Dad died. Dad is dead. Dad is dead.

I wake up in tears. A half hour later I call home. Dad answers.

⁕⁕⁕⁕⁕⁕

The force and vividness of the dream fell away upon confirming that his father was alive and well. But unease persisted: how much did he know about his father? The mock interview question about his black heritage was at heart a question about his father, since his African blood came through his father's side of his family, not his mother's. Throughout childhood, his father had always been in the background, in the shadow of his mother. But now that Anthony was on his own, the presence of his father was pressing in, making itself known—and from an unlikely source: the media.

* * *

In early August 2000 Ervin shaved off his bleached mohawk and flew to Indianapolis for Olympic Trials. The competition at US Swim Trials can be faster and fiercer than at the Olympics because of the sheer number of fast swimmers. Only the top two finalists in every event make the team (except in the 100 and 200 free, where the top six make it because of relay considerations). This means you can be the third-fastest swimmer in the world and not even make the Olympics. A third-place finish at US Olympic Trials—"swimming's version of a Purple Heart," as writer Casey Barrett called it—holds only heartache.

For their races, the World Sprint Team 2000 guys strolled up to the blocks in their black robes with the hoods up like Ringwraiths or executioners. Heads turned. Robes are now a common sight at meets but it was without precedent back then. Gary Hall Jr. also added a splash of color, sporting some red, white, and blue trunks that he got at a Muhammad Ali benefit for Parkinson's disease.

Going into the meet, Ervin was ranked second in the country in the 50 and fifth in the 100. Though his prospects looked good for both events, he recognized the unpredictable nature of the 50 and felt that his best chance was in the 100, where he just needed to crack the top six. And he did—fifth place; he would be an Olympian! With the thrill came relief that he could now focus on his 50 without the added pressure of having to make the team.

A few days later in the 50 free final, Hall raced to a winning time of 21.76, an American record and the second-fastest time in history behind Alexander Popov's world record time of 21.64 from earlier that summer. Touching a mere .04 seconds behind Hall for silver was Ervin. The year before he hadn't even been in the top twenty-five in the country in the event, and he had now just swum the third-fastest time in history. Hall and Ervin, training partners from Phoenix, would represent the US in the 50 free. After the race, an elated Ervin hugged Hall's father. "Maybe we'll be lucky," he told Hall Sr., "and tie for the gold in Sydney."

USA Swimming was eager for an African American swimmer to make the Olympic team. In 1996 hopes had been pinned on Byron Davis, but he narrowly missed the team, coming in fourth at Trials. By 2000 there was a palpable sense of unease in USA Swimming that the color barrier had been broken even in golf—the whitest sport and most rife with privilege—but not yet in swimming. At the 2000 Trials hopes were on Sabir Muhammad, who was also in the 100 free final. But with an eight-place finish, Muhammad missed the squad by two spots, and so the title of "first African American swimmer to make the Olympics" went to Ervin. As Ervin's mother recalled, her son seemed an unlikely representative: "Sabir Muhammad was supposed to be the black swimmer who broke the color barrier. And then Anthony makes the team, this white, blue-eyed kid with blond hair."

The salvo of questions about his race confused and flustered Ervin. He dealt with them in different ways, sometimes by deflecting them with the usual canned platitudes ("I've always been proud of my heritage. It's kind of cool."), sometimes by rejecting the label ("I look like a white person . . . I'm not really black. It's hard to explain."), and sometimes just by expressing his discomfort ("People are trying to pin me down when it's never been an issue for me. In America today I would think that having diverse blood would be no big deal."). He was uncomfortable with his new role as spokesman for black Americans, not only because he didn't know what to say but also because he knew that some people viewed him as an "inauthentic" black. For many, especially those unable to extricate skin tone from ethnicity, the first African American Olympian didn't count because he didn't *look* black. (One can imagine Chris Rock riffing on this: "Have you seen the first black American Olympic swimmer? He's white!") Ervin later tried to compensate by assuming a "black" identity that, ironically enough, was exactly the kind of media-driven stereotype a white suburban kid might have: "My way of dealing with it was to act more 'ghetto.' I took on an N.W.A.-style persona, like, *Fuck the police,* talking in jibe, drinking 40s of malt liquor, etc. I didn't know how to address all the questions. I knew nothing about being African American. I didn't try to learn about African American literature like I did later. Though I listened to some quality hip-hop like Tupac, who often rapped about social justice, I mostly went for tasteless stuff. Often chauvinistic and shitty and about smoking weed. I was more concerned with the display of ego and resisting control by police, women, and authorities of any kind."

Only years later, after studying race and literature, would he develop a more nuanced understanding of the race dynamics at play. But at the time he treated it all as an inconvenience, choosing instead to focus on his swim training and upcoming Olympic debut in Sydney.

Days after Olympic Trials—and after a mad rush to get an expedited passport for Ervin, who'd never been out of the country— the assembled team flew to training camp in Brisbane, Australia. There, by Ervin's own admission, he "cultivated a reputation for extraordinary talent matched only by extraordinary sloth." He'd often stand around on deck in his floral-pattern swimsuit, watching his teammates swim laps, often in excess of five miles for the distance swimmers. Then, before practice ended, he'd jump in, swim a few laps, and take a lengthy shower. He gambled away his per diem at a nearby casino.

Several weeks later, the team flew to Sydney and settled into the Olympic Village, where "every hour of the day was micromanaged to a degree that would put my mother to shame." They wore the same clothes, ate at the same time, traveled with the same luggage, and wore the same swim suits and caps. "You're suddenly shoved into this Corporate USA machine." Anthony remembers Gary Hall Jr. writing, in marker, a short story all over his carry-on, covering every square inch of its surface with sentences to make it his own.

* * *

The 4x100 Olympic freestyle relay is arguably the most exciting race in swimming. Because the US team has the depth of field, it usually rests its top two swimmers and has its third through sixth guys race in heats (prelims). The two fastest heat swimmers then join the top two in finals. They're the ones who also stand on the podium. There's a lot at stake for the prelim swimmers. Before the heat, Ervin and Jason Lezak got into a trash-talking exchange about which of them would advance. In the end, they both did. Little did Lezak and Ervin know, their next shared Olympic experience would be a dozen years later, when they would be roommates at the 2012 London Olympics.

But the person who got the most flak for his alleged trash-talking was Gary Hall Jr. Before arriving in Sydney, he wrote in his weekly blog diary that the Americans would "smash [the Australians] like guitars." This harmless and amusing quip caused a furor in the host country and made "Worst Quote of the Week" in *People* magazine, which Hall later joked was "probably my greatest accomplishment outside of the sport." What wasn't reported was that the guitar-smashing comment was sandwiched between Hall's gushing praise for Australia and Australians and his belief that it wouldn't be an easy victory, even though the US had never lost the event, winning seven consequent relays since it was first introduced at the 1964 Tokyo Olympics. But no matter: Australia now had a nemesis to unite over. If anything, the comment just added more spice to an already heated event. Everyone was revved up for it, but no one as much as the host country.

⚜

I'm nervous but confident. We're going to win gold. In prelims we were only three-tenths off the world record, so everybody knows it's going to happen here. Gold and a world record. There's electricity in the air. The crowd roars as the Australian

4x100 relay is announced, but they'll soon be disappointed. I'm leading off the relay. I put my hands on my hips and take a few deep breaths. At the official's whistle I step up to the blocks. It's premature though—the wrong whistle. The official tells me to step down. Another whistle and I step up with the others.

I dive in. Immediately, out of the corner of my eye, I notice that the Australian swimmer is half a body length ahead of me, dolphin-kicking underwater. I try to maintain my form, but because of the panic I expend my energy too early. At fifty meters I have almost caught the Aussie, but I die at the end of my leg and he pulls ahead of me for the relay exchange. As I haul myself out of the pool it's announced over the intercom that the Australian, Michael Klim, just broke the 100 free world record. This isn't how I envisioned my race.

Neil catches up to Australia by the fifty but then dies at the end, and the Australians regain their lead. I feel our gold slipping away. Jason dives in, gains the lead, and then again loses it in the last fifteen meters. It's like we've all been cursed with the same fate.

Gary is behind when he dives in but he immediately takes the lead. It's looking good, it's looking great. And then, just when it seems like it will be a sure thing, with fifteen meters to go, Ian Thorpe starts closing in. He reaches Gary by the flags. It's deafening. They both lunge for the wall and Thorpe touches first.

The Australians win. We lose. For the first time in history, we lose. The crowd is roaring. It's a world record. The Australians are jumping around, slapping each other, pumping fists. They start playing air guitar on deck, taunting the entire American team.

We lost.

I can't believe it. I stare at the deck. Dream crushed. Silver feels like nothing but loss. I just want to get out of here. In the postrace interview I'm mute with anger. My teammates are gracious in defeat, saying all the right things, congratulating the opposing team, but I say nothing. I don't trust myself to speak.

It was a quiet night for the Americans. Ervin wasn't mature enough to deal with the loss and he had trouble letting go of his anger and blame. He had swum a personal best but that was no consolation. In hindsight, he realizes that he was wearing an "American suit of entitlement" going into that relay. But the loss taught him a valuable lesson on hubris. Winners gain glory, but losers gain perspective. Not to say Ervin was doing too much soul-searching at the time. With one more chance at a gold medal, he spent the next few days meticulously rehearsing his upcoming 50 swim.

Sleep was difficult. Upon arrival in Sydney, Ervin had stopped taking his Tourette's medication, much like he'd done before NCAAs and before Olympic Trials. The excess energy from his taper, the competition nerves, and the biochemical high tide that resulted now that the clonidine was out of his system had left him like a man on fire. Ervin was a handful for the Olympic sprint coach, David Marsh, who once had to go looking for him after he'd been missing for hours one afternoon. Marsh eventually located him in the arcade, "just hyperfocused, playing games for hours and hours, lost in them." For Ervin, the arcade was a way for him to expel his energy. "The only other way was to get on everybody's nerves," he recalls. "If you're filled with energy, you've got to let it out somehow."

The night before the 50 free Ervin didn't sleep at all. His mind was racing, metaphorically and literally, playing out the upcoming swim in all its possible permutations. He watched the sun rise over Sydney. Even sleep-deprived, he qualified for semifinals that evening. He napped in between sessions and placed third in semis, which put him through to the following night's finals. Not one, not two, but three members of World Sprint Team 2000 would be in that final:

Bart and Gary had made the top eight. Two sprint legends were also in the final: the "Flying Dutchman" Pieter van den Hoogenband (best name ever in swimming) and the world record holder in the event, the "Russian Rocket" Alexander Popov.

Between semifinals and finals Ervin remained hyperfocused on his upcoming race. At finals, standing there calmly in his steel hoop earrings, next to his 6'6", 220-pound teammate Gary Hall Jr., and amidst all these other towering, hulking swimmers, he looked out of place, as if his presence was the result of a seeding oversight by the officials.

Ervin was first off the blocks. He remembers nothing of the race. He only knows that he didn't take a single breath until he touched the wall.

<hr />

I look up at the time board and see a 1 next to my name. Gold! I throw a fist. And then I see a 1 next to Gary's name! We tied! 21.98, both of us! I throw another pump. Gary is squinting at the time board, his cap and goggles in his hand. He looks confused. "We did it, Gary, we tied!" I hang over the lane line between us. Eyebrows creased, squinting, he's still trying to comprehend what happened. Maybe the numbers are too blurry for him. He glances over at Hoogenband and looks back at the time board. He throws a fist pump but still seems uncertain. Finally, he smiles in recognition and congratulates Hoogenband, who came in third, just a few hundredths behind us. Then Gary comes over and high-fives me. I lean over his lane line and high-five Hoogenband. The team is going crazy, jumping up and down in the stands. I can't stop grinning. Gary puts his arm around me. Then Bart comes over to my lane and we hug. I can't believe this. It's better than I hoped. We both won gold.

I climb out and throw both arms up at the crowd of thousands, which evokes a roar from them. It's an unbelievable feeling. I saunter over to Jim Gray, the NBC sportscaster who does all the postrace interviewing.

"Anthony, congratulations! I noticed you were blinking prior to the race. Was that your Tourette's syndrome?" He thrusts the microphone in front of me. My grin vanishes and a constriction takes hold of me as I stare into the huge, cold eye of the camera. I'm like a deer in headlights, frozen for the longest five seconds of my life. I can't come up with anything to say.

"Would you like me to ask another question?" Jim says.

I nod mutely.

"How does it feel to be the first swimmer of African American heritage to win a gold medal?"

I give my stock answer and walk away, feeling hollow.

 *Wet, Black Bough*

You come out of the forest with gold and it turns to ashes.
    —Joseph Campbell, in an interview with Bill Moyers

You're still young, that's your fault,
There's so much you have to know.
            —Cat Stevens, "Father and Son"

Millions of eyes were on Ervin when that NBC sportscaster asked him about his black heritage. "I didn't know a thing about what it was like to be part of the black experience." Ervin would reflect years later. "But now I do. It's like winning gold and having a bunch of old white people ask you what it's like to be black. That is my black experience."

But Ervin also knows that there's more to it than that. The question touched a raw nerve, because at a deeper, unintended level, the question was really asking, *Who is your father and where do you come from?* And that made him ashamed. Ashamed, because he didn't know.

Only a decade later, thanks to the genealogical excavations of Rebecca Jozwiakowski, Ervin's half-sister on his father's side, would Anthony learn something about his ancestry. His lineage branched back to two soldiers: the mixed-race American Revolution soldier Shadrach Battles, who fought for the Patriots and survived numerous Revolutionary War battles only to die in penury (see Appendix B), and the Civil War soldier William Slaughter, who as a teenager was killed fighting for the Union cause in the bloody Battle of the Wilderness (see Appendix C).

If Anthony had had a sense of his own lineage back then, he might have felt rooted in something larger than himself. But as it was, he didn't even know about the man closest to him in that long line: his own father. It would be another decade before his father told him about where he had come from and who he was.

Like his ancestor Shadrach Battles, whose military documents curiously listed him as "yellow" under both eyes and complexion, Jack Ervin was also a light-skinned black living in the South. The prejudice came in all colors: "White guys didn't want to be bothered because I was black, and black guys didn't want to be bothered because I looked too white," he recalls. "But I had my cousins. We'd go fishing and hunting." Like both Shadrach Battles and William Slaughter, Jack Ervin also saw combat, but on foreign soil: Vietnam. Though there was military history in his immediate family—both his cousin and uncle were Marines—Jack had never given serious thought to enlisting before the opportunity presented itself. And that opportunity came before a judge, during a hearing.

Some backstory: at the time Jack was living in Delaware, Ohio, where he was, as he put it, "hell-bent for trouble." He worked in the food court at an all-girls dorm, a position that despite the modest $1.30-an-hour pay came with obvious perks, especially since Jack was an equal-opportunity charmer with little regard for strictures against interracial dating. Not everyone was as relaxed about it. One day Jack and his cousin were out with two girls getting burgers and sodas at a Big Boy carhop when two white guys pulled up next to them and rolled down their windows. "Well goddamn, look at that!" the driver said. "Two niggers with two white girls. Ain't that something?" What followed was like a scene from *The Outsiders*. Jack's cousin jumped out of the car, dragged the driver out, and started whaling on him. Jack went over to the passenger door to keep an eye on the other fellow. Once his cousin had knocked the driver to the ground, Jack grabbed the other guy. "Go on," he told him. "Go help your friend up." Then Jack and his cousin went back into their car to finish their burgers. The two white boys left them alone after that, but before driving off they smashed out some lights in the parking lot. When police arrived, the restaurant owner claimed that Jack and his cousin had participated in the vandalism, and so the two of them were hauled off to jail for the night.

The judge had little sympathy during the next day's hearing. He said he had a mind to lock them up and throw the key away. But he told them that if they worked something out with the Marine recruiter in the back of the courtroom, he'd dismiss the case. The main thing was that they get the hell out of town.

His cousin wanted no part of the military, preferring jail instead. But Jack knew that if he didn't make a change, there'd be only jail in his future. It hadn't been his first fight and he was in with a rough crowd. So Jack made his way to the recruiter, who told him that within two days he could be in California, where it was 75 degrees and sunny. "In Ohio the snow was ass deep," he recalls. "I thought, *California? Sounds damn good to me. Where do I sign?*" The recruiter listed him as Caucasian in the Race/Ethnicity slot even though Jack had told him he was African American. He only noticed the discrepancy after he was assigned to his duty station. When he pointed out he was black, the officer replied, "Trust me, you don't want to be black for this."

Jack enjoyed the camaraderie of boot camp and was glad to be in San Diego. But darkness lay ahead: thirteen months in Vietnam. He doesn't talk about that time, and the silence is telling. "I asked myself, *Why am I carrying this baggage?* and so I've let it go," he says, adding that he has to "relive it enough every Friday" when he attends weekly meetings with other veterans. But for Anthony, his unwillingness to share details from Vietnam only demonstrates that he has yet to escape its clutches. Sherry's childhood is Jack's Vietnam: both of them black holes in their past—or at least guarded chests—in which memory must remain locked away. And because Anthony has seen, in both his parents and himself, how bottling away the past only extends and prolongs suffering, he now chooses, for better or worse, to dig up his skeletons and expose them to the disinfectant light of day.

Upon Jack's return from Southeast Asia, he married. But as much as he cared for his first wife, he found himself unable to deal with the family structure. "I didn't know it then," he says, "but my PTSD wouldn't allow me to be a normal person. I had anger issues and was screwing up all around. Depression, anxiety . . . I couldn't talk to anybody." He saw no relief from his dysfunction, so he apologized and left her.

The trauma followed him into his next marriage with Sherry. Though it never fully released its grip on him, upon moving to South Carolina he began attending Friday meetings at the VA where he could broach the subject with other Vietnam vets. Despite his reticence to speak about the experience outside of these meetings, talking has helped relieve some of the war's stranglehold on him. Now Jack Ervin gives the impression of a man at peace with himself, someone who's emerged from the wringer into a more Socratic place of contemplation. After a lifetime of being pigeonholed, his philosophy is that what others think of him is none of his business: "I can't be defined by what you think. If I did that, I'd be lost. I'd be just another idiot out there."

But in 2000 his son Anthony had not yet learned that piece of wisdom. With no clear sense of his own identity, Anthony did define himself by what others thought. And the media had defined him—their story line demanded it—as African American. Yet, Anthony had never asked about his father's past and had only once met his father's parents on a visit to West Virginia. As he was only four at the time, he doesn't even remember his grandparents. Only three memories of the trip remain with him—three that were nonetheless vivid enough to paint his conception of his father's childhood in wonder and fear.

The river is big and slow. You don't go close to it. You don't go close because big snakes live inside. Snakes that swim as fast as Jackie. Big dangerous swimming snakes. Pops says they're called water moccasins. You don't go close to the river.

At night the fireflies come out for playing. They're not really made out of fire but they have lights inside and they switch on and off when they fly. Fireflies don't live in my home. I run after them when they turn their lights on. Pops catches some of them in a glass jar and I keep them like pets. But when I wake up in the morning they don't glow anymore and they don't move anymore.

Pops takes us to his school. It's not like my school. It's dirty and scary and nobody goes now. Pops says it's been closed for a long, long time. The windows are broken and pieces of glass are on the floor. I go in one room and a big black bird is standing on the floor on pieces of stuff. When it sees me it starts to hop up and down and flaps one wing and makes a noise like, *Caw, caw.* I run back to Pops and grab his hand. He says it's a crow and it has a broken wing. I don't like to see it. It looks scared and a little angry. The crow keeps trying to fly but one wing doesn't move and it drags on the ground. It looks at me and says, *Caw, caw, caw.* I tell Pops I don't like it and pull his hand. But Pops just looks at it. Like he's forgot I'm here. I don't like it, I tell him again, and finally Pops nods. "Me neither," he says. And even after we leave I can still see it staring at us, scared and mad.

Fireflies, lurking water snakes, and an injured crow cawing in a derelict segregation-era school. These were the images that came to mind when Anthony tried to make sense of his father's past and his own. His mother's history was a blank, and his father's was of a world he barely knew and in which he never felt he belonged. Even now that he's learned something about his ancestry, he still doesn't feel he belongs: "Whatever my forebears may have been, I am no warrior. If anything, any warrior spirit of my bloodline has been watered down. And part of me wishes I still had it."

Anthony never enlisted or went to war like his father or William Slaughter or Shadrach Battles. But he did compete in the Olympics, and dissimilar as sports and combat may be, there are areas of intersection and overlap. For the ancient Greeks, contests were undertaken in the midst of war: the funeral games of charioteering, wrestling, and the like that take place in the penultimate book of the *Iliad* are as much about invigorating warriors for upcoming battles as commemorating victims of earlier ones. Stephen Crane believed he was able to write convincing battle scenes in *The Red Badge of Courage* despite not having seen combat because he "got [his] sense of the rage of conflict on the football field." Football is the obvious choice, with its lexicon of offense, defense, blitzes, bombs, formations, and ground games, not to mention more colorful recent additions like Legion of Boom, which sounds like an elite special-operations force (or an incompetent explosives disposal unit). And then there's football's crunching bodies on the field and generals on the sidelines and red-blooded flag-wavers in the stands and homefront loyalists in the armchairs, and let's not forget the cigar-chomping suits in the background running the whole damn show. On October 7, 2001, when President George W. Bush launched air strikes against Afghanistan a half hour before the Sunday kickoff of the Eagles vs. Cardinals game, the 65,000 at the Veterans Stadium in Philadelphia erupted in cheers at the announcement. And why wouldn't they? They were already primed, jacked for battle. When the Air Force holds a flyover before every Super Bowl, it's just setting the stage.

Overlap is less apparent in the so-called individual sports like swimming, but it's there. The ideals of a soldier are also those of the athlete: team unity and brotherhood and commitment and sacrifice and perseverance through pain. Instead of boot camp, athletes have training camps; instead of contesting in war, they contest in games. Both sports and military push the boundaries of permissible conduct further on each end of the spectrum, allowing on one end for outpourings of antagonism and aggression and on the other for unprecedented male bonding and intimacy. Both are bound up with national pride and anthems and flags and victory parades. And although nothing compares to the casualties of war—whether civilians, soldiers, or veterans—both athletes and soldiers are swiftly forgotten once their time is up and eyes turn to new heroes.

There's also the odd sense of meaning and purpose that both competition and war instill in us.[25] Some argue sports can generate, or at least approximate, this same sense of heightened significance, without leaving death, disfigurement, and horror in its wake, although this notion has its counterpart among critics who see sports as grooming for war. The linguist and dissident Noam Chomsky once described how as a high school student he questioned why he should care if his school's football team won since he didn't know anyone on it and a victory effectively meant nothing to him. He went on to characterize sports as a "way of building up irrational attitudes of submission to authority and group cohesion behind leadership elements . . . [and] training in irrational jingoism." But even accepting the irrationality of the sports fan's enthusiasm, even finding some theater of the absurd in any athletic spectacle, there's also something to be said, especially in our era of selfies and noncommittal sneering from the sidelines, for letting oneself unself-consciously and earnestly throw one's support behind another person or team. You

---

25 I experienced this during a brief stint reporting on the 2006 Lebanon War. The distant rumble, the power outages, the rooftop view of a thunder-and-lightning storm that was actually air strikes—these all helped impart the feeling that I'd been transported to some other land where daily life was stripped of its superficiality, and solidarity replaced disinterest among strangers. It was disturbingly seductive and intoxicating.

could even call it, allowing for some hyperbole, a spiritual exercise in selfless devotion. And hell, it's possible that rooting for your country in the World Cup isn't prepping you to cheerlead the Third Reich.

When Anthony won gold, he stood alongside Gary Hall Jr. on the top podium and bowed his head as a medal was draped over his neck. Two giant American flags were raised to "The Star-Spangled Banner." He'd done his nation proud. And because of his father's lineage, Ervin's victory carried even more significance, making him a symbol for the changing face of swimming. He grinned on the podium and waved an American stick flag, which someone had just handed him. It was as close to a war hero as you can get in the realm of sports. It's also a comparison Anthony rejects: "I'm definitely no equivalent of a war hero, despite what others may have said I did for my country by winning."

Hero or not, victory's luster was short-lived. The reality soon set in that his gold medal was no carte blanche. He was denied entry to the illustrious *Sports Illustrated* party even with his medal on hand like a credential, though his teammates got in. The drinking age in Australia was eighteen, so he spent most of his time hanging out at bars and nightclubs with a couple of other young Team USAers, Erik Vendt and Klete Keller. Though the swimming portion of the Olympics had ended, the team still imposed a (very liberal) curfew of four a.m.

One night Ervin came back fifteen minutes late. He was given a warning. A few nights later he arrived late again.

◆◆◆

Shit, I'm like fifteen minutes over curfew again. Everett is sitting at his desk in the American House, where we check in. "You're late," he says.

"Sorry, it's only a few minutes. You don't have to report that to Denny."

"I have to," he says, avoiding my eyes.

He *has* to? Everett has been buddy-buddy with me all meet and now he's acting all hard-ass. "Come on, don't do that. The train from downtown was late. All you have to do is let it go."

"No, I've got to." He still won't look me in the eye.

But he doesn't have to do this. He has a choice.

The next day the national team director Dennis Pursley calls me into his room. He tells me he's kicking me out of the Olympic Village and I have to hand over my athlete credentials and I'm banned from participating in the closing ceremony. I can't believe it. I try to reason with him and tell him how the train was late and how I have nowhere to go, but he won't budge. He stares at me unblinkingly. Then everything starts buzzing on me and I start yelling. I'm so so angry. I storm out and start shouting about him to the others in the town house—swimmers, administrators, coaches, anyone around. "Can you all believe this, can you *believe* what he's doing to me?!" And then Denny comes out of his room and we get into a yelling match and I start attacking his character and he says that if I want to appeal his authority I can take it up with the US Olympic Committee judiciary, but that if I do he'll prosecute me to the full extent of his powers when we return to the US.

I call my parents who are now back in the States and I tell them that he's throwing me out just because I was a few minutes late and he's an asshole and nobody likes him and he's going to lose his job, and I'm shouting into the phone so that everyone can hear me, so that *he* can hear me, so that he can realize what he's doing to me. Why, *why* is he doing this to me, throwing me out, casting me out, an authority once again punishing me, ruining what's supposed to be the best moment of my life?

⚬⚬⚬

Though Anthony had been stripped of his credentials, he found a way to sleep in the Olympic Village for a few more nights thanks to two of his World Sprint Team 2000 teammates: Bart Kizierowski put Anthony up in the Polish House, where there was no curfew or doormen; and Gordan Kožulj, who'd already moved out of the Village with his Croatian squad, gave Anthony his athlete credentials. "Back then Tony was talented at getting in trouble," Bart recalls. "I remember being proud that there we were at the Olympics, with such high security, and we were able to sneak Tony in and out of places without anybody knowing." Fortunately for him, Ervin never ran into either Dennis Pursley or Everett Uchiyama, the man who had reported him, probably because he stayed out all night and slept during the day.

Ervin soon moved to a beach hostel, where some swimmers would join him a few days later. He checked into an empty room with three bunk beds and a stained sink. The hostel had been full during the Olympics but began emptying as the Games winded down.

By closing ceremony the hostel was practically deserted. In the next few days the rest of Sydney would follow suit as the nations withdrew their teams. He thought of catching the train back and attending the ceremony with Kožulj's credential, but feared getting caught, knowing all the coaches and managers would be there as well.

Instead he posted up at the bar and watched the closing ceremony on TV.

***

"It's going off," the bartender says. "You just know they're all on the piss. Hell of a party to be at."

"No doubt," I say. "Hell of a party."

I finish my beer and step outside. A crescent moon hangs over the breaking water, a sliver of violence.

I lie down on the plastic frame of a lounge beach chair.

The stars don't give a glittering fuck. It's like I'm back in that treehouse, alone under the night sky. Except this time I didn't run away. I was thrown out. I rattled the cages and the warden tossed me into solitary confinement.

I stand up and walk to the water. The ocean is loud, belligerent. It seethes. I light up a cigarette.

I guess I'm right where I deserve to be. They want me to be the first black Olympian. Well, here I am, fulfilling all expectations, giving them what they want. Anointed black and then treated accordingly!

Maybe not, but the swimming world wants me to be this figurehead for black people and I don't even know what I am. I'm all mixed up. And even now, here I am, a spectator but not a spectator, an athlete but not an athlete. A supposed champion who can't even get into a *Sports Illustrated* party, who's exiled from his team, who's drinking alone at a dingy hostel bar during the closing ceremony. And my medal lying in a heap of dirty laundry. There's the golden truth. There's the glory of it all.

Listen to me, making excuses, blaming others. I couldn't even answer one simple question about my Tourette's. And I know nothing about who I am or where I come from. So I just dodge the question. I have the ultimate opportunity to say something meaningful in front of the world and instead I just run.

I'm a coward.

I head back inside. It reeks of stale beer and cigarettes. On the television Paul Hogan is buffed out as Crocodile Dundee, perched on a float of a giant black safari hat and giving a thumbs-up to the cheering Olympic stadium.

My mouth tastes of ashes. I push my glass toward the bartender. "One more bitter."

In the days after the ceremony, Sydney felt like a ghost town. The nations had withdrawn their teams. The fanfare had ended. The media had moved on to new spectacles. The residents slowly emerged from their shelters and limped through the forsaken landscape like apocalypse survivors, burnt out from the past weeks' invasion of tourist hordes. The only sign of the juggernaut that tore across their city was the litter that blew through the desolate streets like tumbleweed. Flyers and ticket stubs lay torn and strewn about the pavement, plastic bags somersaulted on the breeze. And soon all that vanished too as the convalescent city staggered back to its feet.

The Games were over.

PART III

TURBULENCE

In a Dark Pool

Uneasy lies the head that wears a crown.
                    —Shakespeare, *Henry IV*

I will speak no more
of my feelings beneath.
                    —Alice in Chains, "Down in a Hole"

Upon his return to Berkeley, the Olympic 50 free champion was broke and homeless. Ervin turned down the $83,000 eligible to him in performance bonuses if he turned professional, opting instead to remain a collegiate swimmer. This was partly because of his devotion to his college team and partly because he was still unsure of swimming's importance to him. His friends and teammates let him stay on their couches while he found housing.

The Olympics had taken place in early fall, so Ervin had already missed several weeks of school. The university waived the eligibility requirements, allowing him to take the semester off. He made few practices. One housemate, Matt Macedo, remembers once going to bed while Ervin was playing video games and then waking up for morning practice six hours later only to see him still on the couch, fixed in front of the screen. Ervin lived on a shoestring budget, eating spaghetti almost every night, but his partying didn't suffer. "I never paid for any of it," he recalls. "People gave me all the alcohol and weed I wanted. Everyone wants to get drunk and stoned with an Olympian."

The house was notorious on the block. At one point the neighbors signed a petition to have its residents evicted. The swimmers consequently toned down their parties, but the place could still degenerate into an animal house when there was no morning practice the following day. And many house traditions still stood postpetition, like the partytime law that anyone skunked at foosball had to run around the block naked (women were permitted panties, but no bra). As if to warn against foosball arrogance, posted on the wall was a photo collage of various men and women sprinting down Ward Street in various states of undress.[26]

In the house was a musty old plaid recliner that the housemates wanted to get rid of but didn't know how. One late night, a few of the guys hit upon a theatrical strategy. As the resident couch surfer at the time, Ervin was among them. They pocketed a lighter, picked up the recliner, and started carrying it down the street.

❈

A car drives by as we lug the recliner down Ward Street but the driver doesn't seem to notice. The street's dead. There's no one in sight when we get to Ward and Fulton so we go for it. We drop it in the middle of the intersection and put the lighter underneath the footrest. The fabric catches fast. We sprint back down Ward to the house. After a few minutes we step out again and stroll back up to the intersection. The recliner is ablaze. Others have gathered to watch. We stand off to the side, acting as shocked and confused as the others are. Pretty soon the whole recliner's a giant fireball in the middle of the intersection.

The smoke must be visible a mile away. The flames are leaping up and everyone gathered around is aglow and orange like this is some weird urban campfire. Soon the fire truck comes careening in with lights going and sirens blaring. Since the re-

26 The first night Matt Macedo met his now-wife he skunked her and she ran. One of the finer how-did-you-two-first-meet stories.

cliner's in the middle of the road and there's no wind or risk of the fire spreading, the firemen just let it burn down. They kick back and lean against the fire truck and watch. Only once the flames have consumed the recliner down to its smoldering steel frame do they spray it with that white powdery crap. And then we just stroll away from that charred skeleton, thinking, *Holy shit, we actually got away with this . . .*

A few months later Ervin moved into another swim house on Parker Street. He could only afford the basement room. It was small and dark, with a lone tiny window. It also had an ant infestation problem so he sometimes woke up covered in ants, but at least it was a room of his own. He now had a girlfriend, K, a dancer whom he'd met upon returning from Australia. His first serious partner, she served as a stabilizing force, possibly standing in in some abstract sense for his mother, who'd always kept him in line and who no longer played a central role in his daily life. Despite the partying, he started making more practices. He covered his basement walls with posters of Muhammad Ali and Rocky to motivate him to get to the pool.

Though Ervin aced tests through midterms, he stopped going to class once swim season got into swing. As a result, he failed several courses, burning through his remaining AP units from high school to remain eligible. But he was at a high point in the pool. At the NCAAs in March, the sophomore Ervin won the 100-meter free, tying Matt Biondi's NCAA and American record time of 41.80, which had stood for fourteen years. But it wouldn't be until World Championships in Fukuoka, Japan, when Ervin would swim what he considers the greatest victory of his career.

In preparation for World Champs, Ervin remained at Cal to train. To his surprise, his main college adversary, the South African sprint freestyler Roland Schoeman, flew to California and trained with him over the summer. Schoeman had been the heavy favorite to win NCAAs the previous year in the 50 and 100, but came a close second to Ervin in both. In the 50 free prelims, Schoeman had tied Mark Foster's short-course meters world record; after his finals swim of 21.22 he would have been the sole world record holder had Ervin not out-touched him by 1/100th of a second, denying him both the NCAA title and world record. At the time, Schoeman never spoke to Ervin or congratulated him. But upon arriving in Berkeley he confessed to Ervin his earlier resentment and jealousy, adding he had gotten past those feelings and come around to respect him. "I admired this coming clean," Ervin recalls. "I wished I could have had that kind of strength." By mid-July, when they traveled to Fukuoka, Japan, for World Champs, they had become solid friends. Schoeman and Ervin's rivalry rarely gets press but its duration and competitiveness is remarkable. In 2000 at the NCAA championship finals in the 50 free, only 1/100th of a second separated them. And a dozen years later, in the London Olympics 50 free final, 2/100ths separated them. In those two major competition finals over twelve years, that's a total of 3/100ths of a second, or 1/10th the duration of an eye blink. That's a rivalry.

Earlier that summer Ervin had begun meditating at a Zen temple, which aided him in his races. The meditation was an extension and progression of what he'd learned in Phoenix from Dr. Sommer on the advantages of maintaining focus before races. On the first day of the meet, Ervin set a championship record in the semis of the 50 free. The next night, in the 50 finals, he again beat Pieter van den Hoogenband to take gold. His summer training partner, Roland Schoeman, tied for third, taking his first international medal.

But the most exciting race was the 100 free. Going into finals Ervin was seeded fifth behind the favorites: the event's world record holder Hoogenband and Ian Thorpe, the Australian who the previous year at the Olympics came back in the 4x100 free relay to deprive the US men of gold for the first time in history. Before the race Ervin told his coach that he felt the only way he could win was by going out hard, even if it meant dying in the final meters. Bottom agreed.

At the start Ervin immediately pulled half a body length ahead of the field. When his feet hit the wall at the 50-meter mark, the clock read 22.60. It was an absurdly fast split. Head SwimMac Carolina Coach David Marsh remembers the race: "You'd never seen a guy throw himself out in the 100-meter freestyle like [Ervin] would. He would put himself all out there for a 75 like a great track athlete would for a 400-meter race. And he would allow himself to die, just dieeee. And yet he'd touch the wall [first], and [that] year was the world champion by doing that. He got so far ahead, nobody could catch him."

But no one knew Ervin had won that race when he finished. After he and Pieter van den Hoogenband lunged in unison at the wall and looked at the timeboard, there was no number beside *ERVIN*. Next to *HOOGENBAND* was a *1*. The Dutchman roared and pumped his arms. Ervin stared at the scoreboard, puzzled. From the deck Mike Bottom was yelling that he'd won, that the timeboard was wrong. After Ervin climbed out, the screen showed the slow-motion replay, in which Ervin seemed to out-touch Hoogenband. But only as Ervin was walking down the deck, cap and goggles in hand, was the glitch resolved. A roar went up in the stadium, and he glanced over at the scoreboard and threw his arms up. He had won with a time of 48.33, the fastest time in the world that year and a new American record, ousting Biondi's thirteen-year-old mark.

That night Ervin tried calling K to tell her about the race—his greatest victory yet because it had been so unexpected. No answer. It wasn't the first time he'd been unable to reach her since arriving in Japan. But this time doubt gnawed at him. He called again and again. Her roommate answered once, but said she hadn't seen K. He called others but no one knew where she was. Was she okay? Was she seeing someone else? The thrill of victory dissipated as worry set in, and he slept fitfully. Throughout the following day he kept calling. Suspicions crowded him as he obsessed over the possibility of her infidelity.

His mind was still in disarray that night when he anchored the 4x100 medley relay. In the final meters, Ian Thorpe closed in and out-touched him. It was a demoralizing end to his swims. And it turned out to be far worse even than silver. After climbing out, Ervin learned he had left the blocks prematurely, disqualifying the relay.

Any high from his earlier victories evaporated. He had failed his relay members and the team. And he was convinced K had abandoned, maybe even betrayed, him. He blamed her for the disqualification, resented her for her inaccessibility. He consulted with his roommate, who agreed she'd probably cheated on him, which further derailed him. Yet to the outside world he was still a stud and celebrity. The championships had been widely televised in Fukuoka and the winner of the 50 and 100 was a familiar face everywhere. One swimmer likened it to Beatlemania whenever Ervin stepped out.

As a twenty-year-old, he had already been an Olympic champion, world record holder, multiple world champion, and multiple NCAA champion. He was at the peak of his fame. And he was at a new low.

"Dude, everybody in this bar is looking at you," Bart tells me. It's true, they are. It's weird, I've never felt so many eyes on me before. "We're taking off," he says. "You coming?"

"Hold on," I say. I scan the bar for the hottest girl. They're all staring at me. I crook my forefinger at one and she comes. I can't believe that actually worked. I ask her if she speaks any English. "Little," she replies.

Chad and Bart are shaking their heads, laughing. "Looks like you'll be just fine," they say and leave.

We're not getting far in conversation. Her friend comes over, and she speaks a bit more English. But eventually the friend wants to leave. "So what do we do?" I say to the first girl. And then she just grabs me and kisses me. A little later she pulls me toward the door.

It's sunrise when I leave her place. On the way out she asks if I remember her name. I butcher the pronunciation beyond recognition. She smiles sadly and corrects me. I feel terrible. Only when I get back to the hotel does what I've done really sink in. I cheated on my girlfriend. I slept with another girl. Me, a cheater. I never thought I'd be that guy. And here I've been furious at K for maybe doing exactly what I just did. What a hypocrite. What a scumbag.

The next night we all go to a swimmer's party. I get bored fast because everybody is hitting on swimmer girls and I have no interest. I leave early. As I enter the hotel, the front desk girl is walking in the opposite direction. She just got out of work. I ask if she wants to grab a drink with me at a nearby bar. A few drinks later and I'm asking her if she wants to come up to my room. She's afraid she'll be fired, but I convince her it'll be fine.

Cheat once and it's easy to repeat. The injury is done. It's just piling more damage onto damage. And with enough drinks you can push aside the memory and postpone the guilt.

On the flight back to LA I pop a bunch of Ambiens and get loaded on gin-and-tonics. I hang out with a couple of teammates in the flight attendant alcove where the booze is stocked. After a while they kick us out and we move on to the next alcove and drink there until eventually no one will serve us anywhere on the plane. I reel back to my seat, seeing double.

I wake up hazy, still drunk. As we disembark I'm told I passed out during the flight on the passenger beside me. Apparently I was like dead weight on her. One of the coaches even came over and started slapping me in the face to wake me up, but I was out cold.

After baggage claim, press is waiting. They swarm me with cameras and microphones and questions. I'm groggy, nauseous, half-drunk, half-hungover. I mumble something to them. Who knows what.

Some hero I am.

Upon return to California, Ervin was again approached with an offer to turn pro, which he again rejected. But due to a change in eligibility rules, he was allowed to pocket the prize money from World Champs, which he recollects amounting to "a crisp $60K." The money was like manna, but it didn't alleviate his guilt over those two nights in Japan. He tried to work things out with K, and even flew to meet her in Hawaii, where she was studying. But she could smell the guilt on him, and she kept asking if he'd been unfaithful. He denied it. She in turn claimed she'd been inaccessible while he was in Japan because of a demanding school project. There was no resolution for either of them. It was a cheerless trip. He went skydiving alone because she didn't want to join him. Same with windsurfing. The winds were strong and he couldn't get the sail up: "Failure after failure. That's all I remember."

Back in California, Anthony and K began fighting. "I was so guilty and busted up about Japan that I was toxic," he recalls. "I wasn't good to her." Eventually they broke up.

Bart Kizierowski remembers talking to Ervin in Miami Beach after Gary Hall's wedding in December 2001. "I got the sense he was depressed and lost," Bart says. "Disappointment with success and what comes with it."

Things kept getting worse. Ervin began drinking aggressively, sometimes to the point of blacking out. The worst incident took place at a bar in Walnut Creek, California. One of his teammates worked as a barback there, so he was able to drink despite being underage. One night he randomly ran into K's sister. Even that encounter was enough to trigger memories, and he started drinking hard. The last thing he remembers is guzzling a drink. His next memory is of regaining consciousness in a hospital.

***

I'm on a stretcher, being pushed down a hallway. The fluorescent ceiling lights are painfully bright. My disorientation gives way to panic.

"Where am I? Where am I?!"

"In a hospital," replies a voice. "Just calm down. You've hurt yourself. You need stitches."

I look over. The person talking to me is a cop.

"What the hell is going on?" I cry. "Get me the fuck out of here!"

I'm yelling, freaking out, as they roll me down the hallway. The cop is hissing at me to pipe down. People we pass are looking over at me. I'm just hollering blindly.

After I get stitches the cop cuffs me, puts me in his patrol car, and drives me to jail. I still don't know what's happened. All the cop tells me is that I fell on my face and split my chin open. It's around two a.m. First I'm taken to a processing area. My arms are uncomfortably cuffed behind my back, so I step my feet back through the cuffs to bring my arms in front of me.

"Hey, what you doing!" a cop snaps.

I climb back through them again, but he keeps harassing me. I try to stay calm.

"Can I make a phone call?" I ask.

"Don't worry, you'll get your call later," he says.

My frustration gets the best of me. "Do you know who I am?" I say.

"Who?"

And I tell him, and then he just starts laughing. I'm embarrassed for even trying to play that card. I keep my mouth shut after that.

They lead me into the drunk tank. It's a big holding cell with benches against every wall. In the middle of the room, a thin Scandinavian-looking guy in fancy form-fitting clothing is sleeping in a fetal position on the floor. He's using his shoe as a pillow.

I take a seat. Across the room is some white guy in bad shape. A junkie maybe. He's wearing a hospital bracelet and covered in scabs. He's picking at one of them. Next to me is a guy in super-baggy clothing, sitting more on his underwear than on his jeans. He motions to the guy in scabs and tells me to keep my distance because that guy's got HIV. Then he starts going on about how he's been unjustly thrown into prison.

"Man, this bitch called the cops and had me thrown in here just 'cause she be mad at me. Shiiiiit, they don't question *her* side of the story. 'Course not. They just cart my black ass off to jail."

He keeps going on and won't shut up about it. Everyone else is glum and withdrawn. I touch my lips and they're numb. I must still be drunk. I try to remember what happened at the bar but it's all a blank.

Only hours later do I get my phone call. I call Jackie and tell him I don't know when they're letting me out. He doesn't seem to know what to do, but I ask him not to tell Mom. Then they escort me back to the drunk tank.

While I'm held in there other people are brought in and then released. The well-dressed European guy who slept on his shoe wakes up and brushes himself off. Eventually he's let out too.

My hangover grows fangs as time passes. Only by looking at the right angle through the sole narrow window, which is set in the door, can I see a clock. Time slows to a crawl, reduced to the uniform buzzing of the fluorescent lights overhead. There are about a dozen other guys in with me at one point and then the number tapers off. I keep thinking about that guy picking his scabs on the bench, about how I have fresh wounds. I sit upright the entire time. I doze off like that on occasion but it's nothing resembling sleep.

The following morning they let me out. I've been in there for over twenty-four hours. And who's there waiting for me but K and her mother. *K and her mother . . .*

I have no idea how K found out or why she came, and with her mother of all people. All I know is this is one of the most shameful moments of my life.

<hr/>

Ervin still doesn't know exactly what happened at the bar that night. Though his coach suspected someone spiked his drink with a roofie ("He was a hero to a lot of people and someone wanted to knock him down"), Bottom still made Ervin sign a contract pledging to stop drinking. The abstinence lasted a week or two.

After the jail incident, Ervin and K briefly got back together, although it was really just a pastiche of fights, breakups, and makeups. That fall, after an especially bad breakup, he wrote her a nasty letter. He later apologized, but it was too late. She told him she could no longer deal with his lifestyle and behavior. Ervin was devastated. He even approached her parents in hopes of reaching her through them. They were kind, but the message was clear: K didn't want to see him. "The reality," Ervin now says, "is that I didn't deserve her."

First experiences in love are potent: Eros's first arrow deposits a festering arrowhead, and the wound never heals well. Ervin dealt with the breakup by drowning himself in drinking and womanizing. Through the rest of the fall and into spring he went on a rampage: "I was reacting from being a scorned, broken-hearted lover and began treating women as objects for me to destroy at will," he says. Only in retrospect does he recognize how his psychology was at play. "Essentially, I was trying to deaden the sensation of physical intimacy, which was tied up for me with emotions. And I wanted those emotions to go away."

Warding off sorrow with emotionless sex may be a short-term solution, but as with binge drinking, sickness follows. The aftermath was particularly acute for Ervin, whose sense of identity has always been bound up, for better or worse, with the women in his life. In childhood that was his mother; in adulthood, his girlfriends. "Women totally alter my conception of self," he says. "When I was in a relationship with K, I saw myself in context of being part of a whole." The random parade of females that followed was corrosive: "There was a stream of faces that didn't make any sense to the point that I couldn't even recognize myself in a significant other."

Even though these faces were willing accomplices to his promiscuity, his behavior was shameful to him. His disgust with any woman who cheated on her boyfriend with him stemmed from his own self-loathing: "I find that horrible because I've cheated myself. So I'd treat her and think of her as I'd think of myself, like a piece of garbage." In retrospect, the casual sex now seems "repugnant" to him. "Not that I don't believe it's a livable lifestyle," he adds. "It's just not for me. I can't handle it." That said, the whole Ervin-as-unscrupulous-Lothario perspective may be as much a construct of his fingernail-chewing conscience than anything else. It's just that, for those who aren't innate libertines, any licentiousness can feel like a monstrous moral straying.

Just as his relationship with K had stabilized him, the random hookups only further destabilized him. His sense of self, already confused by the media attention on his race, was further eroded and thrown into question. He was buying into all the hype that he was a talented slacker, and he started missing even more classes and workouts. He now found himself playing out the stereotype of the gold medalist party animal, the champion jock playboy, the shallow star athlete.

In short, he was living a giant, hollow cliché, or more like a whole passage of them.

It goes without saying that time heals all wounds, even a dagger in the heart. To be honest, I know there are other fish in the sea, and when one door closes another opens. But you know what they say: once bitten, twice shy.

K may have an axe to grind with me but it still cuts to the quick that she won't let sleeping dogs lie and let us take out a new lease on life. I'm no knight in shining armor or blessing in disguise, but rest assured I can turn over a new leaf after our trial by fire. And let's set the record straight and call a spade a spade: it takes two to tango. She's not exactly pure as the driven snow herself. Takes one to know one. She left me out in the cold during my moment in the sun in Japan when I was literally dying to talk to her. Mark my words, K, to err is human, to forgive divine. To add insult to injury, she's now avoiding me like the plague even though every fiber of my being is basically chomping at the bit to lay eyes on her. At the end of the day, I'm not asking for red carpet treatment or seventh heaven.

The fact of the matter is, I should stop rubbing salt in old wounds and go with the flow. I may not give 110 percent in training or be the best thing to grace earth since sliced bread, but to be fair, at this moment in time, I'm the big cheese, the real McCoy for all intents and purposes. I've even got money to burn. It's my moment of glory. So *carpe diem*, grab the bull by the horns, full steam ahead! Make hay while the sun shines! Let the good times roll!

Snowball's chance in hell of that . . . I'm skating on thin ice. Life isn't all it's cracked up to be. The naked truth is, I'm down in the dumps and there's no light at the end of the tunnel. Just a stranger in a strange land, weathering out the storm. No rest for the weary.

Oh, cry me a river . . . Pass the bottle, it's high time to tie one on. Trust me, hair of the dog is just what the doctor ordered.

I should keep my eyes peeled for any handwriting on the wall, not that I'd make heads or tails of it. I'm not being funny or anything, but it's all Greek to me.

Clichés aside, after the breakup Ervin started smoking cigarettes, the one vice anathema to swimmers, who rely on powerful lungs the way boxers rely on fast feet. He previously smoked on occasion at parties but he was now smoking a few cigarettes a day when sober. In March 2002, during his taper for the NCAA championships, he briefly quit smoking and took up dipping instead. Even with the tobacco handicap, he swam well at NCAAs, winning the 100 free in American record time and getting second in the 50, a mere .02 seconds behind Roland Schoeman.

Later that spring Ervin moved into a new apartment, which he shared with a roommate. They soon endured an infestation of green flies, which swarmed the apartment for about a week. No matter how much two-sided tape they stuck on the walls and windows, the shiny, metallic flies kept returning. The infestation eventually tailed off and disappeared. But it wasn't until the following year, when Ervin moved out, that he discovered its cause. Upon moving his bed, he found dried vomit caked on the wall and floor. He must have rolled over in his sleep one night and puked against the wall. "So dark and disgusting that something like that could even happen," he says. "And that I wouldn't even notice."

He knew his excessive social drinking needed to stop, so he finally put an end to it. But his remedy was to replace it with solo day drinking. He started putting back a 40 of malt liquor each day. At night he'd smoke weed and play the first-person shooter game *Counter-Strike*. His appetite left and he was losing weight. His motivation to train withered. His coach tried various tactics to revive his enjoyment of water, once even asking him to do nothing during practice but sit on the lip of the pool and splash his feet in the water like a child.

It would make a slick script if Bottom's strategy had tapped into Ervin's initial encounter with water at his childhood Canoga Park pool and rekindled his fascination with it. But life rejects tidy narratives. Ervin soon stopped even trying to wake for practice. And when he did, he would lie in bed in a stupor, staring listlessly at the walls or ceiling. A lethargic gloom settled upon him. At times the murk would lift but these windows of relief grew briefer and less frequent. He moved about his apartment in a torpor and spent long periods immobile, either playing video games or staring off blankly.

As he sank into despondency, he stopped drinking altogether. The alcohol had served to numb the unhappiness and he no longer wanted that balm. "You start to love your own misery and the loss of self-esteem," he says. "You can get high on your own melancholy." He returned to the grunge music of his high school years, this time soaking in the angst-ridden lyrics of bands like Smashing Pumpkins, Alice in Chains, Nirvana, and Soundgarden: "It's like I romanticized feeling bad. Like I was pouring it all over myself, basting myself in it. It's sick." Though he lay off booze, he continued smoking marijuana. Without the stupefying effect of alcohol, the THC threw his already unsettled mind into overdrive. Even under paralysis of ennui, he often found himself ambushed by feverish inner monologues. In this disorderly agitation of the brain, a deluge of questions and anxieties crowded him without resolution or relief.

Such misery. And no end to it. I could ride it out if only I could see a way out. But this fog of grief won't lift. I'm trapped in it. I just keep on screwing up and hurting people. I had such a good thing going with K last year and I threw it all away because I was too insecure to give her space. I cheated, I lied.

And then all this hoopla and fame. I've been built up into someone I'm not. What would I have without swimming? Nothing. I'm worthless for anything else. All I have is this persona as talented slacker. I don't even believe in it and yet I've become it. That's me. The black spokesman who's white. The Olympic hero who's a fuck-up. I'm a zero. I don't want any of it anymore, none of it. This all belongs to someone else's life, not mine.

Nobody understands, and when I try to talk about it I just get flip answers or uncomprehending looks as if to say, *Why are you lying around*, or, *Why don't you get up and go to swim practice*, or, *Why don't you just get out and do things and grab life while you can and suck out its marrow*, and I want to tell them, *Because I feel ill, damnit, can't any of you understand that, can't you just leave me alone, just let me be bedridden? I may not be spitting up snot or shitting water but I'm sure running a fever.*

I just want to hit reset like I hoped would happen a few days ago when I had that allergy or whatever it was that caused the nosebleed and I just sat down on the bathroom floor letting the blood run and it poured all over me and on the tiles and I wondered if I could just bleed to death like that but of course it stopped on its own, not like if I slit my wrist, that would work, but how messy and violent, I wouldn't want that, what's the purpose of all this anyway, why don't I just end it all, what if I do, what would happen, maybe I'd reincarnate or maybe I'd meet a god who would give me some answers or maybe I'd just start over, I mean worst-case scenario the universe would cease to exist and so would my miserable life which is basically just a huge pile of rotting garbage so good riddance anyway, I just don't see the point of any of it anymore, I mean if you just look at it with a cool mathematical mind it makes perfect logical sense to take the next step because if there's a god I can get some answers and if the hell and brimstone preachers are right and I go to hell for the sin of suicide then I don't care because I'm already in hell and if I just reincarnate with no memory of the previous life then great I've succeeded and if there's nothing at all well that's the worst option that's what scares me the most the possibly of extinction of nothingness but even that I'm prepared to because at least there is so god but that's the death I choose over death and please just make it end make it end make it end make it end make it end make it end make it end make it end make it end make it end make it end make it end make it end make it end make it end make it end make it end make it fucking end

This must end.

Any attempt by those in the grips of depression to describe their desolation usually comes across to the comfortably healthy as maudlin and indulgent. As a result, the suffering feels intolerably private and incommunicable, futile to convey. Nevertheless, writers have tried. Ishmael tells us in *Moby-Dick* that he takes to sea whenever he finds himself "growing grim about the mouth; whenever it is a damp, drizzly November in my soul." Dante opens his *Inferno* by telling us that midway through his life he lost his way in a dark wood. Graham Greene, who in his youth had a penchant for Russian Roulette, referred to his misery as a little worm in him that sometimes "starts wriggling." Sylvia Plath also invoked an animal metaphor to describe her anguish: "As if a great muscular owl were sitting on my chest, its talons clenching and constricting my heart."

Poets are among the most susceptible groups to the ravages of mood disorders. And poetry, with its power to rewire meaning and thwart the routine limits of language, is ideal for conveying the smothering darkness and desperation of depression. "I felt a Funeral, in my Brain," Emily Dickinson wrote. "And Mourners to and fro / Kept treading—treading . . . / And then I heard them lift a

Box / And creak across my Soul / With those same Boots of Lead, again, / Then Space—began to toll." Gerard Manley Hopkins wrote of this anguish in his so-called Terrible Sonnets, with first lines like, "I wake and feel the fell of dark, not day," and, "No worst, there is none. Pitched past pitch of grief." Ervin wouldn't encounter Hopkins's poetry until much later in life, but when he did it resonated with him, conjuring up that time in his life when he had lost his way in a dark pool.

When viewed from outside, Ervin's life didn't seem all too bad. He had a full scholarship at a top school, he was exalted around the world for his prowess in the pool, and he had a network of friends and teammates. But depression often descends without apparent cause and can transform a benign world into a malignant tumor. The source of the distress often remains obscured. This is why the question "But why are you so upset?" can be so irritating to the afflicted: to even pose the question is to miss the point. They're upset; the rest is a fool's errand. The writer William Styron, who recounted his spiral descent into suicidal depression, described the acute sufferer as in a "state of unrealistic hopelessness, torn by exaggerated ills and fatal threats that bear no resemblance to actuality."

That's not to say there were no external troubles in Ervin's life. His new roommate had on the sly started dating a girl whom Ervin had just broken up with. She would constantly be over at their apartment, allegedly as his roommate's friend, even though Ervin knew they were secretly having a relationship. While for most people this might be a source of resentment, for Ervin it just seemed an inescapable nightmare, yet another lie and deception, even if not his own, to compound upon others. He had never before sought out professional help so there was no diagnosis of depression. But the diagnostic symptoms were all there: a depressed mood, a lack of interest in pleasure, weight loss, a sense of worthlessness, suicidal thoughts, and an obsession with death.

Shortly after the 2000 Olympics Ervin had stopped taking his Tourette's medication. His symptoms had been decreasing and he found he could alleviate them with marijuana. But though he no longer took clonidine, he still possessed a canister of pills. At regular doses clonidine lowers blood pressure. At higher levels, it can lead to respiratory depression, hallucinations, apnea, cardiac conduction defects, and comas.

For so many years he had relied on those pills to calm an excited nervous system. And now, after a week of deliberation, he decided to turn to them for relief one final time.

I empty out the pills into my palm. There are thirty-three. The most I've ever taken is two. I stare at them for a while. Then I swallow them all with water.

I sit on the bed in a lotus position. I shut my eyes and just start to breathe in and out deeply.

I hear the front door and I open my eyes. I remain in lotus.

The door to my room is open and my roommate glances in. He's with a friend.

"Hey, man," he says, "how's it going? Just came back to grab something." While he goes to get it, his friend waits by my door.

"I just popped a handful of pills," I tell him.

"Whoa, man, that's crazy," he says.

Then they leave the apartment.

I close my eyes again and return my attention to my breathing and to stilling my mind. There's no need for thought anymore. Soon it will all end and I will get answers.

A blanket of heaviness starts to press down on me. As it does, an intense fear grips me that I've made a terrible, terrible mistake. I open my eyes. My vision is clouding over.

I don't want to die.

I panic and shove my fingers down my throat. Blackness closes in on the periphery of my vision. I retch but nothing comes up.

Then, darkness.

 **Brother Saint**

With thy riches hidden in thy being
thou dwellest in a world bare of all shame and show
and thought for self,
in a destitution that never makes thee poor
　　　　　　　—Rabindranath Tagore, *"Poem 63"*

kwan-se-um bo-sal
kwan-se-um bo-sal . . .
(repeat)
　　　　　　　—Korean Zen chant ("one who hears
　　　　　　　　　　the cries of the world")

¹ There is night.

² And the night is without form yet stars move upon the face of the deep.

³ Now one by one, the stars extinguish as night yields to dark.

⁴ And there is darkness.

⁵ And thence out of the void appears a light.

⁶ And as the light approaches, it reveals itself as a man.

⁷ And the man is my elder and as he nears he says, "You ask, but it shall not be given to you; you seek, but ye shall not find.

⁸ "For in these questions no one who asketh receiveth; and no one who seeketh findeth."

⁹ And I groan in the spirit and am troubled.

¹⁰ Then with laughter the man proclaims, "Verily, I say unto you, thou art bound to life. Go forth and bear silent witness."

¹¹ And there is mockery in his laughter, but no hardness in his utterance.

¹² And I realize that the man is but my own self in later years; with such wisdom and understanding and knowledge I awaken.

¹³ And behold, I am alive; and it is so.

¹⁴ And behold, sunlight is streaming through the window and upon the bed; and it is so.

¹⁵ And I see the light.

The handful of pills that Anthony took weren't enough to kill him. Although he felt relief upon regaining consciousness, it came with a sense of futility. "I thought I was depressed leading up to the over-dose," he says, "but when I awoke the next morning I reached a new low, having failed to even kill myself. I couldn't even succeed at that." Yet this time he didn't sink into another quagmire of depression. His incompetence now felt so absolute that it led to a liberating relinquishing of control: "I gave up in the most complete sense. I realized I wasn't that strong and didn't need to be." He recalls having a moment-with-God experience in which he outsourced his strength and began relating his "weaker self" to a greater power, "a power that had it once taken a human form, would be named Jesus." He thinks of the sensation as a kind of ego-death, a freedom from the egoistic conviction that his misery—and more to the point, his self—was all-important. "It was infinite resignation and submission. And with it came total lightness. I was free." The notion that he could find existential answers by ending his life now seemed the ultimate conceit. Seeking answers, he realized, is the work of life, not death.

Despite this transcendent experience, Anthony recognized the severity of his action and the need for outside help. He went to the university health services and began seeing a psychologist, who diagnosed him with depression and prescribed an antidepressant. But Anthony found that the drug caused his appetite to decrease to the point where he was only eating once a day. Since his mood had already been improving before he started the antidepressant, he stopped taking it.

After his overdose he felt the need for quietude, so he began taking long walks and took an internal vow of silence of sorts. It was nothing dramatic, no embargo on speech or any such thing, which would have only drawn attention to him. But he kept to himself. If someone addressed him, he responded briefly in a way that gently preempted further dialogue: "Maybe my roommate and some of my closest friends noticed I was more quiet than usual, but that's about it. I was just within myself, looking out at the world."

He likens the period to a mushroom trip without hallucinations: "I was looking at every leaf on every tree, like I was reborn in a way. Even when out with friends, I was more like a silent observer." His guilt over missing practices fell away. Whereas before he'd been a prisoner of worry and anxiety, he was now free to experience the world unmediated by judgment, unclouded by the obsessions of the self. Now he just let himself be.

During this month of silent observation there was one person with whom he did converse regularly, although *person* isn't quite accurate. It was a voice—the same voice of the figure who spoke to him in his dream after the overdose; it was his older self. In *Darkness Visible*, William Styron noted that some individuals in the clutch of severe depression recount being "accompanied by a second self—a wraithlike observer who . . . is able to watch with dispassionate curiosity as his companion struggles against the oncoming disaster, or decides to embrace it." Ervin's case was different because the doppelgänger appeared not during but after his depression and, instead of observing his fall, spoke to him as a nonjudgmental and prudent elder.[27] But far from being a one-off oneiric visitation, The Voice accompanied him for months: "It wasn't actually auditory. But it definitely came across as a voice inside me. It seemed separate and had a different color from the other hodgepodge of my thoughts. I didn't think it was God. I knew it was my own voice coming from the future with more wisdom. Like a mature older brother. And it became like a conscience."

The Voice never came unprompted, nor was it omniscient. Anthony was always the one who'd conjure it up with a question. But The Voice was always reasonable, and if anything was "someone" with whom he could speak openly, which he hadn't had before. While this may all sound peculiar, and while Anthony himself now wonders whether The Voice was caused by a "psychotic break in the mind to ensure self-preservation," it was really just a few steps removed (admittedly imaginative ones) from the commonplace act of talking things over in one's head. To be more precise, it was a vocalized enactment of mindfulness—the focusing without judgment upon one's sensations, emotions, and thoughts. After all, The Voice never criticized or commanded; it merely observed and helped Anthony check in on his impulses and desires to recognize them more clearly. It resembled the inner dialogue that might take place within a Zen practitioner.

There was more than coincidence to this resemblance. The previous year—after NCAAs but before World Champs in Japan—an afternoon mushroom trip followed by evening bong rips had melted his world into liquid cartoons. He woke up the next day in a state of psychic confusion, feeling like reality had been torn asunder on him. He needed a change.

That was when he noticed the Empty Gate Zen Center.

---

27 At the time he imagined this older self to be in his midthirties, which coincidentally is Ervin's age as this book goes to press.

At least once a week I meditate in the temple. Lotus position is no longer uncomfortable. During one meditation I become aware of a spider crawling up my arm. My instinct is to jerk my elbow and flick it off. But remembering the dharma talk on equanimity, I keep my thumbs and fingertips pressed together at my lap as the spider crawls up my arm. I merely recognize my fear of the spider and my desire for it to depart. After some time, I gently brush it away. I notice I immediately feel relief. The Buddha would not have felt relief. He would view the spider's arrival and departure with equanimity.

Life is suffering. Desire causes suffering. Suffering can end.

Right view. Right intention. Right action. Right speech. Right livelihood. Right effort. Right mindfulness. Right meditation.

Do not kill. Do not steal. Do not speak falsely. Do not cause sexual harm.
Do not take intoxicating substances that cloud the mind.

On occasion I attend daylong sessions. These involve seated and walking meditations from nine a.m. to sunset. During one seated meditation tears start running down my cheeks. I don't wipe them until after the gong sounds. A woman who has also been meditating walks over to me. She smiles and hands me a necklace of wooden prayer beads on a red string. Then she walks away.

To pursue enlightenment is to obscure enlightenment.

Cling to nothing and you can handle anything.

Seeking happiness outside oneself is like waiting for sun-shine in a cave facing north.

Say nothing and saw wood.

After the dharma talk, the Zen master approaches me. In a calm voice he tells me that one's inner quest can at times become obsessive and compulsive, that it can be too much for some people. It seems a guarded way of saying I need to chill out.

What is the sound of one hand clapping? It is the place where truth is.

The tortoise told his friend the fish that he had just re-turned to the lake after a walk on land. "Of course," the fish said, "you mean swimming."

"Have you eaten your gruel?" says Master Chao-Chou.
"Yes," says the monk.
"Then wash your bowl!"

During another dharma talk, someone mentions that an aco-lyte can meditate in the temple, a journeyman can meditate on the mountain, and a master can meditate on a busy street. That's when I decide it's time for me to move on from the temple, to take my practice into the world.

❖

Anthony's meditation practice at Berkeley's Empty Gate Zen Center had aided him in preparing for the 2001 World Champs in Japan. Though he continued visiting the temple upon his return from Fukuoka, his practice started slipping as guilt and relationship stresses consumed him. When he finally stopped visiting the Zen Center, he failed to incorporate his meditation practice into daily life as he'd intended. The world of samsara got the best of him. But in the months after his suicide attempt, he did have a spiritual awakening of sorts, where he brought the discipline of his former temple zazen to his daily life.

During this time Anthony continued to abstain from alcohol and additionally cut out all drugs except tobacco. He couldn't shake off the crutch of cigarettes, though he found a way to assimilate even that habit into a mindfulness practice: "If something ailed me I'd just go outside and smoke a cigarette and let all that go." It was, nevertheless, still a destructive addiction, especially for a swimmer, and would develop with crippling consequences.

The clarity of this period led him to make some lifestyle changes. Recognizing that his approach to sexuality had been harmful—a violation of the third Buddhist precept on sexual misconduct—he decided to go celibate for several months. (He first consulted with The Voice, who didn't think that was a bad idea.) He also felt the need for a more compassionate orientation toward the world. He began depositing handfuls of coins by the gutter and at the base of signposts along less trafficked parts of Telegraph Avenue, where the homeless might find them.[28] He claims this was motivated less by altruism than by a need to shed his belongings and, more symbolically, his attachments and desires. He also took a guilt-free hiatus from swim practices. And he accepted the loss of K with the recognition that loss—of lovers, loved ones, dreams, youth, beauty, everything— is inevitable, and that without accepting this reality, one can never fully embrace life.

During this period, Anthony told only one person about his suicide attempt, and it wasn't the psychologist. It was a Mauritian-born

---

28 In one instance, however, his street charity had less noble motivations. His younger brother Derek remembers them walking at night on Anthony's twenty-first birthday: "This homeless guy had a sweater that said *Fuck Stanford* and Anthony gave him forty bucks."

poet and writer in his sixties named Mamade Kadreebux. Anthony had been introduced to Mamade by the assistant director for student services at Cal Athletics, Mohamed Muqtar, who was on intimate enough terms with Anthony to sense he needed guidance of a less conventional strain. Mamade certainly offered that. A spiritual mentor of sorts in the Berkeley community, sporting a long white chin beard, Mamade would soon become, in Anthony's words, a "Sufi mystic mentor" to him.

Mamade was Anthony's first real exposure to Islam. It was 2002, and in the Islamophobic post–9/11 culture, Muslims came to be equated for many Americans with suicide bombers, or at least with their sympathizers. Although Anthony hadn't vilified Islam, he still "summoned it as this Gothic Other" and approached the religion with some fear and suspicion. But Mamade revealed to Anthony a side of Islam the media rarely presented: one of love, religious tolerance, generosity, and compassion. Every Friday, Mamade opened up his home to anyone of any or no faith for a meal and for music, poetry, and discussions on philosophy, spirituality, and science. Anthony was a regular attendee of these dinner gatherings, which came to be referred to as "The Village" and included individuals as diverse as Nobel laureates and NBA players. In later years, after Anthony had stopped swimming and was broke, he came to rely upon those Friday gatherings for literal, as well as spiritual, nourishment. "Mamade comes across as a scholar," Anthony remembers. "And yet he lives very humbly and feeds the hungry. And I was one of those hungry people." The weekly tradition still stands: a quarter-century's worth of Friday meals.

Anthony began visiting Mamade every day. Whenever Mamade would prostrate toward Mecca, Anthony would meditate in a lotus position. Anthony never prostrated, except once years later, when Mamade gently pulled him down to his knees alongside him. "I remember thinking, *I'm not doing this for Allah or Muhammad, I'm doing this for Mamade.* That was a lesson in being able to honor one who is more than a friend, so that he doesn't submit alone."

But while daily ritual prayer wasn't for Anthony, another of the Five Pillars of Islam intrigued him: fasting during Ramadan. The challenge appealed to him. That November he joined Mamade for a month of fasting from sunrise to sunset. Coming on the heels of the suicide attempt, his appetite was already reduced, and the fasting didn't prove difficult. Each sunset he and Mamade ceremoniously broke fast over milk and dates before conversing on spiritual and celestial matters late into the night. It would not be Anthony's only Ramadan. Almost every year that followed, until he moved to New York, he would fast with Mamade for part or all of Ramadan.

Their conversations ranged over many topics. A well-traveled and educated polyglot, fluent in Creole, English, Spanish, and French, Mamade drew from a variety of literatures and mystical traditions and would freely weave into conversation long passages from writers like Voltaire, Chekhov, Lorca, and Baudelaire, often in their original languages. "He has this uncanny ability," Anthony says. "We'd be talking about something and then he'd pause and start reciting Shakespeare or Baudelaire or Tagore. Right on spot for what we were talking about. I was always blown away by that."

One day Anthony confessed that he had tried to take his life. He remembers Mamade merely looking him in the eye and saying, "It's wonderful that you're here. So very wonderful to have you here, Brother Antonious. Would you like some more tea?" Any wisdom or advice that Mamade did communicate to him came indirectly through literary vignettes and parables. One such story he shared with Anthony was of the first encounter between the Persian religious scholar Jelaluddin Rūmī and the wandering dervish Shams Tabriz. This meeting, of which there are several versions, took place in 1244 in Konya, a town in modern-day Turkey.

THE TALE OF RŪMĪ AND SHAMS

One day Rūmī was sitting with his theological students by a fountain in a small square in town. His manuscripts lay in a stack beside the fountain. A bedraggled stranger walked over to the scholarly circle and asked Rūmī, "What are you doing?"

As the eminent scholar of his time, accustomed to nothing short of reverence, Rūmī was irritated by this vagrant's disrespectful interruption. "Something you cannot understand," he replied.

The man, who was Shams Tabriz, then knocked the books into the fountain.

"What have you done!" cried Rūmī in despair. "You've destroyed my work!"

Unperturbed, Shams replied, "I've destroyed nothing, for you have done nothing." He then retrieved the books from the fountain and showed them to Rūmī.

"What is this?" Rūmī asked, gazing in disbelief at the books, which were all completely dry.

"Something you cannot understand," came Shams's reply.

This experience prompted Rūmī to abandon his scholarly career, relinquishing scholarship for experiential awareness. He spent the next few years with Shams, developing into a mystic and poet of ecstatic verse. The two grew inseparable. Then one day Shams mysteriously disappeared: some conjecture that he was murdered by Rūmī's jealous former students, others that he left unannounced to make way for Rūmī's final stage of spiritual development. Whatever the case,

Rūmī's subsequent grief and mourning led to an out-
pouring of lyrical poetry in honor of his departed mentor and friend, which is now considered among Rūmī's
masterpieces.

Excerpt from *The Diwan of Shams of Tabriz*
by Rūmī (translated by Coleman Barks):

Ode 314

Those who don't feel this Love
pulling them like a river,
those who don't drink dawn
like a cup of spring water
or take in sunset like supper,
those who don't want to change,

let them sleep.

This Love is beyond the study of theology,
that old trickery and hypocrisy.
If you want to improve your mind that way,

sleep on.

I've given up on my brain.
I've torn the cloth to shreds
and thrown it away.
If you're not completely naked,
wrap your beautiful robe of words
around you,

and sleep.

"It's very Socratic," says Anthony of Rūmī's first encounter with Shams. "You think you know something but you don't know anything." The story resonated for him: although his suicidal impulses had been rooted in depression, he had acted upon them precisely because he believed that he knew where his life was headed and predicted all possible outcomes.

Alongside Sufi lore and teachings culled from Mamade, Anthony was also exploring other religious traditions, especially Christianity. He read the Old and New Testaments. One passage that spoke to him in particular was Genesis 19:26, in which Lot's wife disobeys God's command to not look back while fleeing the destruction of Sodom: *But his wife looked back from behind him, and she became a pillar of salt.* Anthony interpreted her turning into salt as symbolizing the way in which regret mires one in the past. A decade later, when journalists asked him at the 2012 Olympic Trials in Omaha if he regretted his eight years away from the sport, he cited Lot's wife: "How do you move forward with one's life if you hold on to regret?" he responded. "If you turn around, you'd be like Lot's wife. You'd just be a pillar of salt. You wouldn't grow. You'd remain stagnant. So in that sense, no. No regrets."

After the Bible he moved on to more esoteric texts of Christian Gnosticism and mysticism, where he encountered the term *agapē*, the unselfish altruistic love for others, even in response to evil. It made him think of how Mamade opened his home to strangers and the hungry. But this expression of *agapē* went far beyond Friday-evening gatherings. In the same building lived the aunt of Mamade's wife Judy. A former newspaper journalist, Aunt Kate, as everyone referred to her, was in her nineties and had advanced Alzheimer's. When Judy had to leave for Oregon for several weeks, Mamade sat by Aunt Kate's side day and night, even though her condition had degenerated to the point where she was unconscious much of the time. In the evenings, Anthony was there too, keeping Mamade company.

◆

The door opens and Mamade greets me.

"It's a full moon and Brother Antonious has come to visit Aunt Kate and me. What an absolute pleasure to see you."

The room is bare. Two chairs, a nightstand, a lamp. In the hospital bed, at the far end of the room, lies Aunt Kate. Her eyes are closed.

We sit for hours, chatting. Mamade occasionally walks over to Aunt Kate's bedside to check up on her. She's long lost her grasp on the world. She's in the transitional phase, between two planes.

"The gift you give her by being here will come back to you from heaven," Mamade says.

"I'm not doing much," I protest.

"Oh, but you are, Brother Saint, you are. And Aunt Kate is grateful too. She may not be able to show it, but she knows."

Brother Saint he calls me. I used to refer to Mamade as Virgil when I started reading the *Inferno*. I thought of him as my guide through the underworld. And then I reached the part where Virgil, after leading Dante through Hell and Purgatory, is denied entry at the gates of Heaven because he was a pagan in a world before Christ. And I thought, *That's not right—Mamade is definitely allowed into heaven.* So I stopped calling him Virgil.

I return the following night. And the one after. The routine is the same. I sit with Mamade and we talk literature and he occasionally goes up to tend to Aunt Kate. It's not every night, but I go often.

And then one evening I show up but Aunt Kate has passed on.

"On a Friday [and] Saturday night, he hangs out with a woman in her last moments," says Mamade of Anthony. "This is the real gold of human achievement, the passion of life standing for hours in a small apartment in front of a faltering woman where life is leav-

ing slowly, step by step, and reaching that eternity that will claim us all. But she didn't go alone."

It was because of these visitations with Aunt Kate that Mamade began referring to Anthony as Brother Saint. The moniker is a nod to St. Anthony, the third-century anchorite and healer whose harsh ascetic lifestyle in the Egyptian desert inspired a monastic movement and earned him the appellate Father of Monasticism. Born to wealthy parents who died when he was eighteen, the teenager sold off his estate, donating the funds to the poor, and took off solo for the desert. As word spread of his remarkable eremitic life, disciples began seeking him out.[29]

Saint Anthony has come to be known for many things: his austerity, his Christlike compassion, his miraculous healings of skin diseases. But what have most caught the imagination through the centuries are the temptations he suffered, some of which, as in this painting by Lovis Corinth, you only wish Saint Anthony had had the weakness of will to have submitted to.

Although the ordeals featuring thuggish thrashings by demons

29 Even Emperor Constantine sent Anthony an epistle praising him and requesting his blessing. Not a man wowed by power, Anthony initially disregarded the epistle. But after pressure from his anchoritic brothers, he finally responded with a benediction for the emperor, the empire, and the church. Though one can only surmise, Anthony probably nonetheless remained skeptical about Constantine and his ambitions.

are far more colorful, one trial that seems more relevant to the twenty-first-century Anthony involves an encounter with precious metals. While traveling across the desert, Saint Anthony came across a plate of silver coins. After a moment of puzzlement, he realized the devil must have laid out the silver coins to tempt him. With this realization, the coins disappeared. He later came across a pile of gold. Recognizing the devilry, he threw the gold into the fire and it too disappeared. Despairing at all these traps, Saint Anthony cried out to God, asking how it was possible for anyone to escape such snares. A voice replied, "Humility."

Like his namesake, Anthony Ervin also withdrew from the world, albeit in a far milder manner. He too sought to resist and avoid temptation. He too heard a voice of wisdom. But as his depression lifted and the trauma of the suicide attempt began to fade over the months that followed, all that changed: he grew more sociable; the voice diminished in strength and frequency until it departed; and the humility gave way as he succumbed to a new kind of temptation—the hubris that, having tried and failed to end his life, he was invincible. That no matter what he did, he wouldn't die.

Unfortunately, this sense of indestructability came at a bad time. He had just bought a motorcycle.

11 *Lethe's Edge*

They are the souls who are destined for Reincarnation; and now at Lethe's stream they are drinking the waters that quench man's troubles, the deep draught of oblivion.

—Virgil, *The Aeneid*

Few people understand the psychology of dealing with a high-way traffic cop. Your normal speeder will panic and immediately pull over to the side when he sees the big red light behind him . . . and then we will start apologizing, begging for mercy. This is wrong. It arouses contempt in the cop-heart. The thing to do—when you're running along about a hundred or so and you suddenly find a red-flashing CHP-tracker on your trail—what you want to do then is accelerate.

—Hunter S. Thompson, *Fear and Loathing in Las Vegas*

I'm coming down the Berkeley Hills, feeling good, sunlight flickering through the trees, no cars in sight, when I emerge from a sweeping turn and see a cop with the radar gun out, looking down the crosshairs straight at me through sunglasses. I pass him going about 60 in a 25 zone. This is it, I'm going to run. The siren wails behind me and my adrenaline kicks in as I open up the throttle. I drop through Strawberry Creek to the back of Memorial Stadium and blast around into frat and sorority row.

Though I'm now in traffic I don't let up. I'm lane splitting, riding the yellow divider between cars moving in both directions. The cop is long gone, he wouldn't chase me through this, but I don't stop, don't even slow down. I'm taking huge risks, not in control anymore now that the adrenaline has got hold of me. Everything is buzzing, I can't let off. I lean left onto Bancroft and accelerate around a red Mustang, overtaking him at three or four times his speed. The driver doesn't see me. He starts to shift lanes because a car is stopped ahead with its hazards on. Though I notice the Mustang moving left, there's nowhere for me to go. Everything downshifts into time lag. I brace and he hits me.

My shoulder takes the impact as I ricochet off the car. I manage to keep the bike upright, but I feel my shoulder dislocate as my arm goes limp and dangly. My right hand is still clutching the handlebar but my grip is weak, useless. I've got the wobbles and am veering straight for the parked cars. Though it all happens within a second or two, it unfolds in crisp slow motion.

Using my torso and core and whatever muscles I can access around my shoulder, I jerk my upper body. My shoulder sucks back into place, and at once I regain use of my arm. Revving the throttle, I kick out of the trajectory, narrowly avoiding what might have been a fatal collision. I'm so freaked out I keep riding at a blistering pace. If I ride to my apartment I'll have to park my bike on the street and the cops might find it. So I ride to a swimmer house nearby and leave it by the back porch, where it can't be seen from the street. I notice I'm hyperventilating as I stash the bike.

I go to the gym and crank through some power cleans, my adrenaline still surging. Then I head to swim practice. The water feels good at first but soon my right arm can't reach as far as it normally does. Lap by lap, my reach shortens until I can't even pull anymore. I climb out and leave without telling Mike.

When I wake the next morning, I can't lift my arm up past my shoulder.

The motorcycle Ervin was riding when the Mustang hit him was a red 2000 Suzuki GSX-R600. He purchased it with prize money he earned in late August at the 2002 Pan Pacific Swimming Championships. The previous owner had wrecked the bike, so he bought it as a rebuilt salvage for a few thousand dollars. There were two reasons Anthony couldn't afford a new bike with the earnings: after qualifying for the national team in the 50 free earlier that month in Fort Lauderdale, he scratched the 100, much to everyone's shock, which meant that he wouldn't be swimming or vying for prize money in either the 100 free or the 4x100 free relay at Pan Pacs.

"Mike couldn't believe it," Ervin recalls. "I didn't want to do it because it hurt too much." The 100 is a far more physically taxing event than the 50, and Ervin "wasn't interested in pain," though he also recognized that "everybody must have thought it was absurd." On top of this, after that same Nationals qualifying meet in Florida, the USA Swimming national team director Dennis Pursley fined him several thousand dollars for violating the USA Swimming Code of Conduct by going out at night.[30] Ervin would have to pay for it out of his Pan Pac winnings, which was galling to him considering he hadn't even won the money yet. "I felt particularly persecuted by this fine because Erik Vendt was out with me and he didn't get fined at all," Ervin says, adding that "Vendt jokingly quipped, *It's because you're black.*"

Although Pursley can't now recall the incident, as it occurred over a dozen years ago, he claims there would have had to have been an objective reason to fine Anthony and not Vendt, such as stiffer penalties due to repeat offenses. "I don't know if he knows this or not, but I actually liked Anthony," Pursley says. "I thought he was a nice guy. He was [just] in a world of his own and didn't seem to have

---

30 Yup, again.

an awareness of where he needed to be. I didn't take that as being rebellious or as a malicious attempt to defy the rules." Whatever the case, Ervin felt like he was being singled out because he was never the only one breaking the rules.

For some time Ervin had been flirting with getting a motor-cycle; after the fine, he vowed to put every dollar of his remaining Pan Pac earnings toward one. A bike came to symbolize a way of escaping those in power. It wasn't that he needed wheels. With his earnings from World Champs in Japan he'd purchased a black Audi, which he nicknamed Vader. But a car offered no promise of freedom and rebellion. And he couldn't outrun the authorities in an Audi.

Not that he didn't try.

⚬⚬⚬⚬⚬

I'm in Vader, driving south on the 5 to Valencia. I'm making good time, zooming down the Grapevine, but just as I'm almost through and into the valley, I pass a cop parked on the shoulder. I'm going 135—about 65 mph over the speed limit. The car can go faster but the governor chip limits its speed. If he nabs me I'm screwed. It's about six miles to the first exit out of the Grapevine. I figure if I make it that far, I can ditch him in town. So I step on it.

Within three miles, the cop catches me. I see him coming in the rearview mirror. Those Caprices are damn fast and they have no governor chip. Game over. I pull to the side and roll down the window.

He tramps over, red-faced, his right hand on his gun. His jaw is clenched.

"Keep your hands where I can see them!" he barks. "Do you have any idea how fast you were going?" His lips are taut, curled back. "I clocked you at 132 miles per hour."

"Yeah," I say.

"Did you see me on the side of the road?"

"Yeah."

He pauses and removes his aviators. His eyes are hard, unblinking. When he finally speaks again, he pauses between the words, accentuating each one. "Then why didn't you slow down?"

"To be honest," I say, "I was hoping I was going so fast that you didn't see me."

The cop's mouth drops and he just stares at me, stunned. He stands there for a while in silence. His lips are pursed, his face twitching under some inner struggle to maintain composure. Finally he quietly asks for my license and registration. He takes the papers and goes to his car.

He seems calm when he returns. "You know I could take you to jail for this," he says.

"Uh, that would be bad," I reply.

He snorts and shakes his head. "I'm writing you up for 120 miles per hour, though you were going faster. Don't do that again. And don't speed the rest of the way."

I toss the slip onto the passenger seat as he walks back to his car. I resume my journey, sighing and muttering, maintaining the speed limit.

I should have been on a motorcycle.

<hr>

For that incident Anthony had to go to court, where he pled guilty to reckless endangerment. Though he had more success fleeing the authorities on two wheels than on four, the motorcycle served more as a means for him to escape his own private troubles. His purchase of the salvaged Suzuki coincided with the onset of his depression, when he'd stopped drinking and started isolating himself. The motorcycle was ideal for that. He'd take to the hills for a few hours to get away from everything. Riding demanded his undivided focus, allowing no leeway for his mind to withdraw into its convoluted interiors.

He had never even sat on a bike before. His first time riding was the day he bought one. He passed the written test so he had a permit, which came with restrictions: don't ride at night, don't carry a passenger, don't ride on the freeway. He obeyed none of these rules. And since he never got a motorcycle license, he continued breaking them for all the years he rode. A license required taking a safety course, which he never got around to.

His collision with the Mustang wasn't his sole accident. He first one was in the fall of 2002, shortly after he got the bike.

❦

I'm east of Berkeley, beyond the hills, and it's getting dark. I can either take the freeways that loop through Tilden Park or the twisties that wind through the hills. It'll be nicer through Tilden. I'll just take it easy.

Hardly any other vehicles out at this hour. I'm feeling good, leaning in and out of the turns, bike purring under me. I take it slow by the drop-offs. No rush.

But it's hard not to open up when you've got all that power available at a twist of the wrist. I don't know the roads as well as I anticipated, and in the dusk I miscalculate and a left turn sneaks up on me. I lean hard into it but end up lowsiding. The bike falls on top of me but the sliders keep most of the bike's weight off me. I skid down the road, the bike and I separating as we slide out. I come to a stop in a bank of decomposing bark and wood bits.

My gloves are shredded and the sleeve of my jacket got pushed back while sliding so I've got nasty road rash on my wrist. Lucky for me, I'm wearing my full leathers. I'd be a mess without them. They're hideous and ridiculously 1980s, with leather patches in the shape of lightning bolts sewn on the back, but they're now the best sixty dollars I've ever spent on Craigslist.

While I'm still on the ground, a truck comes around the bend and pulls to the side. The driver runs over to check up on me. My knee hurts where the bike fell on it, my back feels messed up, and I'm disoriented, but aside from that I'm all right. He asks if I want a ride to a garage in Berkeley. It's either that or wait for a cop to show up, which would be all sorts of trouble since I recently got a warning for riding without a license plate and for carrying a passenger without a license. I couldn't run at the time because I would have endangered her. Fortunately, she sweet-talked the cop and he let me off with a warning. But if a cop comes now and sees that I still don't have a license plate and that I was riding in the dark, I won't get off so easy.

The guy helps me load the bike onto the truck bed. Then he drives me down to a garage.

I feel my back stiffening on the ride down. But only when I step out of the truck to unload the bike and find myself walking like C-3PO do I realize just how messed up it is.

⚜

With a bruised, swollen back, Anthony spent the next few days convalescing in bed. His friend and Cal athletics advisor Mohamed Muqtar, who like others had been warning him about his reckless riding, remembers calling him a few days later only to be forwarded to "an outgoing message that said, *Okay, it happened, now you guys can gloat.*"

Anthony isn't sure precisely when his suicide attempt took place in relation to his motorcycle accidents. As far as he recalls, the timeline is 1) Tilden lowside, 2) clonidine overdose, 3) Mustang collision. But then again, 2) and 3) may be reversed. Or 1) and 2). In fact, the only certainty is that he lowsided before he hit the Mustang. His memories aren't compartmentalized by time but by areas of his life—for example, swimming, depression, mysticism, motorcycling—even if they overlapped. Within each facet of his life he knows the ordering of events, but the worlds they each inhabited were so disparate that when viewed in relation to one another they seem jumbled and disassociated. Whatever the case, when the Mustang hit him, he was either depressed or recently depressed, so when viewed against that darkness, the accident wasn't as traumatic as it might have been. He mostly just felt relieved. But it wasn't from having survived a game of high-speed *Frogger* on wheels. "After the shoulder injury I knew my swimming career was over," he says. "I felt relief I didn't have to worry about swimming anymore."

He continued to train and compete, but in his mind, swimming was over. It showed in his performance. At the 2003 World Championships in Barcelona, entering the 50 as the defending world champion and championship record holder in the event, he again raced Popov and Hoogenband. But there would be no repeat of the 2001 World Champs final in Japan. In fact, there would be no finals for him at all. Or even semifinals.[31]

Those 2003 World Championships would be Anthony's final major competition—at least for the next eight years. After that, he would all but officially retire. Swimming offered him nothing meaningful anymore. But riding did. With his monthly stipend from USA Swimming, he sold his red bike and bought the next-generation model, a 2001 Suzuki GSX-R750. The 750 was a flashier yellow, with more torque and horsepower.

Ervin was still hooked on speed. And he was still fast, in fact faster than ever before. But his speed now had nothing to do with the water.

---

31 His time of 22.74 put him in a tie for seventeenth place with two other swimmers: Salim Iles and (drumroll) Roland Schoeman! His former teammate Bart Kizierowski, meanwhile, tied for eighteenth, also with two others, with a time of 22.75. That's six swimmers narrowly missing semifinals, all touching within 1/100th of a second of each other.

Riding down to LA in jeans and body armor and hovering around 100 mph, I come into a long open stretch with no wind and few cars and trucks—this is the place, time to find out what I can do on this yellow streak of lightning, time to ride that razor's edge—I rev and tuck down as the bike leaps forward and the Gs kick in, that's what this bike is made for, that's the only way it's comfortable, under acceleration, so your weight gets pushed back into the seat where it belongs, not all mashed up in the front where you're up on your arms like in a push-up position—I crouch down as the speedometer turns over into the 110s, 120s, 130s—making myself as small and narrow as possible, tucking down behind the windshield, minimizing resistance—140s, 150s—I come up on a car so I let up on the accelerator and drop to 120 since the turbulence around the car can be unreliable—then shoot past it—130s, 140s, 150s, and climbing toward the 160s when I come upon a semi truck with a cargo trailer in tow—again I let off, even more than before because of the behemoth's denser turbulence pocket—even at 110 and giving a wide berth the wind hits me hard—but I'm ready for it, I've done this enough, I may be a squid but I'm no noob—and soon I'm past the truck too and it's open road again, this time I know I can get it up as high as it will go—130s, 140s, 150s—I stay locked tight onto the bike, hugging it with everything even though my collar is digging in as if I'm being pulled back on a leash and the wind is trying to pry my legs apart—160s—the asphalt is a gray blur streaked with stripes of orange and white from the reflectors and highway paint—170s—now the whine of the engine is all I hear—175—the tachometer is maxed out—176, 177, 177, 177—max speed, I'm at the limit, I'm riding right on the edge—

As I'm approaching LA I realize the engine is so hot it burned a hole through the header—the bike backfires whenever I ease off the throttle—I bum around LA for a few days, then take the scenic route along 1 back up to Berkeley—but you can't get distracted by the sights on the coastal twisties, that's how you go down on a bike: distraction, lack of focus—stray out here and a landslide may trip you up—or a rabbit—or a rogue Bambi—so instead every now and then I just pull over and take in the view and then move on, keeping my eyes on the road—that's the lesson I've learned: always look forward, never back, always keep your attention where you want to go—when the mind strays the body strays, which can be fatal on a bike—here error carries the ultimate penalty—you learn from mistakes fast and hope they're not hard ones—so now when I pass cops with radars I don't even look back—my heart rate barely rises, no adrenaline kicks in, there's nothing to fear because cops can't keep up, they can't weave through the traffic like me, not in those clunky steel cages—I just note them in passing, giving them no more thought than I would a pothole—not to say a motorcycle patrolman wouldn't nab me, but I haven't had the pleasure of passing one yet, and who knows whether or not I'd actually pull over if a cop on a bike tried to run me down—one thing I've learned is that riding is all about knowing limits and riding within them, about calculating risk—sure, I pushed those limits by maxing out on the ride down to LA, but that's the one time I really moved out to the edge on this bike, and you've got to step out to the edge now and then just to find out where it is—no one else can tell you, it's a private matter, you've got to find that border for yourself—of course, there are unaccountables that can come out of nowhere even when you're within the limits—unforeseen gusts, mechanical failures—like the time I popped a wheelie along those vast treeless sweepers up in Sonoma and my chain snapped, that's what I got for riding on a stock chain—but I got lucky because the chain didn't get stuck in the sprocket and send the rear tire into lockdown, which does happen and which would have been nasty—instead I just lost power and came to a stop and pushed the bike down the street to the closest house—and go figure, the guy there just happened to tinker with bikes and have spare parts and he rigged me up a new link for my chain on the spot, just like that—even invited me for dinner—life has a way of working itself out, well, sometimes it does, just like sometimes it has a way of falling apart—who knows, it's all a devil's gamble—all you can do is ride like a warrior, with confidence, with fearlessness, 'cause that's what gives you the best odds of getting out alive—

***

One place Anthony often rode out to was the residence of Della Lorenzetti, a masseuse and sports therapy specialist whom Mike Bottom had introduced him to his sophomore year. But he wasn't riding there for rehab or bodywork. Della had become a kind of surrogate mother to him (to this day he refers to her as his godmother), cooking him dinners, calling him just to check up on him, etc. He also felt comfortable confiding in her. "She became the only person I could really talk to when things with K melted down," Ervin says. "If I talked to other guys they were always like, *Fuck it, dude, go bang other girls.* That was their only advice."

Vivacious and warmhearted, Della opened her home to him, offering strong coffee, Italian hospitality, and an attentive ear anytime he needed it, or even just a safe haven where he could sip a coffee and stare off into space. Anthony and Della grew so close that Mike Bottom would often check in with Della to get a read on Anthony's psychological state.

One reason Anthony could so easily talk to her is because he knew she'd once been down in the trenches too. Della first told Anthony about her own troubled past after he remarked that he didn't care if he lived, that if something happened to him, so be it. "That disturbed me," she recalls. "That's why I told him about my experiences. We all have an appointment with death, but we can bring it on ourselves if we're foolish." Once a manager in the entertainment industry who used to travel with rock bands and ride with bikers, Della had a dark and adventurous side and was no stranger to crazy living. She had lost many loved ones, including her boyfriend, to drugs and violence. When her own life started spiraling out of control, she had an epiphany, what she describes as a life-altering experience of God. Overnight she transformed her lifestyle and turned to Christianity. But she never forgot the dark ledge that Anthony now found himself on. "I know you can go to the end and not come back—a lot of my friends didn't," she says. "I almost didn't."

Della saw echoes of herself and her past in Anthony, and it scared her. She remembers driving behind him at night, watching helplessly as he popped a wheelie and rode a stretch of highway on his back wheel.[32] At times he rode to her house high. "Oh, Della," she remembers him saying when she protested, "you did this too." But while her troubled past made her an ideal confidante for him, it also made her fear for him. "Anthony doesn't know this [but] I called one of my friends and said, *Anthony is probably going to do something to kill himself, and I need to prepare myself for that.*" She also recognized there was only so much she could do. "Then there were times when I said, *I just need to love him for who he is and enjoy the present because we may not have it again.*"

Anthony wasn't pulling as many stunts like wheelies or supermans[33] or top-speed riding on his first bike. Most of that was on his more powerful Suzuki 750. Yet he considered himself a safer rider on that bike. Experience had taught him to know his limits and

---

32 Though she never rode with Anthony, they once rented snowmobiles. "Don't open them up full throttle, they can get out of hand," the guy warned them. But out there in the open fields with Anthony, Della reverted to her older reckless self: the two took off on a tear, opening the throttle, sliding everywhere, until Anthony eventually crashed, flying over an embankment into thigh-high snow.

33 *Superman* is where you lie flat on your belly so that the ends of your legs are sticking out horizontally over the back of the bike. A classic squid move. (*Squids* are newbie riders who ride crotchrockets way too fast and pull stunts like supermans, often in T-shirts, the kind of bikers who whiz by you and whom you expect to find farther down the road at the end of a long red streak.)

ride within them. And experience gave him confidence, which was critical to his riding well.

But all that would change. One night he moved not just to the edge of his limits but way out beyond them. And it started with two hits of acid.

I could have and should have died last night—that's the refrain playing over and over again in my bleary-eyed skull as I lie there, groaning in bed—*I could have and should have died*—what in hell was I thinking jumping on the bike yesterday afternoon right as I was peaking—right as the fractals came on and the walls started breathing and my mind began kicking like a fetus, with the world warping around me convex like in a funhouse mirror— and for some reason I thought this was a *good* time to go out riding into the hills??—remembering how I picked up my Arai helmet and just stood there for a while, noticing, really *noticing,* the red fire-breathing dragon painted on it, the flames so fiery they seemed to leap off the helmet—and then zooming up into the hills—normally so confident and comfortable leaning in and out of curves through alternating patches of sunshine and tree shadows but none of that ease or open-range freedom this time, instead discomfort and inability to gauge distances clearly and just a growing oppressiveness—I wind my way up to the Wall on Grizzly Peak—the Wall a waist-high stone memorial where a biker went over the edge, a lookout point where other bikers hang out for bayview sunsets and remember the fallen—and I park and dismount and even on two feet everything feels unfamiliar, foreign, my body now like some alien vessel out of which my consciousness peers nervously, an uncertain navigator—and if walking is awkward think of what that means for riding, where shifting body position a few inches can mean the difference between taking a corner smoothly at a high speed and your helmet popping like bubble wrap under a sixteen-wheeler—a couple of riders are just wordlessly standing side by side at the Wall, probably just enjoying the burning sky over Sausalito and Oakland and the Golden Gate Bridge, but in my dosed oversensitivity I'm convinced they're actually mourning my death—and suddenly I'm standing there too, hanging my head, thinking, *Shame, shame, he had this gift of life but went and threw it all away by breaking the cardinal moto rule, Know Thy Limits*—I shudder at the, what, premonition?—and that's when I call J, my biker buddy from the auto shop who first taught me something about turning a wrench and who would become my main riding partner once I got my second bike—right away J knows something is wrong—"Hey, man, you sound weird, you all right?"—so I tell him—he's silent for a moment, "And you're on your bike . . . ? Duuuude, that's no good, that's dangerous, can you get down to the shop?"—so I ride down there, nerves jangling, the Wall haunting me—huge relief to get to his shop—I can always count on J, of Chinese immigrant stock but from generations back, not from any recent brain drain, and an ex-con too—but J did his time and put that criminal life behind him and is now just a friendly madman auto mechanic, and a badass rider and fiercely loyal friend to boot— it's after five p.m. so the shop's now closed and no one's there but him—he goes off when he sees me, "Duuuude, you're crazy riding around on acid, we've got to get that shit out of you," and right away pulls out a bottle of vodka and throws down an eight ball of coke—"Come on, let's get you straight"—so we start racking rails, doing lines, which pushes the acid out of my system, or at least out to the periphery (coke not something I usually do or even like to do, just don't care for it really, maybe 'cause the first time I tried it was at a sorority party sophomore year, just me and my buddy and about sixty girls, so you can imagine what that was like . . . talk about chasing the dragon, everything after that was like taking turds), but it does start helping me feel more grounded—and not sure which one of us suggested we go riding but since I'm feeling mighty fine now we hop on our bikes and take the Bay Bridge, aglitter with lights, ushering us into the San Francisco night—I do a few wheelies, and while even this may sound sketchy the reality is it's very hard to spill backward and I'd spent many late afternoons practicing them for hours in an empty parking lot after a few puffs on a joint—but never mind my modest wheelies because J of course is doing sick moves on the bridge, like jumping off the bike and surfing on the titanium skid plates he's installed on his boot soles—so imagine: you're driving along the Bay Bridge in your car, all comfortable and buckled in and nuzzled by AC and surround sound, and suddenly this biker zips past you and then he just JUMPS off the side of his bike (OMG, is this some horrible suicide?!), only to be suddenly waterskiing alongside the bike, sparks flying off his heels like some kind of biker demon incarnate—try to imagine that—crazy jaw-dropping shit, but that's how J rolls—he's not actually a madman, mind you, just a skilled rider who knows how to put on a show—so anyway, we get to San Francisco and go to a bar and drink and order another eight ball and do more lines and then ride back to his shop in Berkeley—more drinking, more lines—then yippee-kai-yay back out to SF again—same deal, different bar—then ride back to his shop in Berkeley—a few more lines, why the hell not—and then zoom back out over the Bay Bridge for a third time to SF, close a club there and it's coming on dawn when we ride back—the plan being to snatch a few hours of sleep and then head out early to a big biker meetup down past Stanford, so as to have the road all to ourselves, with those long sweeping curves through the redwoods—though once I'm in bed it takes a full hour for my spinning mind to reel itself to sleep and by then I'm already starting to feel grim but nothing close to what's to come since the coke is still masking the underlying fear and sapping of confidence that's started to trickle through—

And then awakening to no more trickling for the dam has broken and the horror of morning realization floods in—and so now here I am, lying in bed, pinned and needled by morning light, reflecting in cotton-mouthed dread upon yesterday afternoon and night—in one fell swoop that sense of invincibility that I've been feeling for so long evaporates in a snarling hangover of coke and vodka and acid—never have I binged like that, certainly not in any proximity to a motorcycle—*I could have and should have died last night*—knowing full well I'm not riding anywhere today—knowing in fact I may never ride again now that fear has entered my heart, at least not ride like I once did—because once fear enters, you can never ride that razor's edge again—because 90 percent of riding takes place between the ears, and if when you ride the edge the heart no longer beats softly like that of child, then you're finished, which means I can't ride at all because the edge is why I ride—*I could have and should have died*—I know it in my thudding rabbit heart, I know it in the miasma between my ears, I know it:

My motorcycling days are over.

Fig.1

Fig.2

Fig.
3

Fig.4

Fig.5

Fig.6

the Water Dragon

 **12** *Serpent Skin*

I am a man of substance, of flesh and bone, fiber and liquids.
—Ralph Ellison, *Invisible Man*

A man without tattoos is invisible to the gods.
—Iban Proverb

Bleed in your own light
Dream of your own life
I miss me
I miss everything I'll never be
—Smashing Pumpkins, "Rocket"

Many first-time Olympians head to a tattoo parlor right after they're done competing to get inked with the ceremonial Olympic logo. For once, Ervin chose to go with the flow. The day after swimming ended at the 2000 Sydney Olympics, he rallied a few guys on the national team and they went and got the five interlocking rings of blue, yellow, black, green, and red. Although he wouldn't stop at just that single tattoo, as so many Olympians do, for years it would remain his only one. That ink was about camaraderie, a badge of membership. Situated on the left side of his upper back, his Olympic rings are now the smallest and least striking of his tattoos, although they also happen to reflect the experience for which he's most famous. They would later be rendered practically invisible by a canvas of tattoos that had nothing to do with competitive swimming. But that would not come for another three years, not until after the 2003 Barcelona World Champs.

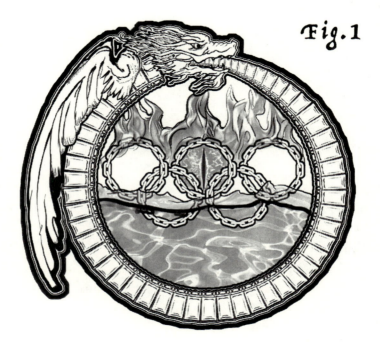

Fig. 1

Every time I travel I move as if in an army, with managers, teammates, trainers. So after Barcelona World Champs I say to hell with it and change my flight to spend some days alone in Catalonia and then Amsterdam. It's my first time traveling solo. I take the train from the airport to Amsterdam Centraal, which from the outside looks like a royal palace, although the surroundings are seedy. A homeless-looking guy approaches me, probably in his midtwenties. He's acting relieved to meet me because, he claims, no one speaks English in Amsterdam. Then he says he's just been robbed and has nowhere to stay and asks me if he can stay with me for one night. When I say sorry, he tells me to fuck off under his breath and slinks away.

I walk toward the center. Everyone is tall, attractive, and riding vintage bicycles. As I soon find out, almost everyone speaks English. I get a bunk in a hostel. Across the street is a coffee shop called Grasshopper. It serves alcohol, coffee, and weed. And there are computer games. The essentials of life. I hunker down there for the rest of the afternoon, smoking weed and playing DotA. I could open a place like this.

The next morning I walk to a tattoo shop. I tell the guy I want a star within a star on my left elbow. I got the idea in Barcelona a few days ago from a backpacker. She was walking away from me, so I couldn't see her face, but on her elbow was a tattoo of a star. I'd known I wanted tattoo sleeves for a long time, but I didn't know where to start. Something about the star caught my eye, drew me in. That's me, I thought, a traveler. I don't know who she is and I don't need to. And people don't need to know who I am. I'd start there and let the other tattoos follow. To make the tattoo my own, I decided on the star within a star.

The tattoo artist doesn't come in until noon and it's only nine so I book the first free slot and head out. After a few hours I wander into a head shop. There are mushrooms on sale, listed by strength. The most potent are tiny ones called Rambo. I tell the guy I want those. He eyes me, sussing me out.

"Where are you from?" he asks.

"USA."

"These are really strong. Sure you want them? Have you had mushrooms before?"

I nod and give him cash.

"Well, just don't eat them all," he says, handing them to me.

He thinks because I'm American I can't handle strong mushrooms. So I open the pack right there at the counter and eat them all. He's just looking at me, shaking his head. Then I walk out.

The mushrooms start coming on as I enter the tattoo shop. A guy is getting his arm done. He has an Asian dragon on his shoulder coming down to his elbow. It looks alive. Fresh tattoos really pop, and not just the colors—they literally pop out because of the swelling that the needles cause—so this combined with the mushrooms make his dragon look 3-D and alive. I know something large like this is the next stage for me. Watching him is like seeing myself in the future, like a higher-evolved, tattooed version of me. When I trip, I see myself in everything.

The session is painful, but the mushrooms give me an unexpected calm and confidence. By the time I leave the tattoo parlor I'm really zooming. The mushrooms start to overwhelm me. That guy wasn't overplaying the power of Rambo. The colorful row houses all jut up weirdly and lean over the canals at crazy angles like crooked discolored teeth. I'm walking through a Van Gogh painting. Standing in a parlor window and suffused in red light, a mannequin in lingerie suddenly comes to life and waves at me. I flinch, recoiling. Next thing I know, there's a whole row of red parlor windows in which half-naked women leer at me like predatory circus exhibits. But there's sorrow there too. A woman's palm against the glass troubles me. I stumble off down bizarre and byzantine side streets. People pass by me, murmuring and babbling in foreign tongues.

Maybe I'm in hell. This rings in my head like a joke, but it feels real too. I need protection. Across the street I see a store called 666. It must be a sign. It's a sunglasses store. Protection against demonic entities. I buy a pair of rave glasses in a light shade of pink. I walk out in them, feeling much better. Now I'm protected in hell.

I walk until night falls.

Fig.2

ight around when I get that tattoo on my elbow in Amsterdam, I decide I'm done with competitive swimming. The star within a star reflects that desire to leave the sport. Since childhood the night sky has represented escape and freedom. As an adolescent, I wasn't just taking refuge in the starry heavens when I fled to the treehouse and stared up into them; I was also taking flight, losing myself amidst the glittering constellations.

The star within a star isn't my only tattoo connected to childhood. The tattoo sleeves I will soon have are rooted in a book from my adolescent reading. In Robert Jordan's Wheel of Time series, the main character, Rand al'Thor, emerges from a gateway to the past, a profound and transformative experience, to discover that his arms have been branded with dragon tattoos. The literary passage, with its transfigurative symbolism, awed me, later inspiring me to get my own tattoo sleeves.

I've been at Cal for four years but still haven't graduated because I lack direction, hopping from major to major, from computer science to cognitive science to biochemistry to philosophy, among other areas. No longer funded now that my four years of college eligibility are up, I leave school with a hodgepodge of credits that don't apply to any single major. With the expiration of my eligibility, I'm able to sign professional contracts. I need the money so I sign with Speedo. One day I'm sitting there on the phone, baked out of my mind, as this agent yaps on the other line about the contract. He has the gift of gab. He bowls me over with words. And finally I can't take it anymore. "Fine, fine," I say, "I'll just take the contract." But four years after my Olympic gold, it's a paltry sum. And I've signed to be a professional exactly when a career in swimming is the last thing I want.

I've been growing out my hair since the summer and by winter start twisting it up into dreadlocks. I also have a number of piercings, including ear plugs and eyebrow bars, although the bars mostly just annoy me because the spikes keep catching whenever I take off my shirt. I haven't officially resigned from swimming, but psychologically I'm done; my piercings, dreadlocks, and tattoos attest to it.

When I return from Amsterdam in the fall of 2003 I start hanging out at Zebra Tattoos & Body Piercing on Telegraph Avenue. I get to know the tattoo artists and their various styles. After several months I ask one of the guys, Les, to start working on my tattoo sleeves. He begins with the left arm, where I have the double star, both because I'm left-handed and because left is the devil's arm, which seems a fitting place to begin. My tattoos on that arm draw from the designs of the Swiss surrealist H.R. Giger, with the anatomy inversed so that the bones and sinews are on the outside. Greenery and water imagery surrounds and entwines the exoskeleton, as well as around the words *Dream of Your Own Life* on my forearm. It's at once an image of torture and torment, in which the body seems destroyed, and an image of strength in the way it conforms to the body like a case of armor.

On the back of my left hand I get a maple leaf, tinged with reds and oranges, as if ready to fall from a tree. But others keep construing the maple as a marijuana leaf. I tire of that pretty quickly so I eventually put a bigger, bolder tattoo next to it of a rose. An ex-girlfriend's sister, who never liked me, later sneers that it looks like a vagina. I'm bothered at first, but then again, most flowers look like vaginas, so rather than let other people's opinions steer my tattooing any longer, I leave the rose as is. People will see what they want to see.

𝔉𝔦𝔤.3

𝕮onsidering how often I hang out at Zebra, I figure I may as well make some money at it. So I get a job there. At first I'm just in the front selling jewelry for piercings, which sucks. Later I'm a receptionist of sorts for the tattoo artists—making appointments, giving estimates, cleaning up the ink, changing needles, sweeping up, that sort of thing. The tattoo artists are good dudes, but they don't let people mess with them. They tell me about one vagrant who came in, saying, "I've got a tattoo, wanna see it?" and then dropped his pants to his knees, with his cock just hanging there. The tattoo was just a little smiley face on his knee. And Reed said, "You motherfucker! Get out of here," pointing at the door, but instead of heeding him the vagrant went ape shit and started kicking in all the glass jewelry display cases. That was a bad move. The entire staff took him out to Telegraph Avenue and proceeded to beat the senseless man into a new order of senselessness, then hog-tied him with duct tape to await the arrival of the police.

They've seen crazy shit working there. And they're full of stories and tattoo tall tales. Like when that white trash kid from the back country of California came in spouting choice words of his dislike for "niggers" and "beaners." No one took kindly to that, so when this racist hillbilly declared that he wanted *BAD ASS WHITE BOY* tattooed on his triceps, they obliged by over-charging him, asking for all the money up front, and carving the letters repeatedly. He whined about the pain the entire time as *BAD ASS* went onto his left triceps and *WHITE BOY* onto his right in Old English–inspired cursive letters. Exhausted, the guy looked at the finished product in the mirror and mumbled, "Fuck yeah," before preparing to walk out. But when he put his T-shirt on, the sleeves covered the first word of each arm, so it just read *ASS BOY* as he walked out of the store, laughter following him.

I only work at Zebra a few months but they are influential ones. The tattoo artists have really lived. Reed has been shot, stabbed, and kidnapped, witnessed murders, and worked for Dustin Hoffman and other Hollywood elite. He's lived around the world and toured the US in various rock bands, one of which, while he worked for Bob Dylan, was the Wallflowers. I grow closest to Reed, for I see him as my rock 'n' roll mentor.

I'm still partying too much and unable to get my sleep schedule under control. Twice in one week I sleep through my alarm. The first time it's a weekday and I show up an hour late. I'm warned. Then a few days later, Saturday of all days, I wake up at three p.m., and I was supposed to be at the shop at noon. When I finally arrive, Reed is just shaking his head, silently saying with his eyes, *What the fuck, dude?* He is punk rock and all, but when a man has to work he isn't going to appreciate it when some irresponsible kid unexpectedly leaves him with a bunch of bullshit to do on the busiest day of the week. The owner tells me he likes me but can't have me showing up late, so he fires me. But I keep hanging out at Zebra, and I'm still friends with the guys who, once the event has washed over, perhaps respect me more for getting fired.

I'm still learning about tattoos and getting inked. And just as nearly everyone in the shop has a chemical dependency problem, whether its uppers or downers, pills or powders, booze or weed, or all of the above, I continue to explore getting tattooed as I started: under the influence.

One time I get tattooed while stoned, which is the worst. All the physical and psychological pain is heightened by the same mechanism of cannabis that turns an ordinary light chuckle into a belly laugh, and the brief moment of personal introspection into a paranoid gyre. But perhaps that is more the effect of the permanent psychedelic stacking that is activated when I am high on marijuana. I've been tattooed on painkillers like Percocet, which I found didn't numb the pain at all and instead made me really irritated. On psychedelics it's intense in a different way, a full and unique experience, whether it is psilocybin mushrooms, LSD, or 2-CB. It's easiest when I'm drunk since the intoxication of the alcohol and the conversation with the artist overpower the pain.

Before Les can complete my left arm, Olmy begins work on my right: a large Japanese-style tattoo of a phoenix, the mythical firebird of self-destruction and rebirth. It coils around the phrase

Bleed in Your Own Light. I like the element of deviance in getting an Irezumi tattoo—it's associated with the yakuza, the Japanese mafia. It is also a nod to Olmy, a guy raised in a hippie commune who in the nineties, after art school, began tattooing in Boston, a city where tattooing was still illegal. Half the time spent tattooing the phoenix takes place in San Francisco at the Hell's Angels shop where Olmy also works. A piece of that shop also went into my skin.

Each tattoo is a time capsule. But what it was yesterday and what it is today and what it will be tomorrow aren't the same thing. When I first got the tattoo of the leaf on my left hand, it was tied into the H.R. Gieger imagery and into a bad pun about songwriting ("the things I *leave* behind will come from my left hand"). But its meaning changed after I went down to my brother's wedding in Hawaii. The sunset ceremony took place beneath a huge tropical tree on the Maui shore. As their kiss consummated the union, a strong wind blew in from the Pacific, raining leaves upon us all. My leaf tattoo is now bound up with that memory too, with, I'm sure, more to come.

Even upon completion a tattoo remains elusive, in flux, just like a memoir. Its meaning changes with time. Because the I of today is not the I of yesterday. And because you see that I with new eyes.

Fig. 4

sually elite swimmers end their swim careers after the Olympics, but Ervin did the opposite. In February 2004, a mere five months before Olympic Trials for the Athens Games, Ervin submitted paperwork to USA Swimming to withdraw his name from the roster of athletes subject to drug testing—a requirement for USA Swimming competitors. It was now official: Anthony Ervin had retired from swimming. His departure voided his Speedo deal and shocked many in the swimming world, especially those who wanted to believe he was just taking time off or in a temporary slump. But those who knew Anthony well weren't surprised. This had been a long time coming.

The one person most gutted by his decision was his mother. To this day, Sherry Ervin sees his departure from swimming as a travesty. "I don't think Anthony realized just what he sacrificed," she says. "I don't think he understands it even now." She feels equally strongly about his tattoos: "I hate them. Hate 'em, hate 'em, hate 'em. He says to me, *This arm is for you.* No, it isn't, I'm not owning that!" She sees no beauty in the tattoos, only an "ugly mish-mosh."[34] Body alterations, she points out, are a desecration of the body according to Judaism. For years after he got his tattoo sleeves she would buy him long-sleeved shirts for Christmas. And whenever he came home for the holidays she demanded he wear long sleeves. "I didn't want to see the tattoos," she says. "They actually hurt my eyes." But Sherry does have two dark secrets regarding his tattoos. The first is that she supported him in getting the Olympic rings on his back, something she now agonizes over, as if her assent had enabled a future ink addiction. The second is that she concedes there's an advantage to his tattoo sleeves. "To be honest," she confesses to me in a low voice, "when I watch him on TV, that's how I find him—by his arms."

By rejecting swimming, Anthony was rebelling against developing his body as an instrument of locomotion. "After being forced

---

34 Unlike Anthony's niece Sophia. Her father once found her coloring her arms with markers. "Look, Daddy, I'm like Uncle Tony," she said, showing Jackie her arms. "I want to live with Uncle Tony."

to constantly abuse my body with labor, I wasn't going to do that anymore," Ervin says. "Years of neglect followed." But while he neglected his body on matters of fitness and wellness, he didn't entirely disregard it. He began viewing his body as clay to be manipulated through artistry, a physical objectification, but aesthetic, not sexual. "It was also a reclaiming of my body, with the tattoos and all. I was giving myself a new skin. I wanted to recreate myself."

During this period he also got a new roommate, who coincidentally knew all about shedding skins. His name was Abraham, after the Old Testament prophet, although he went by Abe. A quiet roommate, Abe mostly kept to himself and was nocturnal like Anthony. He only ate about once a week, although when he did it was an impressive and unsettling sight, as his meals were carnivorous feasts that he preferred not just fresh but alive. An infant when Ervin first got him, the Brazilian rainbow boa initially subsisted on tiny squeaking pink mice whose eyes hadn't even opened yet. Like a modern-day Medusa, Anthony once even smuggled Abe onto a flight to LA by hiding him in his dreadlocks. But it wasn't long before Abe was a four-foot adolescent and Ervin was feeding him adult mice or baby rats. Brazilian rainbow boas are among the most attractive of snakes. They're so named because of the microscopic ridges on their scales, which refract light into rainbows. They're at their brightest after shedding. Dull and faded, the old skin sloughs off like gossamer netting, revealing a shimmering brilliance beneath.

A much-feared and maligned creature in most cultures, the serpent is nonetheless a mythological icon of recreation and transformation. Think of the Ouroboros, the serpent eating its own tail. Or the two serpents that entwine around the rod of the Caduceus, the transformative staff of Hermes, Greek messenger god and psychopomp who guides the souls of the dead. The staff has been co-opted by many in the medical field, who erroneously confuse it with the staff of the ancient healer Asclepius: his rod has only one snake and is thus less visually dramatic. While understandable from a marketing perspective, it's an unfortunate mix-up, considering that Hermes, the Greek trickster god, was a protector of thieves, liars, and merchants, and the escort of the dead to their underworld resting place—not the most reassuring connotation for the infirm.

Ervin viewed Abe through a similar mythological lens, seeing him as his animal totem during those years. A symbol of the creative force of life sloughing off the past, the Brazilian rainbow boa was his slithering reminder that you can only grow by leaving part of yourself behind.

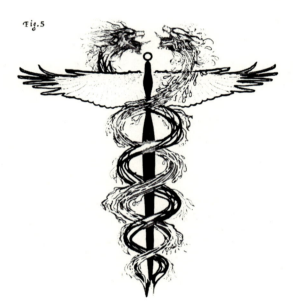

Fig.5

Rent, food, bills . . . I can only coast on savings for so long. So a few months after they fire me at Zebra, I get a sales gig at Guitar Center. I'm working in accessories, selling pedals, microphones, what have you. I hate it. It's all about the upsell. They encourage us to profit off people's passion. The more money you get out of others, the higher your commission. I'm there for four months but I can't deal with its corporate structure anymore. So one day in November I say to hell with it and don't go in. After a few days the manager calls me up.

"You haven't been to work in a couple of days," he says.

"That's right," I say.

"Are you okay?"

"Yeah. I'm just not going to come into work anymore."

There's a pause. It's straight out of *Office Space*.

"Okay, well, take the rest of the week off and let's talk after that."

"Okay," I say.

At the end of the week he calls me again.

"So, have you thought about it? Christmas is coming up. There's good money to be made on commissions. Are you coming back to work?"

"No," I say.

He doesn't call me again. Guitar Center is desperate, but not that desperate. And neither am I.

The next day I'm out with Amir. We walk by STA Travel and see a sign for two-hundred-dollar roundtrip tickets to London over the Thanksgiving weekend. He just split up with his girlfriend and I just quit my job so—why the hell not?—we buy tickets on the spot. At a Goodwill I buy all my clothes for the trip, including a winter jacket for about five bucks.

We bum all over England. I'm subsisting on coffee, absinthe, and Ritalin. Food? Who needs that? In Cambridge I see a guy pissing off a bridge into the River Cam. So much for the refined British. At Cambridge University admissions I ask the receptionist if they accept transfers. She just glances at my dreads and looks away before curtly responding, "We do not accept transfers." In Brighton I see the sun for the first time. It's beautiful by the sea. We celebrate with a bottle of absinthe before stumbling onto a train back to London.

In Camden Town I get a tattoo on my leg of a graffiti-style

skull wearing a crown, or maybe I should say a fool's cap, to remember the trip. It's a shitty tattoo, which I just whimsically chose off the wall. But it will remind me of this period of being foolish and free of all ties. And like the occasional pain in my shoulder, the skull will remind me of the times the Grip Reaper has hovered over me. A crowned skull. A fool's tattoo.

Fig.6

Yet again, I'm broke. So when Mike Bottom presents me with a lucrative opportunity that involves running a few swim clinics along with Gary Hall Jr. for the Japan Swimming Federation, I take it. In December 2004, a few weeks after returning from London, I cut off my Sideshow Bob dreadlocks and fly to Japan. I go for the money and to hang out with Mike and Gary. But while in Japan, finding myself back in the role of an athlete, I'm energized by the enthusiasm I inspire in the Japanese swimmers. I feel an unexpected pull to compete again. I think about Gary, who took several years off after the Sydney Olympics and staged a return in time for Olympic Trials. He not only made the team but also won gold at the Athens Olympics, and he did so while I was peddling pedals at Guitar Center.

But if I swim again, I decide it has to be tied to a cause or charity. Others have given so much to me; I now want to give back. I'm not sure how exactly, but I know it has to involve water. As a toddler I was drawn to water, then fenced out of it. As an adolescent I was locked into it. As a young adult I fled from it. And now I'm considering a return to it, but with a different intention. Typhoon Tokage, the deadliest storm to strike Japan in a decade, just happened two months ago. Water's destructive power has always resonated with me, so I contemplate a charity effort related to flooding. Tying a return to competition to a life-giving effort would be cathartic as well as altruistic. But I still don't know what exactly I can do.

On the flight back to the US, Bottom invites me to join the Cal Berkeley swim team for winter training camp in Colorado Springs. After some thought, I take him up on it. I'm not committing that I'll come out of retirement, but I know the physical conditioning will do me good.

I spend Christmas with my family, mulling privately over whether I should return to competition and, if I do, how to link it to flood relief.

And then, the day after Christmas, the Indian Ocean tsunami hits.

Into the Flood

There were no walls standing, it was as though they'd been sliced off the floors. Only those clay-tiled floors remained, large footprints of rooms, thin corridors stretching out in all directions.
—Sonali Deraniyagala, *Wave*

Give it away, give it away, give it away, now.
—Red Hot Chili Peppers, "Give It Away"

From: Anthony Ervin
Sent: Thursday, January 20, 2005 10:48PM
To: Della Lorenzetti
Subject: i did my best, probably needs some help though

. . . Later on that evening [December 26] I found myself watching TV and news was just getting to the public that a massive earthquake had struck underneath the Indian Ocean and that a resultant tidal wave devastated Indonesia. At this time that was about all the information I knew. I went to bed that night and woke up at 4 AM to catch my flight to Colorado Springs. During the series of flights that eventually landed me in Colorado Springs I read The Alchemist, a novel about pursuing your dreams, among many many other things. The time spent in thought on the

plane after finishing the book cannot be repli-
cated here in this writing, the emotions and
thoughts too powerful to be retained by the
memory of my mind but an undeniable truth in
the memory of my heart. I wanted to give back
to the world in some kind of way, and when I
thought of a way to do so, the earth itself
split open and made this cause an overwhelming reality. Walking off that plane of this
I was sure: I would donate my gold medal, my
most prized possession, to the relief of the
tsunami victims and I would return to professional swimming since I would have to try
to acquire a new gold medal in Beijing in
2008. Sure, I could have taken it as just a
coincidence that less than a week before the
greatest flood devastation of our generation
(and perhaps many generations into the past)
I saw fit to decide that flood relief would
be my humanitarian side project for getting
back into the sport . . . But I didn't want
to respond to it like it was coincidence.
The next couple days, amidst the physical
beating I was receiving in training, I was
glued to CNN and the Internet as the stories
began to unfold of the total devastation the
tsunami had wreaked across several nations.
The body count was rising faster than it was
falling. My heart felt like it was gripped in
a clenched fist as I realized how many of this
rising death toll were only children, innocent lives snuffed out. Amidst the snow that
was falling, the frozen tears of the earth,
there even seemed to be less stars in the sky.
I began to question my course of action. The
sheer catastrophic proportion of the disaster was now overwhelming for me and I felt so
helpless and small, afraid that even giving
away all I had of value would just be a grain

of salt in a sea of help that was needed. But
my heart strengthened me again, strengthened
me with the faith that my donation and whatever inspiration others might see in it, did
matter. And that is the message that I would
like to put out there: everyone can help in
little or large amounts, and that everyone
together can make a difference.

The previous month, a few weeks before the tsunami, the Polish swimmer Otylia Jędrzejczak, a 2004 Olympic champion in the women's 200 butterfly, auctioned off her gold medal, donating the roughly $82,000 proceeds to a charity for children with leukemia. Haunted by the images of devastation in Indonesia, Ervin found her initiative inspiring. "The only thing comparable before that was 9/11," he recalls. "And that was an act of man. This was an act of God. And it had to do with water and drowning."

Mike Bottom remembers from the training trip that Ervin's impulse to auction off his medal was stronger than his desire to swim; in retrospect, Ervin recognizes Colorado was more rehab than training. Back in Berkeley, he consulted with Mamade Kadreebux. "The gold medal is in your heart," Mamade told him. "If you can do something with it, do it. Your gesture will be in gold."

That April, with Della Lorenzetti's help, Anthony auctioned off his medal on eBay. At the end of the ten-day auction, seventy-one bids had been placed. The highest was a $17,101 bid from Anthony Chua, a Philippine swim fan. All proceeds went to UNICEF's Tsunami Relief Fund. One suspects Ervin could have benefited from some PR assistance to better promote the auction: Jędrzejczak's medal had fetched almost five times as much as his. But even she had a bum deal next to the auction of Wladimir Klitschko's gold medal in boxing from the 1996 Atlanta Games: the unknown buyer who bid the winning amount of one million dollars toward building children's sports camps and facilities promptly returned the medal to Klitschko after the purchase.

Ervin claimed, and perhaps even believed, that the sale would impel him to pursue another medal at the 2008 Olympics (even if he'd be "a pretty old man by then," as he told press at the time). But the sale of his premiere swimming laurel seemed more indicative of a deeper desire to shed his swimming identity.

When Mamade heard the auction went through he was jubilant: "Here is someone who can part with fame and glory." But Ervin today downplays his donation, emphasizing instead the untold narrative—that he still harbored resentment for all the sacrifices he made to be a swimmer, and that dropping the medal signified dropping the sport. He recently even referred to selling off the medal as a need to "cleanse" himself, as if the auction were some purification ritual. But the fact remains that he chose to give away the proceeds during a time when he had to sell his car just to cover bills. There may have also been guilt over his sense that he'd been a poor role model. "It's really easy for anybody to be a good example," he told *USA Today* after the auction, "and I certainly could have done a better job in the past. Hopefully, I'm making up some ground for that now." But the guilt continued to follow him after the auction.

<hr />

I've been flown out to the Florida Keys to offer swim instruction at the Race Club, established by the Hall family. I must come across as ungrateful because I've been a total lush. I'm also far more interested in fishing than swimming. One afternoon Gary Hall Jr. and I spear a massive grouper-like fish under a rock ledge. Even skewered by two spears, the fish fights hard. By the time we get the fish out from under the rock, there are clouds of blood everywhere. Sharks start circling. I stab at them with my spear as we make our way back to the boat. Only once Gary gets the fish into the boat does he realize that it is actually a jewfish, illegal to catch. An illegal jewfish . . .

Every free afternoon I fish the Islamorada canal with Takahashi, a Japanese swim coach. I keep hooking the most abominable creatures: stingrays, sharks, barracuda. I lack the prowess to remove the hooks safely, so I just cut the lines and they swim off with oceanic punk rock lip piercings. But my best memory with Tako is when a family of manatees swims up to our canal, the adults covered in motorboat scars. We hose them down. For hours, the manatees roll on their backs, drinking and soaking up the freshwater deluge.

One night I'm woken by a storm battering the roof, a rare occurrence since I've slept through earthquakes and fire alarms. In the morning I step out to see felled trees and streets littered with branches. A hurricane: Katrina. A few days later Katrina destroys New Orleans. Gary asks if I plan to get involved since I've taken up the cause of disaster relief. I just shrug. At night I drink Jack Daniel's from the bottle and read the Mötley Crüe memoir *The Dirt*. I try not to think about the hurricane. I tell myself there's nothing I can do.

Despite airwave chatter in early 2005 that I'm staging a comeback, it's clear as the year goes on that nothing will come of it. My interests lie entirely in music, which now eclipses swimming. Two years ago, when I got that star tattoo in Amsterdam, I decided music was everything. So upon return to Berkeley, I bought a Gibson SG electric guitar. I loved the crunch and snarl of amplified sound and devoted myself to practice.

Mo tries to convince me to get back into swimming. But I insist music is now my thing. So in honor of that choice, Mo takes me to a Counting Crows show at the Warfield in San Francisco. And it's far better than a free ticket.

Mo is friends with the lead singer, Adam Duritz, so before the show he takes me backstage. The bouncer lets me and Mo in through the Warfield's back entrance. I follow Mo through hallways and down a flight of stairs. We make our way to a basement room, and there's Adam Duritz, warming up his vocal chords. *Ah-ah-ah-ah-ah-ah-ahh. Ah-ah-ah-ah-ah-ah-ahh.* Going up and down like that, doing scales.

He sees us. "Hey, what's up, Mo?" he says. Then he looks over at me. "Hey, man, how's it going? I've heard a lot about you." I'm tongue-tied. He's heard about *me?* "Thanks for coming to the show," he continues. I'm still flabbergasted by the whole thing when Adam reaches for a bottle of Patrón. "Want to do a shot of tequila?"

So he pours us both a shot—but not for Mo because he doesn't drink. We knock back the shots. "Hey, man, I have to finish warming up," he says, "but I'll see you after the show." As Mo and I get up, Adam asks what my favorite Counting Crows song is. "'A Long December,'" I say. He nods.

So much for my fear that rock stars are assholes in person. For the encore the band plays "A Long December."

❧⊷⊶⊷❧

Anthony's former Cal teammate and close friend Jeff Natalizio was integral to his launch into music. Natalizio not only gave Anthony his first acoustic guitar but also first got him excited about playing electric. Natalizio remembers once hammering on some basic pentatonic power chords, amplified and with distortion. "Anthony was just looking at me amazed," Jeff recalls. "I said, *Dude, it's just a trick.*" Kindred spirits, Jeff and Anthony were bound by water, ink, and music. And, of course, deviance: Anthony remembers once driving through Berkeley with Jeff in a '71 Chevy Nova. "We're bumping and blasting hip-hop and we stop at a light next to a couple of black dudes in a Cadillac. They look over at us. Fools that we were, we were drinking and driving. So Jeff and I both lift up 40s at the same time. For a second they just stare at us and then they lift up 40s too and all four of us start hooping and hollering." It would be Jeff, as his artist alter-ego Frank Zio, who would later design Anthony's logos during his 2012 AE 2.0 reinvention. While Anthony was swimming 2012 Olympic Trials finals, Jeff was getting Anthony's skull logo tattooed on his ankle. "I felt like I had to get it before he swam," Jeff says. "To put the permanent mark on me, to show that I believe."

⊷⊷⊷⊷⊷

I begin seriously playing guitar and getting inked at the same time. Tattoos may represent permanence, while playing music is by its nature transient, but both come from the same desire to reinvent myself. I don't stop partying but a lot of the macho stuff gets turned on its head. I start moving away from things that were classically and conservatively masculine. Even the role models in my rock music aspirations are often androgynous innovators like David Bowie, who constantly pushes boundaries and reinvents himself.

The music I've listened to has always been bound up with my identity: angst-driven grunge when trying to form a sense of self under parental authority in junior high; mellow R&B when I chilled with my Asian posse and dreamed of wooing girls as a high school senior; ghetto rap when questions on racial identity plagued me after the Sydney Olympics; a return to nostalgic alternative rock and grunge when I was down in a hole as a Cal upperclassman. Even before I saw the Counting Crows at the Warfield, I saw the band Zwan there. The lead singer, Billy Corgan, also fronted Smashing Pumpkins, and their album *Siamese Dream* had been my favorite as a teenager. The show woke me to the power of live music, especially the song "Mary Star of the Sea." The song opened with a dreamlike lullaby music box sound, then shifted into progressive rock, and then kicked into distortion, the lights simultaneously flaring up and illuminating the Warfield's ornate vaudeville interior. It was titanic. The lullaby ended and I was in a rocket ship, taking off. The music wasn't in my ears, it was a sonic leviathan resonating through my entire body.

As early as junior high, listening to my brother's albums like the Pixies, Red Hot Chili Peppers, and the Smiths, I wanted to be a rock musician. But in high school I had to choose between swimming or playing trombone in band, which wasn't exactly rock 'n' roll. Though my friends had guitars, I'd always been too nervous to play them and couldn't afford my own. My musical side was consequently aborted, like a tree's dominant branch that had been struck by lightning. But after that Zwan concert, the music and lyrics spoke to me anew.

As a competitive swimmer I channeled my energy through the water. Now I want to channel my energy through people. The power of music over me was there as an infant when I squealed with delight as my brother pushed me in the stroller, blasting Michael Jackson; it was there when I fumed all weekend at a swim meet as my nonswimmer friends rocked out at a Megadeth and Iron Maiden concert; and it was there when Billy Corgan's melodic distortion resurrected me at the Warfield. To be able to evoke that sensation in others seems to me the ultimate high. That's not to say that I'm not interested in any other highs: I'm still thoroughly exploring psychedelics.

2C-B isn't normally as heavy a psychedelic as mushrooms or as cerebral and visual as LSD, but if you rail it through your nose it comes on fast and intense, even though it burns like hellfire. But today I take it orally because I haven't slept in thirty hours and snorting seems like a bad idea. I promptly pass out facedown on my friend's bed. I wake up to find myself inside a Monet painting. My friend tells me that while I was passed out on the bed my 'fro looked like a giant coral waving in a sea of watercolors. Only when the visuals let off do I put on a Doors album and walk downstairs.

On the wall along the stairwell is a poster of Jimi Hendrix's head against a starry background. I stop in front of it on my way down. It's always been a trippy poster but now the stars around his head are swirling, some trailing stardust, others throbbing and flickering. Jimi comes to life, his head hovering and pulsing in the ether. He eyes me. I break the silence. "Jimi," I say, "do you know that here on earth you're a legend?"

Jimi is chill, unperturbed. "It don't matter, dude," he responds. "Here in outer space everyone is a legend." Then he recedes back into the poster.

I bought the sixty doses of 2C-B with the intent to sell them, but I've been going through them, doing the overwhelming majority myself and occasionally giving some away to friends. Over a three-month period I'm dosing three or four times a week. It's a wild time. Just got my star tattoo in Amsterdam and my yellow GSX-R750 moto and an electric guitar and what seems like unlimited 2C-B.

Then I meet Omar Gusmao. Holy shit can Omar shred. Not only can he solo like a motherfucker, but he understands how to jam and connect with others. He's all about the groove and the feel of music. I learn so much just from watching him. That summer, after they fire me at Zebra, I move out of the Ashby House—the 2C-B House, as I've dubbed it—and move into a summer sublet on Regent Street with Omar and another friend, Mike. The girls who sublet to us have no idea as to the scope of their blunder.

We store our empty beer bottles in neat piles in the garage. But instead of recycling them, we get into an impromptu game of garage bowling one night, hurling beer bottles, trying to knock the top ones off the stack. Within hours we've shattered every bottle and trashed the garage. A cop later comes knocking on our front door because of the broken glass in the street.

The situation in the apartment isn't much better. We stay up all night smoking cigs, jamming, and playing cards and video games. Omar and I share a bedroom. A sock on the doorknob means *Girl on Premises*. But even when sock-exiled, neither of us venture into the living room. That's the rat's room. The rat has had the living room ever since Mike brought home that huge loaf of bread. Omar and I came home one day only to see this enormous rat pop out of a three-foot loaf of bread on the kitchen counter and scamper into the living room. The rat chewed out a tunnel through the loaf, burrowing right through the plastic wrapper and down its length. When I peered in, I saw a little highway of rat shit running the length of the excavation. The fucker ate and shat his way straight through the loaf. So we just slammed the door to the living room and gave the rat his own room. We didn't even call the landlord. We didn't want to deal with it. Besides, it's not our furniture.

Only Attila, the Hungarian water polo player, has ever braved the living room for any length of time. He needed to crash at our place for a few nights. He said he'd take the couch. "You don't want to go in there," we warned. "That's the rat's room." He just laughed at us. Evidently, rodents don't unnerve Hungarian water polo players. Especially ones named Attila. Eventually we went in and found the rat dead in the trash can. The poor bastard climbed in looking for something but only found his doom.

Here in the sublet, living and jamming with Omar, I'm breathing and dreaming guitar. The music gets me high, high to the point where I'm tapering off the drugs. There's still weed, of course, and I'm addicted to cigs. But I don't feel as much interest in other substances.

Not that there's no recreationals floating around or that I never touch the stuff anymore. Like that time I got stopped by cops while tripping on LSD because they thought I matched the description of a robbery suspect. Though I was fried, I kept my cool and the cops let me go. Or like the night a few of us are hanging at the Rat House and Omar does too many lines of coke. One minute he's there chilling with us, then next thing we know he's wigging out. His arms contort, his elbows lock into his torso, and he starts making these horrible gargling sounds. We're all panicking, grabbing him. "O.G., you alright? . . . Omar!" No response. He just sits there, convulsing, his eyes rolled back, whited out. We're all freaking out, wondering what to do . . . maybe call an ambulance? "Somebody, give him a guitar!" I shout. So we thrust a guitar into his arms. And Omar is hunched over the instrument like some cripple in leather pants with big wild hair. At first his fingers are just clutching and clawing at the strings, but soon he gets some rhythm. Slowly, he starts rocking himself into a more upright position and his eyes roll back down and a few moments later he's shredding, and just like that he's snapped out of it and is tearing it up along the fretboard.

In that moment, watching Omar solo his way out of an overdose, I know he's destined for greatness.

❖

Now a full-time rock guitarist based in Los Angeles, Omar shakes his head when recalling that period: "We were pushing the limits to see how much we could do before we cracked. Thank God we didn't." It was a time of letting go. Or as Omar put it, a time of "zero fucks given," an essential phase because by letting go of everything you can discover what you ultimately care about.

After that summer sublet, in the fall of 2004, Anthony and Omar moved in with some other guys into a house in the Kensington hills overlooking Berkeley. They formed a rock band, Weapons of Mass Destruction, playing everything from melodic Zeppelin-esque rock to funk to punk to reggae to metal. Omar, the main talent behind the band, played lead guitar; Anthony played rhythm guitar and arranged songs; Jeff Natalizio was on bass; Tim, a water polo player, handled the drums; and they recruited a local guy, Josh, for vocals. They cooked together, played together, partied together. It was one of the best periods of Ervin's life. He was in a rock band.

⚜

The oppression of my former swimming identity loses its hold on me. I am no longer Anthony Ervin the Swimmer, but Tony, just another guy in a band. Omar is the first person in a while who knows nothing of my Olympic history, not when he first meets me and not for a long time after. This was virgin territory for me. Water has always been my terra firma. As a swimmer, I never lacked confidence behind the blocks. If anything, I felt jaded. But behind a guitar, I was insecure and inexperienced; it's what kept me from playing as an adolescent. When I talk to artists or musicians, the concept of trying to compete is terrifying, but expression is easy. Their attitude is, *If others don't like it, they can fuck off.* For me it's the opposite. I was never intimidated to compete, but baring myself on stage is terrifying. I'm scared of doing it poorly or having it received negatively. My skin isn't thick enough. But the reality isn't half as terrifying as I'd imagined. I love it. And I never miss a band practice session.

As a teenager I often fantasized about playing music for an audience. That dream's time has finally come. In fall 2005, the year after we form, Weapons of Mass Destruction lines up our first show: a college house party at a swim house.

* * *

This is it, here we are. We stand with our instruments, exchanging glances. The crowd assembles around us, blue Dixie cups in hand, swaying with booze and with the music that's still playing over our sound check. There are cute girls everywhere. The atmosphere is similar to the college party I was at a few weeks ago, when this short, pretty undergrad walked over to me moments after I arrived and said she wanted to show me her tattoo. "But we're going to have to go somewhere if you want to see it," she said, eyeing me meaningfully. She had piercing blue eyes, a fierce owl-like expression, long dark brown hair, and a beautiful round ass. "Can I drink my beer at least?" I asked, knowing I couldn't resist her if I tried. She held me by the elbow as I finished it. It wasn't until we arrived at my apartment that I realized how drunk she was. She didn't even remember my name and was thrashing wildly, hair in her face. I wasn't going to have sex with her like that. So we just made out and dry-humped for hours. By dawn she seemed to have sobered up and even remembered my name. She still wanted to do it, so I reached for a condom and started wriggling out of my boxers from under her because she was straddling me. "No," she said, dismounting me. "I want you to fuck me from behind as hard as you can." At first I just stood there, slack-jawed, as she bent herself belly-down over the edge of the bed. That wasn't my style, but I couldn't very well say no. I gave it my best. A few hours after I'd passed out, I was woken up by a head between my legs, my vision flooded by sunlight. I craned my neck, looking down the length of my body. But the girl between my legs wasn't the undergrad. "What . . . ?" I moaned, trying to sit up. "What's going on?" She lifted her head up. It was my neighbor, whom I'd never even hooked up with before. The undergrad was gone. "What . . . " I said, stunned, "how'd you get in here?" "Jeff let me in," she said, and then lowered her head again. And so did I, allowing myself to be woman-handled twice in one morning.

That night had started at a party like this. But it's the last thing I should or want to be thinking about right now. A guy from the house staggers up to the mic, bottle in hand. "Here they are," he yells, "the Weapons of Mass Destruction!" Then he stumbles off into the crowd. They're so primed, they're already cheering and hooting and yelling despite knowing nothing about us. Tim leads us off, tapping out a four-count with his drumsticks, and we slam into our instruments together. The blast of music sets off the room as the audience erupts into a swarming, writhing throng. Playing music always lifts me, but evoking this feeling and response in others sends me soaring, the force and energy of this crowd acting upon us like bellows on fire. Jeff is bent over his bass, his body rocking and head stabbing back and forth in communion with his bass line, while Omar is coiled over his guitar, eyes shut, in thrall to the music, murmuring and moaning like some leather-clad dark mage in the violent grips of incantation. I'm just standing wide-stanced, trying not to get swept off my feet by the frenzied onslaught, my forehead veins throbbing as I thrash at my guitar. So overwhelmed am I, deluged by this shuddering intensity, that I'm messing up all over the place. But no one seems to give a damn, and who knows, maybe they don't even notice, they're all too pumped to give a shit about technicalities like accuracy, not while under this raw animal channeling of energy—hell, not even just animal, more like primal, or make that primordial, cause this feels like the stuff goddamn solar systems form from and perish into.

The crowd is right up in our faces because there's no platform or stage, the audience encircling us like some roaring tribe on the charge, a surging mass of bodies with wild glittering eyes and flailing arms and swinging hair and dripping faces and drenched shirts and who knows by now what's beer and what's sweat. Our set ends but the audience will have nothing of it, they're jacked up, chanting, "More, MORE, MORE!" so the other guys decide to play a few covers. I play the Rage Against the Machine song "Bulls on Parade" with them but don't know how to play any of the other covers, so I just set my guitar down and step into the audience, where strangers grin at me and slap me on the back and right away put a beer in my hand. It's all very casual, this is no Fillmore or Warfield, there's no fog machines to shroud you in smoky otherworldliness and no mirror balls to transform the walls into a swinging orb of cheetah skin and no lighting rigs to cast down pyramids of light from the ceiling and no monstrous sound systems to send music throbbing up from the floor through your vibrating legs and core and no strobe lights pulsing red through your eyelids when you shut your eyes to be engulfed by the music—there's none of that, because this is just a house party with a bare bulb hanging from the ceiling and some modest amps, but no matter because when Omar busts into the opening riff to the next song, more cheering goes up and drinks slosh about and the floorboards sag and thud under us and a great tumultuous wave of energy floods the room.

I want to do this forever.

Nothing is forever. In December, just as our band is gelling and getting its playlist together, our lead singer quits and takes a job in LA. It's a blow for me. Though I recently sold both my car and motorcycle (I never recovered from that coke-fueled Bay Bridge all-nighter), I'm almost broke again because I'm not working. I'm barely eating and I start to shrivel up. For breakfast I slather weed butter on sliced bread. I'm wasting away—smoking a pack a day and down to 150 pounds. My sorry financial and physical state, along with the lead singer's departure, has me in a rut. Though the band's status is uncertain, I'm still playing guitar, and songwriting helps me from slipping into depression again.

In January I talk by phone with my former Olympic teammate

Erik Vendt. He's now working for a New York City swim school cofounded by Lars Merseburg, my former Cal teammate and captain. Vendt suggests I contact Lars to do the same. I call Lars and he is unambiguous: "Come on over."

I'm still hesitant. I've lived in California my entire life and never even visited New York. I'm still undecided when I fly later that month to the island of Curaçao off Venezuela to teach a swim clinic for triathletes and swimmers, including the neuroscientist Oliver Sacks. I like the energy and demeanor of the New Yorkers in attendance, especially Doug Stern, the swim and triathlon coach who is running the clinic. When Doug advises me to go for it and move to New York, it's the final impetus I need.

A few weeks after returning to Berkeley, I move my belongings to Della's house. They don't amount to much. I've sold off my car, my motorcycles, and, of course, my gold medal. And with a duffel bag and an acoustic guitar, I board a one-way flight to New York City.

"The Wanderer"
song by Anthony Ervin, circa 2005

With cold-blooded hands you unearth the old roots of your home.
There were roses so lovely but thorns dig deeper than you know.
So you turn and you wave like a tree in the fall as you leave
Then the sky opens up and the wind carries you to the sea.

There you meet a man fishing. Is he more than he seems to be?
And when he does speak, then you don't know just what to believe.
"Forever we have, but we never will know when we're free."
Again asking why: just the way that it has to be.

Tripping and falling, I've long had the cares to be spared.
[Backup: Is this path leading nowhere?]

Churning and turning on this road that will never end.
Am I wandering all alone?
Am I wandering all alone?

14 *The Chrysalis*

All is flux.
> —Heraclitus

An ending fitting for the start.
> —The Libertines, "Can't Stand Me Now"

The city is blanketed in snow when I arrive. Lars and Erik are waiting at a bar. One minute I'm lugging my guitar through snow and cold and the next I've entered a warm, faux-tropical bar with palm trees. Welcome to New York City.

I crash on Erik's couch for the first few weeks. New York is an intimate city. Everything is so compressed and in such close quarters that when something happens—a crime, an accident, whatever—it feels like it happened just next door. Lars shows me hidden gems around the East Village: dingy stairwells descending into plush speakeasies, unmarked doors opening into swanky lounges with chandeliers and velvet couches, quiet cafés with backroom stairs leading up to punk shows.

One day Erik tells me that a few years back, right after the 2003 World Champs ended, a few guys on the team trashed the hotel rooms after checkout, even tossing furniture out the windows. Dennis Pursley was furious, but no one confessed or volunteered names to him. Erik says he just clenched his jaw and muttered, "Anthony Ervin." I laugh to hear it. I was backpacking around Catalonia at the time. Denny must have figured that out eventually because I never heard anything from him about it.

Erik moves out so I have to find a new place. I've started casually seeing an artist and sculptor. She's creative and gorgeous and has directed her passions to the arts, which I find extremely attractive. But gradually my phone calls start coming later and later in the night. I really like her, but when she confronts me on where it's going, I shut down. I fear the intimacy. She offers to let me stay with her for a bit, but I run off, afraid to give us a try. Instead I move into a one-bedroom in Fort Greene, Brooklyn, with a friend I meet through Lars named Cydney, who generously offers me a spot on her couch. In return I reciprocate with chores like cleaning and watering the plants.

New York City is the first American port of call for music coming out of London, and I reconnect with the British bands of my youth like the Cure and the Smiths. The most influential contemporary band for me now is the Libertines, with their raw, quirky, dreamlike, heavy-lidded tunes. I adopt the current hipster look of proto-eighties postpunk fashion: skinny black jeans, white, red, or black shirts, horizontal stripes, and Chuck Taylors. When I save up some cash I replace my black overcoat, which is more suited for an investment banker than a wannabe rock 'n' roller, with a black leather jacket purchased from one of the stores lining Orchard Street.

One night I'm at a Mercury Lounge show when a small girl with Manic Panic red hair (I soon learn she was the actual model on the Manic Panic hair-dye box), alabaster skin, candy apple–red lipstick, and a lacy black dress catches my eye. A hulking, sweating, balding, khaki-wearing square has her and her copper-haired friend cornered, though they're clearly uninterested, looking off into space. So I stroll up to them—a greasy, tatted scoundrel in a ratty thrift-store shirt—only to be met by smiles and bright eyes. The sweating, nine-to-five desk jockey retreats. The two of them turn out to be the queens of cool of the New York music scene. The one who caught my eye, Eva Chavela, is a rock artist with the most gut-wrenching scream that defies her striking looks, while the other, Jenny Penny, works for a young music management company and seems to know about every great emerging band years before they break out.

I never hook up with either of them, but Jenny Penny occasionally lets me crash at her Lower East Side place after late nights. One night I go back early to her place to rest for a few hours and stumble out of her bedroom in the early-morning hours into a party that she brought home. There I am, milling amidst strangers in my boxers like a barbarian, when I see M, a beautiful creature with dreamy eyes and an easy, blissful smile. She's long-limbed and lithe, yet curvy. A dancer in her youth, her movements are graceful and elegant. On June 6, 2006 (6/6/6), as counterpart to her Catholic upbringing, she performs in a "black Mass," where she walks nude onto a stage and is bent over an altar as a human sacrifice. After her throat is mock-slit and her fake blood is poured over communion crackers, M walks to the edge of the stage and inserts a bloody cracker into my mouth. It's hard to one-up that as a first date.

Eva's boyfriend Ryan plays bass in a postpunk outfit named Blacklist. A huge fan, I get Ryan to convince Eva to let me play bass in her group, though I don't have a bass or even know how to play one. I buy the cheapest left-handed bass I can find, which happens to be hot-pink. Like some idiot punk rocker I walk into my first band rehearsal at the dingy grunge dungeon Ludlow Studios with this hot-pink bass. I think we sound pretty damn good, but Eva seems over it after a few practices. So I stop calling and begin jamming exclusively with Lars—he on drums, me on guitar and vocals. And as I phantom out of the goth rocker scene and start jamming just with Lars, I also phantom out of M's life. If I'm good at anything besides swimming, it's jumping ship.

Although Lars had offered Anthony a position at Imagine Swimming without hesitation, others had discouraged both him and Imagine's other cofounder, Casey Barrett, from hiring Anthony, claiming he lacked dedication. But Lars was sure he'd be an excellent instructor. "And not just because of his decoration of medals," Lars says. "I knew the kids would be drawn to Tony because he has a kind face and he's different." His tattoos also made him "like a superhero" to children.

Though Anthony had had no formal training in teaching children and Lars had to "explain to an aquatic genius" how to teach the basics, Anthony had a gift for conveying to children how to feel the water. "He was demonstrating some things better than Casey or I could," Lars says. "Like how to do a flip turn properly. Children are such a blank canvas that if you show them the proper way, they have it. Teaching is multidimensional and he understands that complexity. When he's on and focused, he has such a natural rapport with children and people."

But Anthony wasn't always on. Once while coaching Imagine's swim team, the Manhattan Makos, Lars saw him sitting on the pool deck reading *Moby-Dick*. "I think he almost did that to get a reaction. I was fine being his older brother, but I didn't want to be his parent." Fortunately, Anthony didn't need to be told more than once. "He was a bit confused, and that's okay," Lars says. "We were all lost souls at that time, so we related."

Anthony's moods fluctuated at the pool. One day he would be engaged, the other aloof. Lars could sense the internal conflict. It was as if somewhere along the way he'd suffered a psychic wound, either from outside or self-inflected. "Probably both," Lars says. "Then again, we're all wounded and damaged. We tell ourselves love heals all, but that's just what we tell ourselves. We still stay wounded."

Swim lessons are stabilizing, but even after my dual life of swim instructor by day and goth rocker by night ends, I can't keep my after-hours habits separate from work. At first I smoke pot before lessons, but that only makes me paranoid instead of more mellow and playful with the kids. So I stop that. But even clearheaded, the lessons can cause me anxiety. Some children are terrified of the water, and I can't help but absorb their stress and fear.

I have one lesson with two five-year-olds who are opposites. One is strong and capable but afraid, and the other lacks ability and strength but is fearless. The brave one will jump right in and sink with an arm straight up. I have to haul him up, water shooting out of his nostrils. The scared one fights and digs his fingernails into my arm so hard that he draws blood. He uses all his energy thrashing at the water to pull himself out of it instead of letting himself relax in it. It's amazing to see him loosen up, lesson by lesson, until he's soon placing his face in the water without fear, swimming longer distances, and then playing underwater, completely at ease. It's inspiring to see a kid buckle down and find courage while trying to overcome a fear of water, just as it's awesome to see the confident one learn his limits and expand them. One day, watching the two of them so absorbed in play underwater that they're oblivious even to my presence, it hits me that somewhere along the way I lost that sense of play. I even had that playfulness as a college swimmer when I was experimenting and exploring new ways of moving through the water, but somewhere I lost it.

It's been about six months that I've been on Cydney's couch. It's a beautiful one-bedroom brownstone, and she's a great roommate. But one night I bring back a swim coworker I'm dating while Cydney is out of town and we have sex in her bed. I do a poor job at covering my tracks because when Cydney returns, she asks me if I slept in her bed. I tell her what I'd done. And she tells me I have to move out.

Now a Dallas-based consultant, Cydney Roach says Anthony is mistaken, possibly out of guilt, in thinking he had to leave because he brought someone back. Rather, she claims, it was because the landlady once saw Anthony tearing up the stairs, yanking on the stairwell newel posts as he ran, and slamming the door behind him. Anthony's uncouth demeanor and savage mistreatment of the refurbished stairwell traumatized the landlady, who from that day badgered Cydney about making him leave.

Though Cydney paid for rent and groceries, he contributed in other ways. "Nobody on this planet can clean a bathroom like Anthony Ervin," she says, describing how he'd garb his Speedo before climbing into the bath. "He would detail the grout between the tiles, shine the chrome, get all the nooks and crannies in the toilet that even I wouldn't clean. It was a work of art." His swim gear wasn't exclusively reserved for WC duties. During one of her weekly Sunday barbeque gatherings, Anthony came out to water the plants in his swimsuit. He later returned with "a giant bowl of blueberries, which he was holding down by his blue Speedo," offering the berries from guest to guest. "He thrives when he's in the spotlight," she recalls. "He could be moping around the house, and then people come over and the performer in him comes out."

Despite such antics, she also remembers that he was often in a low place and struggling with a number of issues relating to his purpose and identity. "Tony will free himself to go to the depths or heights that a lot of people won't allow themselves to go," she says. "A lot of us do it in the narrow confines of what society tells us we can do. He just goes for it. He doesn't care if he looks depressed or angry or blissed out or disheveled or whatever." Another issue that came up often was his relationship with his parents, especially his mother. "He would be on the phone with her, and would come off either elated because she was happy with him or in the depths of despair because she wasn't."

⚬

After Cydney's, I find a sublet in a Bushwick warehouse over a print factory, off the Jefferson L stop. Aside from the factory, the Brooklyn warehouse has been converted into apartments, but it's run down and scummy. It's the only place I can afford. It's a hub for musicians, so a live band is playing somewhere in the warehouse almost every other night. The gentrification has yet to spread, so there are plenty of down-and-outers around too. My new roommate upstairs just got out of jail. He's strange, quiet, and stoic, and just does push-ups and pull-ups all day. One of my roommates is a theater actor. It's a rough neighborhood. When I stumble home from the subway late at night, the streets are dark and near deserted, with no police presence.

Not long after I move in, Imagine Swimming shuts down for the summer so my income dries up. I visit my parents in South Carolina and return with several cartons of cigarettes. I sell the cigarettes individually in the warehouse to cover food costs. There's a tortilla factory nearby, so I subsist mostly off cans of beans, tortillas, and cheese. And of course there's always cigs, which keep food costs down.

In one of the warehouse free piles I find a white spaghetti-strap dress. It must have once been the wedding gown or formal dress of a very tall woman. It fits me, so I wear it for the hell of it and start walking in and out of the various rooms in the warehouse. It's all dudes and nobody has much to say about it. They don't really care, but they also don't really want to look at me. They seem uncomfortable that I'm in a dress.

It's my first time cross-dressing, though I've worn makeup before. Last summer, while in the Florida Keys, I caught a ride to a Miami mall with Gary and his wife Elizabeth. While they were off doing chores, I went up to a cute saleswoman at a MAC Cosmetics store and started flirting with her, saying I wanted to try on makeup. A few other employees came over, intrigued. They laughed and were about to apply some, but their gay male counterpart stepped in. "I better take over for this, ladies," he said. They watched as he applied glittery blue-black shadow over my eyes. "I'm gorgeous," I said to their laughter, looking in the mirror. Then I bought the eye shadow and headed off into the busy Miami mall—not only in black jeans, black T, Converse, ratty hair, and tattoos, but now also with an overwhelming amount of eye shadow and liner. Everyone in the whole damn mall was staring at me, eyes widening if I met their gaze. The attention made me nervous so I sped through until I finally reached Elizabeth and Gary. Elizabeth went bug-eyed like everyone else, but Gary just chuckled. "So why'd you do it?" he asked. I had no good reply. I told him I just felt like it. Same reason I wore the dress in the warehouse.

At the end of the summer I move out of the warehouse and deeper into Bushwick to a row house near the J train Halsey stop. The neighborhood is so sketchy the landlord can't even rent out whole apartments; he just rents out individual rooms on Craigslist to the desperate. The train is above ground and next to us so you constantly hear it thunder by. On the next corner is a liquor store where the clerk sits behind Plexiglas and a motel that charges by the hour. Prostitutes work the corners.

It's a random group of characters. There's the addict—I'm not sure what he does besides heroin. There's the Israeli contingent—one of them is way too innocent for our neighborhood: he gets mugged one day after walking back from the subway at two a.m. while listening to his iPod. New York isn't for him. He eventually hightails it back to the Tel Aviv beaches. But his longhaired, tatted compatriot is right at home here: he smuggled a brick of hash up his ass from Tel Aviv to New York. He smokes that ass hash for months. And then there's my med school buddy Shivesh, who claims Othello is the ultimate hero and Achilles is the first rock star, and who gives me a book on the cosmos about wormholes and parallel universes and the fifth dimension that boggles my mind, and who tells me the wildest stories over six-dollar fifths of vodka about treating wasted drug addicts in the Bed-Stuy hospital where he interns—the weird humanity one encounters in the middle of the night in a shitty Brooklyn hospital. His stories blow me away: people dying in the waiting room, nurses banging med students in the closets. There's the sixteen-year-old girl who came in with a bruised leg, complaining of pain. The moment the scalpel touched her leg for the biopsy, the skin split open, black from some flesh-eating disease. They amputated but it was too late. Then there's the night I found Shivesh chain-smoking Newports with shaking hands after assisting on an open-heart surgery where the anaesthesiologist skimped on anesthesia because he was an addict who was feeding his own habit. The patient's eyelids had fluttered open only to look into the eyes of Shivesh and of the surgeon hovering over him. Then he looked down, only to see, with widening eyes, his own exposed heart. His head fell back and he flatlined, dying on the spot. But Shivesh's most disturbing story is of the 300-pound guy who comes in with bowel impaction. His large intestine was all twisted up, so he couldn't shit. But he kept on eating. His intestine didn't rupture as they often do with older people who have brittle intestines. But the shit still has to go somewhere, so in younger people it gets backed up into the small intestine, then the stomach, until eventually they're vomiting feces. "This guy was in pain for a day," Shivesh tells me, "and because he was in complete distress we had to hold him down to treat him and put a tube down his mouth. And one of the interns got the vomit in his mouth, which was a biohazard—"

"Enough," I interrupt. "I don't want to hear any more. I'm going to bed."

I fly back briefly to California for a Cal Swimming fundraiser over Halloween weekend. I pack the white spaghetti dress from the warehouse. At the gala, all the men are in tuxedos, but I'm wearing a leather jacket over a polka dot shirt. After the gala, I change into the white dress, put on eye shadow, and strap on a ceremonial Samurai sword like a drag queen out of *Kill Bill*. I pop a couple of ecstasies and head out with Lars to a house party in the Mission. The girls at the party are all over me. All I have to do is glance at a girl and smile and she'll come start talking to me. That's never happened before. And it's not necessarily anything sexual. There's something liberating about that, about being freed from the usual mating games. Maybe I'm unthreatening to them or maybe I'm a curiosity. Whatever it is, I love it.

Cops eventually shut down the party. Lars heads somewhere else, but I hang around outside, waiting for Omar, who's driving over to pick me up. While I'm standing there, alone, a group of wasted delinquents walk by. One has a problem with how I look.

"You faggot! Fucking faggot!" he yells. He's trashed. His face is twisted up with hate and aggression. He won't let up.

The ecstasy is coming on hard, so on top of being bug-eyed, I'm also glassy-eyed and clenching my teeth. My heart starts thudding. He's only getting more hostile, so I put my hand on the hilt of my katana blade and put one foot forward in a fighting stance. The sword isn't sharp, but it's full length and has a metal tip. I wonder if I'll have to run him through. But the guy's friend sees me shaking, my hand on the hilt and the crazy glint in my eye, and he puts his arm on the guy's elbow. "No, no, no, no," he says, holding him back. Finally they leave. I'm so shaken up that I hide in the shadows of a building's stoop. A few minutes later two girls pause nearby on the street. I call out to them from the darkness. They look in my direction, startled.

"Who's up there?" one of them asks, frightened, squinting in my direction. When I tell them who I am and what happened, they ask me to come down out of the shadows. As soon as they can see me properly, they start bubbling over and cooing. "Aww, you're the most adorable drag queen I've ever seen!"

Their ride soon shows up and they say I can join them but I stay. Omar arrives shortly after that. He folds over in half, laughing, when he sees me. We party through the night. The following morning I catch a ride to Mike Bottom's house in the Oakland hills for his two-year-old daughter's birthday party. It's all part of the same night out, just that the sun came up. I haven't slept and I'm still in my white dress when I arrive, my face smeared with makeup. I get up on the fireplace mantle and sing a happy birthday song for Mike's daughter that I originally wrote for this cute girl in Williamsburg. That New York girl didn't appreciate it nearly as much as they do.

***

That memory still makes Mike Bottom laugh. He didn't know why Anthony showed up at his daughter's birthday party in a white dress and didn't ask: "With Anthony, sometimes you don't want to hear the full story." But like the tattoos, Anthony's cross-dressing was another way of shedding the old skin and reformulating his identity by rejecting the conventional image of a dominant masculine athlete. At the same time, the fact that he was still rebelling against the idea of himself as a swimmer suggests that the desire to swim still maintained a hold on him.

That winter, he started getting wet again. He began attending

Masters workouts with Elliot Ptasnik, now the head coach of Imagine's swim team. An investment banker–turned–passionate swim coach who can unfathomably maintain a hops-and-barley diet on a consistent five hours of sleep without ever getting sick, Elliot would soon become one of Anthony's tightest friends.

Elliot had first met Anthony in Erik Vendt's apartment back in the spring, shortly after moving to New York: "I walk in at one or two p.m. and there's this figure on the floor. Just passed out. Hardwood floor. No pillow. I just step over him to the couch and I'm eating Skittles and watching the Discovery Channel with Erik. And this dude is just sleeping there. An hour goes by and Erik—he's intense and kind of aggro—goes, *We've got to get this fucker up: kick him.* And I'm like, *Uhhhh?* He's like, *Fucking kick him!* So, BAM, I do. And this guy gets up and fixes his glasses, which are all crooked, and he sits down and grabs some Skittles. And he's all skinny and has this 'fro going and is wearing baggy balloon pants and I'm just like, *Whhaaat is going on here?* And I later found out it was Anthony Ervin."

Elliot and Anthony entered some Masters competitions in 2007. At one meet, Anthony had a good 50, Elliot recalls, but got disqualified in the 100 backstroke: "He forgot how to do a flip turn. He turned over at the flags and just started swimming freestyle." Anthony was still a smoker at the time, and Elliot remembers how later "somebody on a blog wrote something like, *I saw Anthony Ervin before his race smoking a cigarette outside in shorts and a leather jacket.*"

My enthusiasm for training quickly wanes. The frigid New York City winter, the dawn commute from Brooklyn to Manhattan, the lack of training facilities . . . these all get my spirits down. I fly home for Christmas and as soon as I enter, Mom lays into me about how I've made poor life choices, how I've walked away from my talent, how it all could have been so different had I only done things differently. I just shut down and check out. I sleep all day and stay up all night, watching sci-fi horror B movies and popping narcotic pain meds left over from when Derek had his appendix removed. I sit with a six-pack of beer and take one OxyContin and drink one beer. Then another OxyContin and another beer. The first time I ever took opioids was on a Malibu beach, and I remember the sun melting into the water and feeling like everything was right with the world. But this time it's only deadening. The sun comes up and I'm still awake, feeling nothing.

With food costs mounting now that he was swimming again, he fell behind on rent payments for his Bushwick room. One day he packed his things and bailed (the enraged landlord, Edwin, told Anthony's former roommate Shivesh to let him know if that "deadbeat" ever returns). Anthony moved in with another Imagine instructor, Ben Selby, who let him stay on his couch in his Upper West Side one-bedroom for several months. "Tony was the classic New York couch surfer," Ben says. "The first time I met him he was sitting on Lars's balcony, looking all melancholic, strumming the acoustic guitar." At the time Anthony still had the glam-punk vibe going. "When he went out at night he'd wear eyeliner," Ben recalls. "He was into skinny jeans before skinny jeans were cool. And really tight shirts with short sleeves that showed off his tattoos." One day Anthony asked Ben if he wanted to join his band. Ben played no instruments. "I said I could be the singer," Ben explains. "And he said, *No, I'm the singer*. But after a while he was like, *Fine, you can be the singer.*" The entire conversation had taken place in the backseat of a taxi.

An editor at *Spin* magazine also joined the band and, in Anthony's view, promptly took control. "Suddenly I wasn't singing *and* I was being told what to do," he says. He never envisioned being an accessory, so he quit. The band, which would later become The Miki Doras, exists to this day, playing regular shows in Manhattan and Brooklyn. The only remaining original member is Ben, who's still the singer and recently even tattooed *M I K I D O R A* across his knuckles. "Tony was the original founder," Ben says. "He also came up with the main riff of our best song, 'Uptown Downtown.' He wrote that on my couch."

As the threads of Anthony's life began unraveling—the music, the swim training—he also withdrew from swim lessons. He told Lars he couldn't teach anymore and holed up in the apartment. Ben remembers him staying on the couch all day—no training, no Miki Doras, no Imagine: "He would just sit at home and eat cereal and watch cartoons. One day we were sitting on the couch. I didn't have the balls to say everything I wanted to say face-to-face, so I wrote him a long e-mail on the couch. And he's sitting next to me. He didn't say anything, but he responded. The gist was, *Man, you've got to stop being so sorry for yourself and down in the dumps. We live in a great spot, a great city, and you have all this talent.* And he wrote back something like, *I like being moody. That's my nature. I like dwelling in the darkness.* And I said, *That's fine, but not here.*"

Ben felt that by letting him stay longer he'd only be enabling him. So he told Anthony he had to leave.

With nowhere to go, Anthony turned to Shivesh, who was still at his old Bushwick spot. Shivesh said he could take the couch, so he moved back there on the sly. Shivesh Kumar, now a practicing doctor in Las Vegas, sensed that Anthony was far unhappier than the previous year. Anthony had seemed at his happiest, at least back then, when surrounded by people who had nothing to do with swimming. "We didn't judge him," Shivesh says. "He was enjoying the adventure and seemed at peace that he didn't need swimming." Those who knew him as an athlete were always urging him to get back in the water and not completely squander his talent. The failure when he did try only further depressed him.

Like Anthony, Shivesh was a Libertines fan. One day he casually mentioned how shocking it was that the lead singer, Pete Dougherty, who was in and out of jail at the time, could self-destruct like that when he had so much potential. "Dude, that's so easy to do," Ervin replied. That was a telling moment for Shivesh: "I remember thinking, *I'm just a normal guy, trying to build something up. Tony is coming from a different world than me.* He understood exactly why Dougherty could have done that. He obviously knew something about self-destruction."

I'm not in a good place. It's easy to appreciate why. I can see my glass ceiling: teaching swimming to a top crowd. I can have a pet music project that my friends will like and make a scene around that. But that's my limit. To advance beyond that I need to start finishing things that I've started. First things first: I need to finish my degree. I'll get an English bachelor's and study poetry. It'll also help me become a better songwriter.

Since I can only do so much remotely, I move back to California in March to reenroll for the fall semester. In San Francisco I stay with Amir on his couch. He's finishing law school. I'm out of money but don't know what to do for work. I'm barely eating, just smoking spliffs and cigarettes and playing *DotA*. A few months later Amir's roommate's girlfriend moves in. "Emma doesn't want you here," Amir tells me the next day. "Sorry, man, but you have to either start paying or leave."

I'm homeless again. Mike Bottom hooks me up with Johnny, an old-timer friend of his who lives in Berkeley. He puts me up until I find a job and get a place. I'm terrible at finding work. I just walk into places with my feeble resume, which except for Imagine is empty since I've never held a job for more than a few months. No one calls back. Finally, I give up. Johnny has a great library, so I stay in, reading his collection and eating his food. And then one day Johnny says, "That's great you're reading, but you have no job and I don't see much happening on your end. I'm going to have to ask you to move on to something else."

Kicked out again. I'm totally worthless.

Ervin's friend Amir, now a lawyer based in LA, says that of all the times he can remember, Anthony's "absolute low point" was while he was on his couch in San Francisco: "He never left the house unless we went out together. He was ridden with angst about his future. No plan. He couldn't figure it out and that was really scaring him." Ervin's aimlessness, compounded with "no ambition at all," created a human couch slug. "For him, ambition was getting through the day," Amir says. "I think it all goes back to accomplishing so much at an early age and how easy it came to him. Yeah, he put in hard work, but everybody else on earth who puts in the hard work doesn't get as far."

Homeless once more, Anthony was short on options. His brother Jackie and his wife Theresa said he could stay with them in Los Angeles for the summer. "We were concerned, because Anthony wasn't taking care of himself," Jackie says. "He wasn't bathing, wasn't washing his clothes, wasn't paying attention to if he ate or not." But the housing offer came with conditions and stipulations, which made Anthony hesitant.

He had also been in contact with a friend in New York, Jarmin. A former college gymnast who was a Berkeley classmate, Jarmin had known about him when he was still swimming. But she didn't meet him until years later, after he'd quit swimming and she'd left gymnastics. One night she ran into Anthony at a punk show. "I thought, *What are* you *doing here?*" Jarmin recalls. "*This isn't where you're supposed to be. Athletes don't hang out here.*" They nevertheless hit it off.

"We were both figuring out who we were as post-athletes. He was definitely rejecting everything sports related."

⚜

Though my relationship with Jarmin occasionally crosses beyond friendship, it's always casual. She later moves to New York for graduate school, so I see her a few times there. But at my going-away party in Bushwick, the day before I fly back to California to re-enroll, something more intimate takes hold. I've been working on these sad acoustic songs. When I play them, she claps and smiles, the first girl to like my music.

We continue texting and talking after that night. And then in late June, my mentor, the triathlete coach Doug Stern, dies abruptly of kidney cancer. Distressed, I call Jarmin. She offers to fly me out for the funeral, saying I could stay with her if I want to spend some time in New York. So I do. And so begins a three-year relationship. I bounce between Jarmin's place in New York in the summer and during holidays, and co-ops in Berkeley for the school semesters. For the first couple of years, I share dorm-style doubles or triples.

The one time I have a room to myself is when I rent out the living room of a Berkeley one-bedroom, but it comes with a catch: the man has four pet rats that roam over his lofted bed. He lays there in bed, watching something on his laptop, while rats crawl all over him. His sheets and blanket are covered in little brown rat turds.

⚜

In New York City, Jarmin helped Anthony set up a suit-and-tie internship at an SEO-optimization law firm. He kept his tattoos covered, except for when he showed up one day in a short-sleeved button-up, shocking everyone in the office. He hated it. So one day, as he'd done at Guitar Center, he just stopped going. "Half the battle is just showing up," Jarmin would tell him. "Who cares if you hate it? Just show up!" But her words fell on deaf ears. "He was a self-proclaimed antihero," Jarmin says. "And that was a way for him to shirk the responsibilities of the hero. Maybe unconsciously, maybe sometimes consciously."

Despite such employment flubs, being in a relationship, even an undefined one, again proved stabilizing. Anthony remains convinced he would never have completed his bachelor's degree without her. In her presence he was happier, more confident. In the fall he began his English coursework at Berkeley. Hardly any of his prior undergrad courses applied to his new major, so it would take five semesters to complete his degree. But he didn't mind the protracted process. Anthony had gone into his literature courses with a utilitarian mindset, thinking they'd help him improve his song lyrics.[35] Instead he found something better.

⊱────⊰

As far as fundamentals, we've barely changed since the origins of the written word. My initial motivation to develop myself as a songwriter seems a paltry impulse next to this journey into myth and humanism. The literature envelops me, cocooning me in its chrysalis. I feed upon it, maturing, stretching, morphing within its silken chamber.

Medieval literature is my thing. The oldest text I read is *Beowulf*, the Seamus Heaney translation. The tale of a heroic age long gone, back when there were still dragons, monsters, and heroes. *In off the moors, down through the mist beams, god-cursed Grendel came greedily loping.* Beowulf isn't a hero just because he kills monster. His greatness lies not just in brawn but

---

35 Not that studying poetry to write song lyrics is the epitome of pragmatism.

speech. The strength of rhetoric and diplomacy. I take stock of my life in relation to the heroic-age virtues of courage, honor, and good deeds. *Behaviour that's admired is the path to power among people everywhere.* Don't care about power but yes to good conduct . . . I have work to do.

I struggle with *Paradise Lost* because of Milton's argument for free will over predestination. *For so I form'd them free: and free they must remain.* Thinking I control everything is too big a burden. It's crippling to think I'm in charge of my destiny. I need to believe that forces—the will of the gods—are acting through me. But I'm drawn to Satan, Milton's own Augustinian confession. *Non serviam.* His own personal *Crime and Punishment.*

It's not all heaviness. There's Chaucer's raucous characters in *Canterbury Tales:* the bawdy adulteress who sticks her ass out the window in the darkness for a cheeky kiss, and the Wife of Bath, a powerful and independent straight-shooter at a time when women were so oppressed. And there's redemption: the allegory in *The Faerie Queene* that one can err and wander off course, but through suffering emerge to find the right way.

Then there's the Bard. Fucking genius. The enchanted ending of *The Winter's Tale* sticks with me—how even after all the damage that the berserk king of Sicily causes, there's still the compassionate possibility of forgiveness. I think of the friendships I've strained, the generosity I've exploited, the bridges I've torched. *Do as the heavens have done, forget your evil; With them forgive yourself.* There may be hope for me yet.

But it's the literature on race that touches the tender spot. I've always liked knowledge, but self-reflection troubles me, and these readings cut too close to home. A course on "passing"—on being classified as one race but accepted as another—changes everything. You're mixed, and while you may be able to exist in a white world, you're not white even if they might see you as one. And because of your privilege, many African Americans resent you and won't always accept you as black. I realize that the claim that I bore responsibility toward African Americans was more about white people conceiving me as black. But I'm mixed race, and if my responsibility lies anywhere, it's there. When I look in the mirror, I see neither a black man nor a white man. That's the tawny-gold truth.

Even so, one text haunts me: *The Autobiography of an Ex-Colored Man* by James Weldon Johnson. It's about a talented young biracial pianist who intends to elevate the black race by composing groundbreaking ragtime music. But when he travels south for research he witnesses a brutal lynching that terrifies him so much that he drops his dream and returns north, where he passes as white in security and comfort. The book's closing lines ring in my head: *When I sometimes open a little box in which I still keep my fast yellowing manuscripts, the only tangible remnants of a vanished dream, a dead ambition, a sacrificed talent, I cannot repress the thought, that, after all, I have chosen the lesser part, that I have sold my birthright for a mess of pottage.*

In turning my back on my swim talent for a mess of pottage, I can't help but wonder: *Is this me?*

Anthony took off the spring semester of 2009 and spent the year in New York, living with Jarmin and working with Imagine. At the end of the summer, the two of them flew to San Francisco. With two master's degrees behind her, Jarmin had applied and been admitted to a PhD program at UCSF. Anthony, now beginning his final year at Berkeley, had yet to finish undergrad, and there was a competitive sense that if he didn't pursue a graduate degree he'd be left behind in their relationship. Also, his advisor, who was the director of the master's program in Cultural Studies of Sport in Education, urged him to apply.

So Anthony decided to go for it. He filled out the application forms and took the GRE. Everything was in place, the future looked hopeful. And then things went bad.

I begin graduate school. After breaking up with Jarmin, however, doubt takes root, and I feel lost and confused as to why I am here at all. I stop attending classes and for a month sit alone in my room, smoking and wasting away. But fear of repeating past failures allows me to muster some strength, and I return for the final weeks of Derek Van Rheenen's class. I commit to writing the final paper: an autobiography of my life in sport.

The essay is thirty pages of skeletons, a confession of all the terrible things I've done. Things I've never told anyone, not even myself. All that I've buried. The self-loathing, the escapism, the way I fled the sport. All of that is out now, swirling around me, howling fiends freed from Pandora's box.

But I welcome their release. The readings from the last few years have given me eyes and wings to better understand my actions. I may not like what I see, but I can understand my behaviors better now. And I know I need to make a change. I have a handle on my drinking, but smoking I've never been able to shake off. Smoking has always been at my side, a haggard, limping, wheezing, baggy-eyed pusher, blowing death down my throat. I've tried quitting before but never succeeded. This time I will.

I smoke my last joint while writing my final paragraph. I e-mail the paper. Then I step outside and light my last cigarette.

PART IV

THE RESURFACING

 *Meditations*

The past is never dead. It's not even past.
—William Faulkner, *Requiem for a Nun*

It's over. Will tomorrow be the same?
—The Moody Blues, "Dear Diary"

The autobiographical piece, grueling as it was to complete, forced Ervin to confront a submerged past that had been wreaking havoc on him. The act of looking squarely into the mirror was cathartic and transformative. He'd never done anything like it before. The voice in the piece was unforgiving, the self-reflective gaze unflinching, the writing empty of the sugary platitudes and banalities common to athlete memoirs.

Under another professor, Ervin may never have written so frankly, but his professor and advisor, Derek Van Rheenen, had become a mentor, one of the few people Anthony could open up to. A former professional all-star soccer defender, Van Rheenen had firsthand experience of the straightjacketing athletes face. As a closeted gay soccer player in college, he dealt for years with jock culture's discomfort with homosexuality. It was only after his return to graduate school that he was able to openly embrace his sexuality.

"Anthony's journey is more of a metanarrative of all our journeys," Van Rheenen says. "It's just being played out under the lights. It's about his coming to terms with who he is and what's important to him." Anthony in turn now credits his studies with giving him a consciousness to understand the social pressures underlying some of his past behaviors, like the partying and promiscuity, which he attributes in part to the "culture of hypermasculinity around being a champion jock and the culture of excess pathologically linked to it."

Van Rheenen, who came from a family of intellectuals, always defied that "brainless jock" stereotype despite being pigeonholed by it: "Athletes are often represented in media portrayals as vapid individuals behind a performing body. What's particularly interesting about Tony is his social conscience and critical eye. He can be a model for others who aspire to heights both athletically and academically." The wholesale dumbing down of athletes in the public imagination, he adds, is even more prevalent with black athletes: "One of the things I feel lacking in popular culture around athletics is the construction of the public-intellectual athlete. To me, Tony is the symbol of deconstructing social constructions like athlete/intellectual, black/white, for a greater understanding of reality."

That act of turning inward was not only illuminating for Anthony, but also, as the weeks passed, psychologically fortifying. So he thought it beneficial to continue taking stock of his life. A month after turning in the personal narrative, he began keeping a journal. Though only spanning a few months—from January to March of 2011—the diary entries reveal a mind looking inward with trepidation, only to be pleasantly surprised.

Excerpts from Anthony Ervin's 2011 Journal

1/20/2011
A couple days returned from NYC where I spent time with old friends, working out/swimming, and reacquainting myself with my sport. But perhaps I am getting ahead of

myself, for the time between finishing my personal narrative for Derek's class and now has had a profound effect on me.

The narrative focused on alcoholism, but what does not get enough mention is the effect of smoking marijuana and cigarettes. Smoking dope is highly entertaining in the basest of senses. Simply put, I can smoke dope and sit doing as close to "nothing" as possible. Were I not high, I would surely be bored and feel compelled to do something. Moreover, being high is exhausting to the brain. In addition, the lungs are damaged, which coupled with latent development of nicotine addiction, had a profound effect on my ability to use my body.

This focus on "smoking" as a form of undoing came to me when i was visiting my family over christmas. I remember having a huge fight over the phone with my mom—she was laying into me mercilessly about choices i've made over the last ten years—and finally having enough, stopping her to say, "if this is what it is going to be like when i visit, i don't want to go." Perhaps it was my pleading tone, but she immediately relented and promised to never bring it up during my visit—a promise she kept.

Derek picked me up from the airport. I was surprised he wasn't immediately pulling out a cigarette. I commented on it, and he said he was trying to cut back. Furthermore, he told me mom and dad had both quit smoking. I was surprised and pleased, myself being 5 days off cigarettes. Nicotine withdrawal is a total bitch, and the first few days often show a very ugly side of myself to others (i was in withdrawal when on the phone with mom). But i was glad to know that breaking the habit was something the whole family was going through. For the first time in memory, the whole family is on board. Even Derek had his last cigarette a couple days ago, making the seal complete (i need to remember to call him, see how he is doing).

It was not just the cigarettes. By being with family I knew I could avoid smoking dope. It is so easy in berkeley to surround myself with people who enable my use. "Misery loves company" goes the maxim, and it cuts to the bone. As enjoyable as being high seems, for me it became my strongest coping mechanism and escapism from responsibilities. It was tough, knowing that to a degree I would have to ostracize myself from these friends for a time (forever?) and reconstruct my social base.

I began jogging on my mom's treadmill, perhaps out of boredom more than anything. Then i was asking my dad to take me to his gym where i could pump a little iron. Then I was going to the gym with Derek to talk to kids in the neighborhood swim program before swimming a full mile. Not once did my mother or father talk to me about the disintegration of my semester or what i would do come the new year. I had some whiskey with my father the night before my flight and told him how i was feeling, about the smoking, about my body, about going to nyc, and about wanting to be proud of myself again. "Son, I want nothing more than to see you rise again before my time here is done." For the first time in as long as i can remember, i was a bit sad when it was time to fly away. My father's words echoed in my head as i flew across the country.

Back in Berkeley i actively avoided any situations that might tempt me to get high. I went to the pool and was shyly working up the courage to ask the women's coach if i could do some workouts with her, but before i could muster it, she asked me herself! "I would love to, Teri!"[36] I said. "Be here at 6 am . . . don't let me down." I was there in the morning. The ladies kicked my ass, but i felt no shame.

It is quite amazing; I remember just a few months ago my chagrin at having to walk the block and a half to campus. I rebuffed invitations from friends who lived on the north side of campus (a 20 minute walk), simply because the thought of such a journey exhausted me. Now, such tasks seem trivial. Of greater importance is pushing myself beyond my own expectations when working out. When this happens, as it did today, I feel surprised; for so long i believed that "giving up" and general sloth were built into my character.

1/22/2011

After hearing of the impending descent into JFK airport, i open the window shutter (i always fly window so i can lean on the side and avoid getting my knee banged by carts and people) to gaze at the lit majesty of NYC. Immediately, I feel wonder and awe, as i do every time i fly here. Inspiration, hope, vitality. Hard to explain why i would feel this, but i do. A warm welcome from the trains, which i know how to navigate better than BART, and I reunite with a Cyprian-American friend[37] in SoHo. We talk and drink Scotch, catching up on life. I tell him about my figurative "turning over of a new leaf," and he tells me about learning tango while living and writing in Buenos Aires. It is Friday night, but we both have early days at the swimming pool teaching and coaching, so

---

36 Teri McKeever, head coach of the Cal women's swim team and head coach of the 2012 women's Olympic team.

37 Your humble narrator. The modern-day word is Cypriot, not Cyprian, although considering a secondary, archaic definition of Cyprian means "licentious; wanton," Anthony may have been onto something.

we go to sleep—an unexpected luxury: my own personal air-mattress.

In the morning I take the subway to a pool on the upper east side where I jump into the water for a workout with a fellow former Olympian. Oddly enough, she is heavily tattooed as well, and recounts to me stories of hearing about my retirement and sojourn into tattoos and rock'n'roll and thinking it was "super fucking cool." I smile, but am internally torn about never believing in my own status as a role model and my ability to influence others.

After workout, I see the "Manhattan Makos," a club team I helped nurture and start. I haven't seen them in nearly 2 years and am pleased and inspired by their improvement and their excitement upon seeing and actually remembering me! I lead them through a dryland routine of push-ups, sit-ups, squats, lunges, and even some yoga i just learned. Their form is terrible, but they keep going. I feel myself fatiguing, but I can't collapse in front of the kids, so i muster the perseverance! The kids jump in, and i'm yelling GO relentlessly, voice booming around the tiled acoustics of the indoor pool. After the workout the parents caress me with their words and questions: are you here for good? oh, studying the culture of sports in education? the kids have grown, haven't they? I am all smiles and feeling great as I leave with one o' my best friends and head coach of Makos, Elliot P.[38]

1/23/2011

I spend the week walking through the snow, slush, and ice of manhattan between morning workouts and afternoon coaching with Elliot. When I can, I swim before the

---

38   The same Elliot who kicked him awake on Erik Vendt's floor.

kids' afternoon workouts. I lift with Elliot and Jean "The Machine," a poolside assistant and lifeguard. Jean is Puerto Rican with bulging biceps and pecs, and perfectly manicured hair and eyebrows. He leads us in the weight room, and his form is flawless—I see why they call him the Machine. Elliot crushes as much weight as Jean, but his form is wild and it looks like he is taking out life's aggression. I push and pull maybe half the weight, but I feel no shame, and actually feel quite good about myself. No late nights, and with a premeditated melatonin, by 10 PM I am easily falling asleep. I find myself waking, refreshed, on my own just minutes before my alarm.

Over the weekend, I go to Princeton, NJ where a massive age-group invitational is taking place. A few parents' and coaches' eyes bug-out at my sleeve tattoos, but I do my best to ignore it. Not once am I stopped and questioned over my authenticity as a coach (a latent fear of mine).

Despite this being the first meet of the season, there were 80 percent best times across the board, including multiple first time Junior Olympic qualifiers. I am all laughs and smiles, delivering regular high-fives. Only one girl, M, does not perform equal or better than past performances. She has been in a slump since the summer. She is quiet and reserved after each race. I am torn between trying to tell her about a slump i had at her age and saying nothing. My heart breaks for her because I know she is genuinely trying her best and is confused why her efforts bear no fruits.

After the kids turn in for bed, the other coaches and i make our way to the bar. M's dad proceeds to fill us with beer and whiskey. He, of course, wants to talk about his oldest daughter and her recent plateau. He thinks she is not working hard. He says, "M is going to be undersized her whole life, and on top of that is Asian—which means she needs to work 15 percent harder than her peers."

I am a bit intoxicated at this point and say, "That, sir, is quite racist," which earns a laugh from all. My experience about over-driving parents takes control of my tongue and I argue for giving her time. Too much pressure before she is ready to improve, either physically or mentally, and burnout is inevitable. Of course, he doesn't want to hear that, which is understandable. He wants to see his daughter happy.

After four hours of sleep, the other coaches and I wake up hungover and head to the pool. My brain is floating, but I am attentive to the needs of the kids, making sure they know when they are racing, what heat and lane, and what their goals should be. Giving high-fives afterward and ruffling wet hair.

1/24/2011

Flying back to Berkeley, there was no part of me remaining in NYC. My last visit, all I could think was, i want to move back to nyc right now! but this time around, i was ready to be back to pursue the path i had chosen. Of course, I have a slough of tasks and anxieties: financial issues with the university, my rotting crown (another financial issue), clearing up "incompletes" from last semester, organizing my internship, etc. ad infinitum. Not long ago these issues would have been extraneous to my simple mind and its sense of responsibility. Now it seems ordinary and natural. But i digress.

I went to the pool to talk to coaches Dave and Teri, of the men's and women's team, respectively. These two have shown me nothing but support over the years, and that certainly did not change once I asked to be part of their teams. I had anxiety that new feelings and motivations were just a temporary product of the holidays and New Years, but i accepted this possibility with a mantra of "day by day."

I stepped on the scale at 160 lbs—I've gained 10 since Christmas, and I am glad for I have certainly been eating much more (food bill going through the roof!). In the weight room, however, my feats were dwarfed by the awesome muscular builds of the super-seniors-and-beyond. A short sprint/anaerobic workout followed. I'm getting grief over my red cap . . . I need to find a Cal cap soon.

I had a relaxing weekend: saturday waking early-ish for breakfast and writing, a hike through the fire trails with a loquacious 19 year old i met in school (she tells me about her first and recent drug experience and i do my best to realign her thinking and feeling with my experience and wisdom without coming across as overtly didactic); sunday morning the same, dryland and swimming, and computer games with my "old" stoner friends. They are smoking around me and come across as silly and stupid as they laugh at total mundanities. They attempt to offer me weed. After my refusal, one friend says, "we'll just keep pressuring you until you buckle." I don't want to deal with always saying no. If they're to remain friends, they have to expect and know that i am no longer smoking and that our friendship is not held together by only dope.

And now, it's finally TODAY, Monday the 24th, and I woke up at 545 to go swim. 4k meters with the women (and boy do they make me look bad!). Afterward, the sun is up and i'm feeling good. I delay breakfast so i can talk to my coaches (yes, now it's "my" coaches). My plan is to train with both the gents and the ladies, 6 days a week (however, no double workouts . . . yet). I wish to continue yoga Thursday evenings. It would be easy to jump right in just with the men, but over these years I have taken in a lot of femininity in trying to understand and navigate the big city. After what i discovered writing that narrative, i want to be a friend of the fems; i don't want them to be just sex objects, because i do enjoy their company, mentality, and beauty. Not to mention, training with Teri and being surrounded by the young women is both progressive and hot. Hah!

Breakfast and (here I am) writing. I think I will try to make dance class with the ladies before the first day of Professor T's class. But first, a shower and some lotion (chlorine wreaking havoc on my skin; tattoos looking faded; face a mess).

1/26/2011

Classes began this week. Can i operate on a high level both academically and athletically? That would be the dream that always seemed unattainable, a dream that contradicts the asceticism and specialization of elite athletics.

I did the reading for class last night. It took me over an hour to read 30 pages: too slow. Perhaps it's the fatigue. My body certainly pulls a lot of my conscious energy to greater awareness—constant flexing of muscles, grasping or touching a triceps or pectoral, clenching a fist, orbiting scapulas along the back, or simple deep breathing—all using the forebrain, i'm sure. This may turn out to be a drag on my higher brain functions, a drag away from critical thinking.

Yesterday I was working on the body in the presence of the ladies. I found the shape and strength of their bodies beautiful (though when i was their age, i was repulsed for some reason). They motivate me with the ease of their regimentation. Far less chaos or need to repeat things as with the men.

First was the weight room, where Nick helped me. Gratitude—I'm still dumbfounded why I get attention, and I feel no little anxiety that I pull coaching attention from the ladies. The only outlier amongst the ladies is Natalie. She worked through her exercises fast, moving around and through the rest of the girls, and thus setting herself outside them.

Into the pool and a quick few thousand. Seriously, the ladies just GO during interval sets. They put the men's team to shame (at least, the sprint group). I gas and get lapped. After the interval set is a short anaerobic set, where i should excel. But i'm still pooped, mentally as much as physically from the interval set, and I'm disappointed in my performance.

Strangely enough, after the set, i feel compelled to join the men for their abdominal workout. I can almost smell the testosterone in the air, causing a spike in intensity at a cost of form . . . but I think I need a little of this, though wary of too much.

This morning, 6 am with the men. Chillaxin' long swimming to warm up. I feel good power doing the distance-per-stroke set; not fast, but good flow.

Had my usual breakfast at Café Med where I was joined by Ward. We talked fashion and literature. Since I don't have much to read until Amazon delivers, I may pick up Marcus Aurelius's Meditations (stoicism, and a personal account of the Platonic route to being Philosopher-King), a short work oft recommended by Ward. It strikes me that when younger I was so impassioned, yet clueless as to where all this raw energy was going. Now, I want a sense of balance, so that instead of letting the energy lance out like lightning, I radiate like the sun.

2/4/2011

It is Friday and I am closing my 2nd week of swim training. Teri and Dave, in particular, are treating me with what seems like a "silent leadership." In 40 minutes starts the men's dual meet against USC. I may be doing an exhibition swim. Last week's exhibition at the girl's meet I consider a success: 20.98.

My next post should be dedicated to Max Weber, a man whose writings have occupied much of my mind of late.

2/9/2011

I submitted my FINA/USADA e-forms this morning. It's "official." There was some momentary hesitation, pondering my expectations for entering the arena. Do I feel I can win? No. Do I want to win? I wouldn't mind, but t'would be unreasonable to fantasize. Training this morning showed that I can keep up with the team when going fast . . . all except Nathan, who absolutely crushes everyone. I want him to win it all. Where he already is seems beyond my talent. How well does the rest of the country size up to him? Is a relay spot achievable for me?

Perhaps these are old goals and old ways of thinking to ask these questions. I got back into swimming to reclaim my own legacy and a future in the sport (not as a competitor). What else should I be learning, and what can I build in the future? This should be the question of most importance, but it's open-ended and significantly less pressurized.

Let me shelve swimming to talk about grad school. The dept. of education is overwhelmingly fixated on trying to educate those with no education. Whether it's looking at urban schools and their misery (black kids) or student-athletes (revenue sports/black kids), the gap between the floor and the ceiling seems huge. Is the goal to close this gap? How are we measuring this gap?

Do i feel white guilt? No. But during class and reading I do feel some moments of shame for my privilege, while simultaneously envious of those who have more. There is a fixation on what I don't have but want, of formulating some way of climbing higher, etc. And yet I feel as stuck in the middle as I've ever been and will be, eyes gazing upward and onward at a horizon yet to come. Do I turn and look back? On occasion—but that whole pillar of salt thing . . . too much sodium is bad for the diet.

2/21/2011

Swimming and School; that is my life. I've put on almost 20 lbs now, and believe (with a larger food budget) I can reach my goal of 180—to then be leaned out to 175 of pure power. I swam at the Cal v. Stanford duel meet; 20.55 and thus shaving time at every attempt during this self-styled "pre-season." It felt good, and the atmosphere is positive from both gendered teams and coaches. Of course, being my harshest critic, I remember that i finished high school with a 20.2.

On the school front, I feel I'm being lazy. One project at least seems to be warmly received: the athlete image initiative to portray student-athletes as Philosopher-Kings, or as embodied and intelligent heroes/heroines.

2/26/2011

Life is good. Swimming and eating, tutoring and reading, and even a date with a young hot girl. Also, I hope to finally be out of the financial murk—of course, by taking out more loans. I made an appointment to finally take care of my rotting tooth—more money for better health, a good trade, yes?

With Urban Ed, and even with Professor T's class, I am supposed to try to answer the question of how to close the "achievement gap." It's difficult. First, there seems to be a lack of understanding in the culture as to why underprivileged populations (economic/racial) should try to achieve academically. The case is easily made that it's actually "white achievement," and that such merit is not all-encompassing. Well, what is black achievement? Or yellow achievement? Or brown achievement? Every culture seems to have a different standard of how they value achievement and what's worth achieving. Can there be a general standard for achievement on the "tan" side of things? The dream of equality is as yet completely amorphous. No one knows what it would actually be because it has never existed. Equality is a pursuit and a fight—that is how it has translated into existence, and it only occurs when one realizes they are in a grossly unequal place (re: 2011 Arab revolution).

3/18/2011

It's cold and rainy. Root canal this morning—not pleasant, but not awful either. Lifted too hard and i think my shoulder is hurt.

Strange day because of 2 people that reached out to me. Agent D[39] is the first, who must have heard I am swim-

---

39 Swim agent (a rare species, but such creatures do exist).

ming again. He wants me to call him. I haven't decided. What would I say? I suppose the truth? (whatever that is). I don't want a public announcement of any "comeback." It would be more fun to swim masters under the pseudonym "Queequeg Turambar."

The second message i received today is from Jarmin. This is the first time in 15 months that she's contacted me, citing some article about drugs in the co-ops as reminding her of me. That made me very sad. I almost cried.

16 *The Year of the Water Dragon*

*Adopt the disposition of the octopus, crafty in its convolutions,
which takes on the appearance of whatever rock it has dealings
with.
At one moment follow along this way, but at the next change
the color of your skin:
You can be sure that cleverness proves better than inflexibility.*
———Sixth-century BC elegiac poet Theognis

*don't chase that carrot
'til it makes you sick
what do you think you're gonna prove
just let it dangle
'til it falls off that stick
that's when you make your move*
———James McMurtry, "No More Buffalo"

When I start training again in early 2011, there's no intent to return to serious competition and vie for another medal. I just need to replace smoking with something else. Weight training and swimming seemed natural alternatives. Smoking pot and cigarettes turns out to be my Kryptonite. Once I stop the lung abuse, my body just resurges and comes to life. But even when the impulse to smoke is gone, I don't want to stop swimming. It feels good. The pool, a prison for much of my youth, is now a sanctuary.

Though I do a few exhibition swims, and though I take Teri's advice and reenter the drug-testing pool, I'm still hesitant about how competitive I want to be. But that changes in late March when I go to men's NCAAs in Minneapolis.

March 24–26, 2011
University of Minnesota Aquatic Center

It's barbaric in the Cal section. No other university has alumni representation like us. Last year Cal almost won, so in this year's lead-up to NCAAs there was a huge alumni swell. E-mails were sent out, urging all to attend: *This is the year, after three decades, this is the year Cal will win!* Alumni have flown out not just from across America but from all over the world, a Cal bear migration to Minnesota. We've taken over a whole section of the stands, painting them gold and blue. By the second night we're not only chanting for our swimmers, but even roaring when no Cal swimmer is in the finals. There's no other squad of alumni like us. A horde of boozy pillagers. Hooligan invaders amidst alarmed swim parents.

It's a dude storm. The Charge of the Brohirrim. The alumni have left their wives back home and for one weekend are reliving their college years. It comes at a cost. After spitting his drink all over a bartender's face, my friend Mark gets dragged out by his foot, laughing, and dumped into a pile of snow. Another alum, in his midfifties, falls and cracks his nose, later showing up at finals with his face all bandaged. And then there's Jafari, who gets shoved by a friend, trips on ice, and has to go to ER to get his shin splinted. He shows up that night on crutches, animal that he is, leading cheers.

For the final event, the 4x100 free relay, we just need sixth place or better to clinch the title. As long as we don't disqualify, we'll win. Jeff Natalizio is wearing his white pants, bare-chested, swinging his Cal shirt like a lasso over his head, and roaring.

Our section is covered in gold Cal placards. Even with safe relay starts, Cal crushes the competition. Tom Shields, who swims third, pulls away in the final twenty-five yards into a clear first, which Nathan only extends.

We're NCAA champions for the first time in thirty-one years! I charge down to the deck even before the trophy is handed. I clear security right as the team is jumping into the pool. Only after I've jumped and hit the water do I think, *Oh no, what am I doing?* Just because I've started to train with the team doesn't mean I'm *on* the team. That's when I know my competitive spirit is back. I want to be part of this energy and excitement. I want to race again.

✦✦✦✦✦✦✦✦

Both Teri McKeever and Dave Durden, the Cal head coaches for the women's and men's teams respectively, welcomed Anthony to their practices, but neither had any idea initially what to make of his desire to train. Durden at first assumed the swimming was "maybe just cathartic" and a way for Anthony to get back into shape (which it was). But after the 2011 NCAAs, Durden could see that Anthony wanted to get back into competition.

Cal swim star and twelve-time Olympic medalist Natalie Coughlin thinks the desire may have been there even earlier, at least at some deeper level. She remembers her surprise when she first saw Anthony at one of the women's practices back in January. She asked what he was doing there. He said he didn't know: "But he kept coming. So I kept asking. And he'd say, *I don't know. I'm getting in shape.*" But as time passed, Natalie got the sense that he had his sights on Olympic Trials: "I think deep down he knew he was going to do it, but this was kind of a crazy goal knowing his past. I think he knew to keep it close to the chest."

Anthony has always had a close relationship with Teri McKeever.

She remembers him back when he seemed to be "a half-step behind [and] almost overwhelmed" with juggling swimming, school, and social life. But the Anthony who returned was far more mature and confident, "someone more comfortable in his own skin."

Most startled of all by Anthony's return to the pool may have been his 2011 roommate, Ward, who only knew him as a "gutter-punk intellectual" and never an athlete: "Our apartment was fucking disgusting. If you consider Hemingway's aesthetic of a clean, well-lighted place, it was the exact opposite. It was dim and dirty. And out of that shithole, Tony started waking up again at five in the morning, working out, getting back into it. This English major, chain-smoking, intellectual type . . . It was inspirational for me, because I'm like, *If this dude can turn it around, no matter how pathetic I am, there's hope."*

You needed hope living in that co-op. Ward's previous roommate had overdosed on heroin and had to be rushed to the hospital. Anthony replaced him, moving in the next day.

It helped that Anthony happened to be in one of the best places in the world to train. He had top coaches, weight trainers, and physical therapists at his disposal. And he had the top American sprinter as his training partner: Nathan Adrian, the NCAA champion in the 50 and 100. Though there was competitive tension between them at practice, they pushed one another to improve. "They may not have that kumbaya moment where they say, *Listen, I appreciate you,"* Durden says, "but I absolutely believe they do."

And then of course there was Natalie Coughlin's presence. "Natalie makes us all better," Anthony says. "She has nothing left to prove. She can learn from us to a degree, but she's so advanced, the net benefit is to us."

If Anthony was to compete again, he had to have his shoulder examined. Doctors soon determined that his biceps tendon had been stretched when his shoulder sublexed in the motorcycle accident. Since his right biceps was thinner and frailer than it should have been, the shoulder might still occasionally sublex. But with weekly rehabilitation, he could still swim again at a high level.

Those were busy days. He began weekly physical therapy. He supported himself through a variety of jobs: coaching in the Oakland Undercurrent swim program; tutoring students on campus; and working the will call counter for music shows at the Warfield or the Regency. And then of course there was coursework and swim training.

❖

5:00 a.m. Alarm. Snooze once. Coffee. Oatmeal.
5:40 a.m. Walk to pool (15 mins).
6:00–7:45 a.m. Swim practice.
8:00 a.m. Walk home. Eggs over greens w/feta. Hydrate.
9:00–11:00 a.m. Class.
11:15 a.m. Light lunch.
12:00–1:30 p.m. Weight training.
2:00–2:30 p.m. Bagel sandwich.
3:00 p.m. BART to Oakland.
3:30–6:00 p.m. Teach/coach Undercurrent swimmers.
6:00 p.m. Chicken skewers at Chinese spot.
6:20 p.m. BART to San Francisco.
7:00–10:30 p.m. Work will call at Warfield.
10:30–11:00 p.m. Watch end of show. Drinks.
11:00–11:45 p.m. Food with Shane and co.
12:00 a.m. BART to Berkeley.
1:00 a.m. Sleep.

This isn't, of course, my daily routine, but such days aren't uncommon. Even though my lightest day is grueling next to my former life as a nocturnal couch sloth, I'm nonetheless happy and optimistic, riding high. My greatest challenge is finding the time to eat since my food requirements are double if not triple what they were back when I did nothing and measured time out in cigarettes.

The tutoring and coaching drops off, as they do in the summer, so I soon fall behind on rent. Teri suggests I race in December at the Elite Pro-Am in Oklahoma meet, which offers cash prizes. I win the 100 free in a time of 42.65 and get second in the 50 with a 19.41. With the prize money, I pay my back rent.

After the meet I call Dave Durden and ask if I can join the men's team at the Colorado Springs training camp. The training there pays off. At the Austin Grand Prix in mid-January 2012, my 50 free time slingshots me in the rankings to second-fastest American in that event. Olympic Trials are five months away. The media begins to buzz. And just like that, it is real and it is on.

Even when I amp up the training, I keep coaching in Oakland. It keeps me grounded. The best kids to coach are the pleasers—the ones who work hard, don't complain, don't quit. They're usually girls. The hardest to deal with are the kids who don't want to be there. Then there's another category: the kids who do nothing in workout and then just fly in meets. What to do with them? I realize I was a crossbreed of the two: the kid who resents being there and the kid who cruises through practice but lights it up during races. The worst combo. Certainly *not* the kid who aims to please.

How much of this attitude has spilled out into the rest of my life? I think back on all the jobs I've half-assed or quit when things got hard or undesirable. Like Guitar Center: abandoning it without even giving notice. I could have met some great musicians and artists there, but instead I was indifferent, needlessly rebellious. Or the office job in New York that I stopped going to one day without even an e-mail or phone call. Just not giving a shit. So terrible.

It's surprising how many people have welcomed me back

with open arms this year. They've had no reason to. Just like the friends over the years who took me in, fed me, supported me . . . they had every reason to give up on me long ago. If I hadn't gotten myself together when I did, how much tolerance would there have been for my irresponsibility and vagrancy?

It makes me ashamed. I owe so much. Time now to give back.

In Book IX of Homer's *Odyssey*, Odysseus recounts how he and his crew entered the cave of the Cyclops Polyphemus, seeking his hospitality. Polyphemus's response was to snatch up two men, smash their heads against the rocky ground, and chow down on them, an act which is up there in the Top 10 list for Worst Host of All Time (along with the Red Wedding scene from *Game of Thrones*). As part of his escape plan, Odysseus plies Polyphemus with wine and tells him, "My name is Nobody. Nobody, my father, mother, and friends call me." After Polyphemus passes out, Odysseus blinds him by driving a blazing sharpened olive branch into his eye. When the other Cyclopes rush over at the sound of his cries and ask if anyone has attacked him, Polyphemus responds: "Nobody, my friends, is trying to kill me by violence or treachery." So the others shrug and leave.

This linguistic maneuvering is a classic Odyssean ruse, implausible as it sounds (a Cyclops's strength of mind must be inversely proportional to the size of his eye). It takes the standard camouflage tactic and amps it up to a protean 2.0 version: evasion not through blending into the environment but through transformative identity-shifting. It also happens to be an escape tactic that Ervin had resorted to, whether consciously or not, as a way of slipping free from external pressures and attempts to pigeonhole him.

As a teenager he simply absorbed these pressures, lacking the pliancy to evade or the will to upend them. When heralded in 2000 as the first African American swimmer to make the Olympics, he had no way of responding except with stock answers. Dropping out of the sport a few years later was his prison break from the Cyclops's cave: rejecting the primary identity that the world expected of him was an act of radical self-assertion. As with Odysseus's adoption of the Nobody persona, Ervin more or less abandoned the name Anthony, the signifier for "Olympian Swimmer," and became Tony,[40] a more neutral name that gave him the invisible autonomy he desired. He purged swimming from his life, auctioning off the gold medal. For a period he even mistakenly believed that he had lost his silver, though it was in his parents' possession all along. "His silver medal wasn't lost," Sherry says. "*He* was lost." New friends only learned through others that he'd once been a champion swimmer, often months or years later. One sportswriter for the daily *Santa Clarita Valley Signal* tried in vain to track him down for an interview on his postswimming life. When he finally made contact through e-mail, he told Ervin he'd become his White Whale. "Don't you know what happens to Ahab?" Anthony replied. He then quoted Dante's *Inferno*: "*Lasciate ogni speranza, voi ch'entrate.*" (*Abandon all hope, ye who enter here.)*[41]

The Nobody wordplay stunt is only part of Odysseus's plan. To escape the cave, which is sealed shut with a giant boulder, Odysseus lashes himself and his men under the Cyclops's sheep. The next morning, when blind Polyphemus lets his herd out to pasture, running his hands over their wooly backs, he misses the men, who are hanging udder-like from their underbellies. The literal blindness of the one-eyed Polyphemus is a metaphor for his deeper blindness

---

40 His mother detests the diminutive "Tony," which she associates with a guy with a handlebar mustache shouting in a ghetto Bronx accent from a flophouse window. (Anthony says friends would call home looking for "Tony," and his mother would reply, "No Tony lives here," and hang up.) Hence, in her presence I only refer to him by the maternally permissible Anthony. That's also why I only use "Anthony" in this book. There are times for risk-taking and times for thinking of one's neck.

41 It should be obvious by now that Ervin has a quixotic penchant for the dramatic and for seeing giants in windmills.

and tunnel vision—his inability to see or keep up with the fluid and chimerical adaptations of a boundary-crosser and chameleon like Odysseus.

Though Ervin sloughed off his swimming identity, he didn't consciously resort to subterfuge like Odysseus. "I never lied about my swimming past," he claims. "There just was never a reason for it to come up." Unlike Odysseus, he didn't have to lie. Since he didn't conform to the conventional image of an athlete, he could live unrecognized in the open. It was less that he was Odyssean than that others were cyclopean—blind to the possibility that this tatted, chain-smoking, skinny, black-clad "shitty rock 'n' roller," to quote a friend, was also a former Olympic champion. Not that they had any reason to view him otherwise. His athletic past was irrelevant to his present self. If he ever felt like Ralph Ellison's invisible man—one whose real nature others were unable or refused to see out of prejudice and preconception—it was while he was a swimmer, not after: "People who first knew me as 'Anthony Ervin the Athlete' could only see me from within that framework. Anything else I did was peripheral."

Even his Wikipedia page was often meddled with, sabotaging any sober efforts to identify and describe him. I found some noteworthy edits among the endless Dead Wiki Scrolls of the Anthony Ervin page history. One was the February 11, 2008, addition at 06:31 of the phrase "and he is one long, hard, throbbing piece of wonderful," followed by its swift deletion four minutes later. Another was the addition on February 3, 2011, of the sentence, "He currently has some unbreakable age group records," which survived the Anthony Ervin page for almost two months, until an editor on April 1, perhaps putting in overtime and on April Fool's alert, recognized the absurd conceit and purged the word *unbreakable*. But the gold goes to Anthony's 2007 edit that he made himself, described as "nonsense" in the editor's remarks; it stood as the official Wikipedia biography for Anthony Ervin for forty-eight hours:

Anthony Ervin
From Wikipedia, the free encyclopedia

Adrift in the ethereal plane for 7,777 years, Tony (as he is better known) shrugged and tore a hole into our reality. He was immediately attacked by 13 ninjas. When the first ninja met Tony's eyes he simply exploded like a blood sausage. The other ninjas screamed and tore out their very eyeballs, vowing to never mess with him again. So the legend goes . . .

In his earthly existence, Tony enjoys swimming, sleeping, playing guitar, and singing. He is an Olympic champion in swimming and sleeping, but his musical abilities are second rate at best.

"Nonsense" as this may be, it's in many ways more revealing than the standard script you might find on his bio page today; it's a giant middle finger to the inflexible tenets of Standard Narrative—the orthodox account of Anthony Ervin, of records and championships and medals, of predictable biography, and above all of rote reality which, as the bio states, "Tony" shrugged off after 7,777 years of Odyssean drifting by tearing it open and welcoming in another dimension. It privileges fantasy and imagination, reconceiving his daily grind as mortal combat against faceless ninja killers. It's the manifestation not of Anthony the athlete but of the adolescent imaginaire who sought escape from the regimentation of his home and swimming through fantasy books, where he could look through the eyes of heroes and villains while roaming amongst dragons, wizards, and gods.

Ervin left swimming because he needed to wander in the wilderness and explore other parts of himself. But now he was reversing the equation. He was returning to swimming, but without forfeiting other elements of his identity. He might never be a rock star, but he could still be a rock 'n' roll swimmer profiled in *Rolling Stone*.

Even the classics had a place in the sport at press conferences, where he could drop literary quotes. Sportswriter and co-owner of Ann Arbor's Literati Bookstore Mike Gustafson was heartened by Ervin's return to racing precisely because he felt Ervin was bringing this much-needed new artistry and identity to the sport: "I'm not sure why there's not more of a fusion with sports and art. I get the sense when Anthony tweets out Shakespeare quotes before his race that it means more than beating the guy next to you. That's such a black-and-white approach to competition."

Though Odysseus escapes the Cyclops's cave through deception, his departing statement is of revelation. As his companions frantically row away, he yells back, announcing himself as Odysseus of Ithaca. Not only does he endanger himself and his companions solely to reveal his identity, but he also later suffers for it because the Cyclops prays to his father Poseidon for troubles to rain down on him. Yet for Odysseus, whose name means "he who gives and receives pain," the risk and suffering is worth it. Matters of honor, pride, and identity trumped all in Ancient Greece.

For years Anthony felt like he was boxed into a cave. In response he resorted to role-playing, name-changing, retreating into the shadows. But invisibility eventually proved too passive and self-destructive a tactic, and the time had come for assertion rather than evasion. His return to swimming on his own terms was his brazen declaration to the Cyclops over the water.

⊶⊷

May 26, 2012, Willard Park, Berkeley
Jolly Roger grins down from up high. Mom bought me the kite after my undergrad commencement in 2010. She told me she wanted to get me a gift. We were walking past a kite shop in the Embarcadero at the time. So I chose this kite. A cartoony red and black pirate, with skull and crossbones.

That night after graduation I was drinking whiskey at an Irish bar with Dad. He's always been smooth and easygoing, but that night he seemed torn up. There was something in his eyes and the cast of his face. I'd never seen him like that before. He told me about Vietnam, how it messed him up for years. It was the first time he'd talked to me about it. And it brought him down to earth for me: he's just coping with things, doing his best. Both of my parents have tried to do their best with me. My life trajectory and mistakes are mine, not theirs.

I flew the kite that year on my birthday and the next year on my birthday and now this one. Not sure why, but it's become a tradition. I've never flown it any other day. The kite makes me think of my parents. With Mom I once felt oppressively tethered to her. But now I feel that the string between us connects rather than confines. I am who I am because of her. And with Dad, I now feel his story and lineage extending out, tugging upon me from a distance. Like the kite, they connect me to something larger.

A mother and son approach me. She asks if her boy can try out the kite. I offer him the spool, but his eyes are wide, intimidated. The kite is too much for him alone. So I hold the spool for him. And he pulls on the string, feels the tug from the kite, high up in the sky, fluttering full and proud in the breeze. And he looks at his mother and grins.

In the Chinese zodiac, 2012 is the Year of the Dragon, considered the most potent of the twelve signs. Every sign rotates through five elements—metal, wood, water, fire, and earth—which means the same sign and element appear only every sixty years. 2012 happened to be the Year of the Water Dragon, a paradoxical merging of a fire creature with the water element, signaling a time of transformation and upheaval. It was an apt year for Olympic swimming, and a mythologically auspicious one for Ervin to return to the world stage.

When he made his 2000 Olympic bid, Anthony was a Tasmanian devil of rowdiness and tumult, a swimming savant whose self-awareness in water was equaled by his social artlessness; twelve years later, he had swung to the other side of the pendulum as an exemplar of discipline. Going into Olympic Trials, he cut back on work to focus on training and rehabilitation. He cleared his schedule, aside from one music show and one coaching gig per week. The founder of the Oakland Undercurrents swim program, Ben Sheppard, arranged for Anthony to run some swim clinics so he could make up the lost income.

The meet organizers at USA Swimming didn't hold back for Olympic Trials. American pizzazz and excess was on full display in Omaha, with strobe lights swinging amidst the darkened arena and neon-pink lights and cascading green waterfalls of light and award ceremonies with gold medalists emerging godlike out of the floor on a mechanized elevating podium and company logos everywhere and announcers egging on the crowd to, "Come on, let's make some NOISE!" and hissing ten-foot walls of fire blasting up off the deck after every record-breaking swim, emitting a heat that could be felt in the stands.

The first of Anthony's two opportunities to make the team didn't pan out: he failed to advance beyond semis in the 100 free. A boy collecting autographs stopped Anthony the next day on his way to the pool. "Are you fast?" the kid asked, holding his pen out. "Not yet," was the reply. The boy nodded and lowered his pen. Anthony wasn't trying to evade an autograph. He'd merely given an honest answer, at least by his own estimation.

Had that boy asked him a few days later, he would have gotten an autograph. Anthony not only won prelims but also semifinals with a personal best time by two-tenths of a second. He was seeded first going into the final. But, of course, nothing is certain in the 50.

The Anthony Ervin entourage at semifinals and finals of the 50 free included, among others, Lars Merseburg, Casey Barrett, and Elliot Ptasnik, who was sporting a black shirt he'd made for the occasion that in hot pink read, *TONY ERVIN IS ROCK AND ROLL.* Anthony's parents were sitting right below us.

There's plenty to be nervous about in a 50 free race, especially in an Olympic Trials final: there's little to no margin for error. A bad start, a bad breakout, a bad finish, and your gold medal can turn into no medal. Compound this with the injustice that, despite year-round competitions and world circuits and Grand Prix, swimming only exists to the nonswimmer public once every four years. Being sick or injured or just off during Trials or Olympics can make the difference between international acclaim, sponsorships, and a book deal on one hand, and history's memory hole on the other. Compare swimmers to, say, high-ranking tennis players, who get four Grand Slams per year in which to vie for glory and who, within each match, have dozens of games and hundreds of points in which to recover from their errors. Not so with a swimmer, and even less so with a sprinter. Screw up once and you may well be screwed for good. And it's not as if those who do come out on top are set for life. Try to imagine a scenario where a top NBA player like Kobe Bryant takes a job teaching basketball for thirty dollars an hour after leaving the sport; yet I know several swimmers of comparable achievement who have done exactly that.

If you're a fervent fan, this period immediately before the race begins is when your stress levels are in the red zone: the point when you're trying desperately to convince yourself that none of this really matters, not next to life, love, family, etc., that it's just a damn race, just one of millions of races that have taken place and will go on taking place until the end of the human species, that no matter what happens the sun will still be there tomorrow. But though you know these things to be true, they don't *feel* true: the hairs on your arms are sticking straight up and your heart is throbbing from somewhere inside your Adam's apple. It may all be irrational, just as rooting for your home team may be irrational, but there's an invigorating activation of glands and caveman fibers inside your body in these moments. Normally squelched by antiseptic day-to-day life, these primal howling-at-the-moon aspects of our being can now emerge. You'd be hard pressed to find such a mass display of human passion in one place outside war and genocide. Screaming and howling in public is generally frowned upon, so sports offer us a socially sanctioned place where we can all do it together without killing each other.

We empathize with athletes for the pressure they face before important races, but spectators are an ignored, invisibly suffering bunch (except when fan-suffering is exploited to boost TV ratings, like in the World Cup, where cameramen revel in the ironic pathos of fans with colorful painted faces who look like they've just been told their dog is dead). There's more jitters and overactive bladder activity in the stands than behind the blocks, where autopilot mode and prerace routines help keep nerves at bay.

Every hyperstressed spectator copes with these tensions differently. Some turn to trash talking, others to prayer, while still others, perhaps lacking faith and/or feeling hostility, seek alcohol's balm. But booze can also backfire, as it did for Elliot twenty minutes earlier when, blinded by nerves and a beer-fueled craze, he threw a fist pump and yelled out, "YEAH, Coach Troy!" to the head Olympic coach Gregg Troy after his Florida Gators swimmer Ryan Lochte touched third in the 100 fly. It was a genuine gesture on Elliot's part because it was a personal best time for Lochte, but it was also obviously, at least to those of us unfortified by four pints in one hour, a disappointing finish: to qualify for the Olympics in an individual event you must place first or second, so to come in third is to be first loser. Elliot's shout-out came a split second after the mustachioed Troy—who in heated moments looks like a cross between Gary Oldman in his more dynamic personas and Super Mario after eating the fire flower—cried out, "Damnit!" while slamming his rolled-up heat sheet against the balcony rail. The brief stormy glance he then cast back in our direction instantly sobered Elliot, the alcohol suddenly operating on him as the depressant it really was.

The time had come. The 50 free Olympic Trials final. Silence, then: "Take your mark." The starting signal went off and the bleachers erupted. Anthony was behind off the start, as expected, but gaining every meter. Casey was the first to call it. "Yes!" And then we all saw it too and jumped to our feet, roaring, as Anthony closed in on the leaders. "Yes, yes, come on, yes! Come ON! YES!!"

He pulled ahead in the final meters, charging into the wall, head down. He didn't win—he was 1/100th of a second behind Cullen Jones—but the order was irrelevant: top two is all that matters at Trials. He'd made the team, and with another personal best time: 21.60! It was hard to believe that the same guy who just a few years ago said he couldn't imagine even swimming a thousand yards freestyle, and who had last qualified for the Olympic team a dozen years earlier, would again be an Olympian.

❖

During the ceremony, it's Gary Hall Jr., of all people, who drapes the medal around my neck. Then I make my way down the deck, giving high-fives, almost walking past emcee Summer Sanders, who pulls me back for the postceremony interview.

I'm buzzing with energy, barely able to contain myself. After a few questions, I grab the microphone out of Summer's hand. "You know," I say, turning to the audience, "it's been an incredible journey, but the journey continues because I'm going to Londooooooon." As the crowd roars, I extend my arm straight out by my head and drop the microphone, keeping my arm extended and fingers spread apart for dramatic flair until after the mic hits the deck. Cullen Jones, who is waiting nearby for his interview, throws his head back in laughter. Summer Sanders, meanwhile, just stands there, hands out and palms up in a flabbergasted *WTF?* pose. I raise up both arms, prompting a roar from the delighted audience, and take off on a celebratory run down the deck, slapping hands with spectators as I jog by them.

 *Still Water*

We are not now that strength which in old days
Moved earth and heaven, that which we are, we are;
One equal temper of heroic hearts,
Made weak by time and fate, but strong in will
To strive, to see, to find, and not to yield.
                    —Alfred Lord Tennyson, "Ulysses"

London Olympics, 50 Free Final, August 3, 2012
I'm here at the Olympics but my Games are over. Fifth place. No medal. I'm left only with the memory of a terrible start that will haunt me for days, for weeks, for who knows how long . . . After yesterday's semifinal swim, where I came in third despite a poor start and finish, I really felt like I could pull it off and win finals. Alas, Fortuna shone elsewhere.

I just want to hole up by myself. As I walk back to my room in the Olympic Village I start receiving texts that a dinner has been organized for me at a Thai restaurant. It's my only chance to see the friends and family who flew out to support me, since some are leaving early tomorrow. But if I go to the dinner, I won't make curfew, which could have major repercussions as it did in 2000 in Sydney when I was thrown out of the Olympic Village and had to watch the closing ceremony alone at a beach hostel. For months now I've obeyed every rule, wielding a moral certainty in my behavior and abstaining from even the smallest indulgences that might derail me. So far I've been nearly flawless on that front. And now here I am, in a possible refiguring of that fateful moment when I went out in Sydney and got busted because I was late, because I broke the rules. I don't want that to happen again. I won't miss closing ceremonies this time.

When I arrive at the apartment, my roommates, Jason Lezak and Eric Shanteau, both team elders themselves, don't bring up the race or ask how I'm dealing with the fallout. It's the elephant in the room. But they're also not treating me as pitiable or pathetic. They're behaving as they always do with me, like bros, cracking jokes, talking to me like I'm a normal dude. That's when it becomes clear to me that the people waiting in that restaurant are too important to me, that I'd be a fool and a slave if I didn't see them just because of a curfew and whatever that curfew may mean to the administrators. The rules of family and friendship trump all. Maybe that makes me dishonorable to the code enforcers, but does it make me dishonorable to my friends and family? What matters is not the letter of the rules but the spirit. And that means not disturbing those swimmers still competing. That's what's important. If I get in trouble and the overseers send me on my way as they did in Australia, I'll find a way to deal with it graciously.

I put on street clothes and make my way out of the Village, navigating what feels like an endless series of security checkpoints. Eventually I'm spit out into the teeming mass of a crowded mall. For the first time in a while I'm not an athlete. I'm not quarantined in the Olympic Village in uniform. I'm wearing a gray shirt and jeans, just another passerby in a bustling swarm of strangers. Here I'm as invisible as all the selves I've left behind—the lonely kid with the tics, the pyrotechnic delinquent, the broke couch surfer, the suicidal wastrel, the Zen Buddhist, the crotchrocket squid, the dreadlocked guitarist—selves I've left behind but whose shadows still linger with me.

The world is returning to me, or maybe retreating from me, in a way completely foreign to everything that's led up to the race. The isolation I felt after the race now takes on a new form, one of cold urban anonymity. But whereas some people find this variety of urban isolation alienating, for me it's welcome right now. No one here looks upon me with pity. Their eyes just pass over me, they don't know or care who I am. In this moment, it's unexpectedly liberating. I'm unburdened of responsibilities, of the media, of obligations to be a mouthpiece for this or that.

I've prepared at a higher level than ever before. No partying, no drinking, no skipping practices. But this time there was no victory, at least not in terms of merit and domination, which is how I formerly understood victory. That kind of success was corrosive. It brought out demons in me, made me the protagonist of a script others had written, like an actor miscast to play the hero. At the Sydney Olympics my identity was constructed upon that version of success. And later I paid for it. To have now tried my hardest and not won is a humbling new experience. Maybe it's even a new kind of victory, overthrowing my former concept of success as merit and conquest and replacing it with something deeper and weightier.

But as I arrive at the restaurant, Busaba Eathai, I'm overcome with fear. Fear I failed to live up to hopes and expectations, fear I've let everyone down, fear I'll have to deal with their disappointment and sadness. Walking earlier from the pool to my room, I felt ashamed. I almost used the rules as an excuse to not go out. But here I am.

When I open the door and see so many people—my mother, who through the incredible grief of her childhood would never abandon me or fail to bring me home no matter how lost I became; my father, who maintained confidence and conviction in my strength even as I cast myself into danger over and over; Mike Bottom, the coach who cared more about the kid in search of himself than the Olympic champion, who invited me into his home even after I cast aside his original purpose; Della, a kindred spirit who never stopped praying for me or opening her home to me no matter how dark the night; my friends Lars, Amir, Elliot, Conz, all who stayed by my side through the light and the dark, always sharing joy with each other; and many other people from all the years—when I see the way all their faces light up, the fog lifts, and with it the rush of so many memories in that moment, and I have to forgive myself for all the shame I've carried, the bad choices, the abuse, the harm I've caused those I love. I know it's from ignorance and pride, and that all it makes me is human. What have I actually suffered? As I look into humanity, I have not yet suffered. It all still lies before me, in a future I cannot help but race toward. But what I do know is that I'm alive, my existence affirmed in these smiling, cheering faces. The cheers and celebration are not supposed to be about proving myself over others, but giving my all despite the limits of my humanity. My awareness expands beyond this room, to the many who have helped this foolish human, and I well up with gratitude for all these blessed people who have been so tolerant of my mistakes and waywardness. I stand humbled.

 *Epilogue*

Everything in moderation, including moderation.
—Oscar Wilde

For a year now Ervin had been refuting the image of the dissolute, disobedient, slacker teenager by eschewing cigarettes and recreational drugs, attending practices, working hard, eating well, and foregoing nocturnality. He had become an athletic paragon of the Apollonian ideal—focused, orderly, disciplined. As a result it rocketed him back into the international spotlight and made him a media sweetheart as the "reformed bad boy," which in a Manichaean society like the US is the media ideal: now that the gelding knife of redemption has done its task, all the juicy naughty bits can be served up without tarnishing the golden image. But with Ervin's final race over, he was confronted with a simple question: what's the point of temperance and discipline once their purpose has passed? With Apollo's duties now over, Dionysus was stepping in.

As soon as their events are over, many Olympians proceed to do the polar opposite of everything that got them there, and with equal energy and commitment. It's like the confined high school kid off on a tear at college orientation—same story except amped up and involving individuals way more experienced with their bodies. Newton's third law of motion plays out in all sorts of interesting ways at the Olympics, especially when the equal and opposite reaction happens all at once and involves thousands of rested, tapered, and toned young adults in the best physical shape of their lives. One needs only a rudimentary knowledge of physics and physiology to grasp just how and why the Olympic Village transforms as the Games progress from a squeaky silent military barracks into a giant international set for a dorm porn production. And of course London—with its Victorian-era history of contradictions, where social decorum and antisex crusading coexisted with a thriving underbelly of immoderation and kink—was a welcoming city for the athletes to momentarily flee their glossy, role model–Olympian personas.

Once Ervin made the decision to join the rest of us at dinner, he knew he'd have to break curfew. Exactly how long past curfew didn't matter: bureaucratic regulations deal in black-and-white, not gray. This was just as well, because Amir, who arranged the dinner, was all fired up to head over to The Box Soho, an exclusive, recently opened cabaret nightclub in the Soho district, where he'd finagled a VIP table for a small group of us. Anthony looked apprehensive as Amir tottered in front of him, whiskey in hand, saying playfully: "As your attorney, I advise you to go to The Box with your buddies." Back then Amir still had the same frizzy Medusan black hair and excited eyes that cartoon characters get upon accidentally grabbing a live wire. His go-to outfit was Converse sneakers with a vest and tie, and he was fearless in approaching and confounding potential corporate sponsors, who were more accustomed to dealing with slick Wall Street–type attorneys and managers than wild-eyed Dr. Gonzos. But Amir was uniquely suited for engineering colorful gigs, like VIP table service at The Box.

It was futile for Ervin to resist our collective will to debauchery. An hour later we were standing outside The Box. There are always between two and four bouncers in front at any time. The bulk of them are Muscle, usually your typical overgrown, thick-necked, stony-faced doorman with a buzz cut and crossed arms wearing a black oversized trenchcoat and cheap clunky black shoes, the latter a giveaway that he never dresses up or looks so badass outside of work and is probably just some earnest Slavic farmhand who thought he'd try out his fortune in the wider EU world. Aside from all the Muscle, there is the Lord of Admission with the last word on who gets in. He's neither Eastern European nor muscular, but rather a suave, slender Brit who commands a kind of St. Peter at the Gate authority to all those who crowd around him, seeking his approval and admission.

Without pause Amir rolls up past the lines of swanky people to the stylish gatekeeper and whispers into his ear, pointing at Ervin. A moment later Muscle is parting the red rope for us to the covetous gaze of a blond trio in stilettos who still haven't been granted entry despite sporting push-up bras and combing their fingers through their hair every time Muscle or St. Peter approached them. Little did we know then that it's near impossible to gain admission to The Box on the weekend as a single guy or a group of men if you're not an Olympian or a celebrity or royalty, or unless you're willing to pay in the hundreds or even thousands for table service. It also helps to know St. Peter, who rather modestly goes by Joe, a name whispered with apprehension and reverence in line, although not everyone remained awed, like the one outraged guy who jabbed his finger in the air at him and blasphemously shouted, "You are *nothing!*" after St. Peter turned him and his girlfriend away from the pearly gates.

Inside everything glowed red and pulsed, with gilded mirroring and plush carpeting and golden horn–blowing Eros sculptures mounted on the rococo walls and even an upright piano upon which lounged a four-foot nude Aphrodite. The speakers throbbed with house music, so the cumulative vibe was something like Tiësto spinning in an opulent nineteenth-century bordello. Our first bottle came out at once and the mood, which was already at a buzzing pitch from the restaurant drinks, quickly got feverish. It was strange to see Anthony uncoil and let loose. For over a year now he'd been leaving early anytime we went out, ordering sparkling waters to our whiskeys and pints, and now here he was, throwing in the Apollonian towel and going for broke with the rest of us. As he later recalled, shaking his head when asked if he remembered details from a street brawl later that night: "We gave over control to Dionysus. We were just players, puppets in the play."

We were on our second bottle when the burlesque acts came on. The Box is known primarily for two things: 1) a royalty and celebrity patronage that has included Prince Harry, Zara Phillips, Princess Eugenie, Emma Watson, Kate Moss, Bradley Cooper, and Rihanna; and 2) its controversial shows, which have included things like a survivor of Thalidomide[42] doing a burlesque act that involved throwing off his arms along with his clothes, as well as more explicitly sexual performances that probably shouldn't be described here in detail, but let's just say that our night had an Olympic theme and the closing act involved some inverted gymnastics by a drag queen whose stage partner then used her as a human torch-holder by planting the Olympic flame down where the sun don't shine. Not everything is so shocking—there are also astonishing feats of acrobatics at The Box like the man who hopped upside down on one hand and later did a headstand upon a basketball that was perched atop a makeshift pyramid of bottles and plywood boards—but there certainly was a fair amount of staple raunchy burlesque, like the woman who smoked a cigar on stage (not from her mouth), as well as just plain old weirdness like a man wrapping his package in tissue paper and setting it on fire, or a transwoman, wearing a loose-fitting microskirt with nothing underneath but her flappy bird, twerking inches from the gawking faces of uncomfortably aroused males, or the onstage dinner couple where the woman held up an unopened bottle of beer and her dinner partner promptly thrust his arm into a giant vat of Crisco (skip to the next paragraph if you're squeamish) and then, standing up and turning around so everyone had an unobstructed view of his backside—and to a chorus of groans and gasps from the audience—plunged his arm forearm-deep up his own arse, retrieving a bottle opener like some desperate prisoner contraband-smuggling tactic.

42 A sedative drug withdrawn a half-century ago after thousands of mothers gave birth to disabled babies with stunted limbs.

At some point in the debauchery, Anthony turned to me. The tension from his face was gone, replaced by astonishment: "Whatever it is I thought was ailing me, I'm doing all right." The only person in our group who was indifferent to the acts was Lars, who watched it all unmoved and said in deadpan Germanic drawl, "I've seen as much in Berlin."

Once the final act ended, culminating in the aforementioned triumphant and terrifying planting of the Olympic torch, the space erupted into a thumping dance party. There must have been a fair bit of pill-popping because there was a touchy-feeliness in the air that made for easy transitions into fondling/makeout sessions in one of the VIP alcoves and on the couch upstairs. As the night went on it only got sloppier, with girls sitting slumped with skirts hiked up almost to their hips and the tops of their hosiery showing and guys stumbling around with the kind of dazed, slackjawed expression you'd otherwise find on someone who's just been smashed in the face with a shovel.

Whether because it was so early in the morning when Anthony returned to the Olympic Village or because the guards were mellower, he didn't get in trouble for breaking curfew. But someone else did that night: the 200 back gold medalist USA swimmer Tyler Clary, who was later fined thousands. The irony is that he was meeting with the owners of the club Chinawhite to set up for the following night when he was slated to deejay for his fellow swimmers in a Team USA bash celebrating the final day of competition. To this day Anthony hasn't forgotten the officials responsible for punishing him at the 2000 Olympics, so he interprets Clary's subsequent preference for racing cars over swimming as an expression of resentment against the swim authorities: "He was trying to do a good thing for our community and he was penalized for it."

The following night's party at Chinawhite—another exclusive and lavish club but without the burlesque or transgressive mystique—was the launch of a weeklong Dionysian phase for the rest of the swimmers. Michael Phelps was elsewhere that night, but Ryan Lochte was present, along with most everyone else on the team, so it was enough to draw the paparazzi and make the online gossip rags. After months of training and sobriety and pressure and focus, for all these honed physical specimens to be let loose in the VIP section of a club where one of their peers was deejaying and where bottles of top-shelf liquor were always within arm's reach was nothing short of savagery. A tall blond Scandinavian athlete liaison who had mistaken me for a Team USA member bought a platter of shots for Anthony and me and, after making us knock back three in succession with her, ripped the top of my shirt open with both hands[43] and proposed a threesome, at which Anthony turned to me with the expression of a lemur. It was one of those parties where others have to fill you in on some of the details, and whatever memories you do have are disassociated and weirdly detailed random flashbacks. For example, I distinctly remember reflecting on the nineties TV advert catch phrase "Abs of Steel" while dancing with one of the women's team swimmers but don't remember spilling half of two mixed drinks down the front of Lochte's shirt after knocking into him on a bar run (and neither did he when I apologized a few months later). It was pure pillaging on all fronts, with ice cubes being passed mouth-to-mouth like Chinese whispers and all sorts of other exchanges and zestful interactions that you'd expect from prime thoroughbreds who've been penned up for months and finally put out to pasture, details of which can't be shared out of respect for the athletes' Olympic blood oath, *What happens in the Village stays in the Village,* the spirit of the maxim still prevailing even outside the Village.

That said, Anthony claims the Olympic Village, at least for Americans, isn't nearly as universally licentious a scene as it's reputed to be—its notoriety perhaps due to hyperbole from horny journalists projecting their fantasies onto their work. Amir and I did visit the Village with him earlier that day and, considering all the media reports about the record-high numbers of condoms supplied, had hopes of seeing some balcony action or even just some passing window nudity.

---

43 The actual fabric, not just the buttons.

But it wasn't all that unlike an empty college campus during summer break with a high population of international students who'd left their national flags hanging from their windows. The only notable sight of any shock value was the McDonald's in the athletes' food court.

On the final day of swimming in London, the day after the 50, I'm finally able to cheer in the stands without the pressures of competing. It's not about me anymore, it's about those now swimming. No longer under the microscope, I'm free from all responsibilities except supporting the team. The atmosphere is charged, electric, crackling. We roar from the stands as we win both the women's and men's 400 medley relay. During "The Star-Spangled Banner" in the relay victory ceremonies, I fiercely sing the last three words in the line, "And our flag was still there!" in a higher octave. This pumps up the others, who bellow out the rest of the anthem. It feels so good to be part of it and even lead the musical charge. I wasn't able to participate like this before my race. It takes such an emotional toll to watch finals that I was always resting in the Village. Only this last day am I free of the burden of racing. In retrospect, I wish I'd gone to other finals. It would have helped me escape my head.

Being here feels like when I walked into the dinner last night, when my narrow individuality was subsumed within the community of family and friends. Cheering and singing with the team, celebrating relay victories, I no longer feel myself as Anthony Ervin but as a member of a collective—a teammate, an American. We're all together, one voice singing our anthem and fight song. It's a proud song, and in such moments it's earned pride. That's not to say the sublimation of the individual into the collective can't lead to terrible things. As Samuel Johnson said, "Patriotism is the last refuge of a scoundrel." But the flag and anthem needn't be used as a wrapper in which to hide one's misdeeds. I'll wave the flag and roar that anthem and chant *USA! USA!* as loud as any jingoist, but that doesn't erase the unpleasant social and political and economic baggage we carry. I won't say America is the "best" country in the world, because that makes no sense. Maybe one can talk about the best swimmer. But even that is tied to temporality. You're the best only for that moment and then it's past and you must prove it again. In my experience, being the best is awesome for a second and then sucks.

But even if the US isn't the "best" country, it's still *my* country. I didn't choose to be born in the US, but I choose it as my favorite. And I'll die an American, even if in a faraway land. There's a shared bond among all swimmers in getting where we are, and one can broaden that out to all Americans. Of course, ultimately this extends out even beyond nationality. It's less about nation than community. I celebrated with my friends from other countries who did well, and I tried to be there for those who didn't. Friendships transcend borders and performance.

Now that my race is over, I feel light again, even if it's tinged with disappointment. It's liberating to be in the stands, relieved of all expectations. This year has been harder and less fun than last year, when I first returned to swimming and no one, not even I, expected anything of me. Last year was my high. I was still in the shadows then, flying under the radar. The last six months I've been sighted and saddled with responsibilities. Not that I don't want them—they're essential to the productivity I want of my thirties. They may stress me, but that's just how it goes. And the pressure that comes with being a professional and a teammate pays off when I'm in the stands like this with my team, fused into something greater than myself.

It's so different now from Sydney. There, I was the champion but unhappy. The media expected me to speak on behalf of the black experience, even though I'd never thought of myself in black or white terms before then. I'd been cast into a mold and I had no control over determining who I was. Or at least I lacked the capacity and consciousness to do so. And then I was thrown out of the Village. This time it's been the opposite: USA Swimming and its staff have been nothing but supportive of me.

There's no medal this time, but there's camaraderie. Sure, the media have positioned me within the "rock 'n' roll comeback kid" story line, which is just another construction, but that's no big deal. No real outside forces are at work. Not to mention my skin's thicker. And I'm not a hapless victim anymore to the culture of excess that comes with being a champion jock.

I'm still an outsider this time, but only because I'm older and my road has been unusual. I may look different because of my ink, but even tattoos are no longer rare. I don't feel alienation anymore, just identity. The identity of someone forged between black and white, yet living a life uniquely outside them in the overlapping spaces.

The next afternoon I'm in the Hilton lobby when a woman approaches me. After the usual *Is it true you're an Olympic gold medalist?* shtick she asks how I did. "I came in fifth," I tell her. "I'm sorry," she replies. It's happened several times in the last few days. I try not to let it bother me. She's only perceiving the surface notion of success that society and the media project. And in all fairness, it's easier to grasp than the deeper sense of success, which is subtler and has more to do with what Melville described as "the ungraspable phantom of life" than with medals and podiums. It's important I maintain this perspective. It's easy to sink back into the default understanding of success and failure, to see my fifth place as a flop after such a successful and unexpected year. I have to be vigilant not to sink into a Charybdis of private gloom.

Her comment still weighs on me when I leave the Hilton with Amir and Constantine. The sky is the gray of an overboiled egg. I'm walking just in front of them, about to cross the street. I glance left, as I habitually do, not noticing the *LOOK RIGHT*➡ injunction painted on the asphalt to warn foreigners that in this land people drive on the left. Then I step off the pavement and into the street. A loud warning cry from behind causes me to spin my head around. Just to my right I see a red double-decker barreling at me. I lean back hard, throwing my hands up in a surrender pose, barely pulling back in time as the bus shoots by me, the driver slamming on the horn. A gust of air hits me as the blaring bus passes within inches of my face and chest. Amir's phone falls from his hand with a clatter. We're all frozen in place as the driver brings the bus to a stop, clearly also rattled. Amir and Conz are looking at me as if they just saw a ghost. After a few seconds the red bus pulls away, leaving us standing there, petrified and wordless, pulses thudding.

Just like my start in the final, it all happened in under a second. My balance and reaction may have failed me on the blocks, but not on the street where there was more than a medal and glory at stake. I was inches and milliseconds from a meaningless death.

For days the specter of death haunts me. After having come such a long way, from having dove down into the blackest gorges for years and soared out of them again to become invisible in the sunny spaces of a London sky, I know the darkness awaits me, tempting and challenging me to continue finding myself again and again and again.

Berkeley Marina, May 26

The snowy owl hovers high overhead, gazing down with golden eyes. Anthony bought her earlier today at a kite shop. Minerva, he calls her. A birthday gift to himself.

There's more wishful thinking than truth in the transformation-and-redemption narrative. His slumps still come, bouts of gloom when he wants to drop everything and withdraw. But he now has an ally: self-knowledge. It's telling he chose an owl, the symbol of wisdom, for his kite. You can't change who you are, but you can change how you are. So when the winds change, you can do what you know you need to do to stay aloft. To keep yourself from nosediving.

Elliot and I toss a Frisbee. Anthony is off on his own, gazing up into the blue. Beyond us all, the bay glitters, its waters spilling forth and renewing themselves within the Pacific, evaporating as mist, thundering down as rain, surging as rivers, heaving as oceans, always in flux, chasing new places, ever restless, ever turbulent, ever unconstrained.

THE END

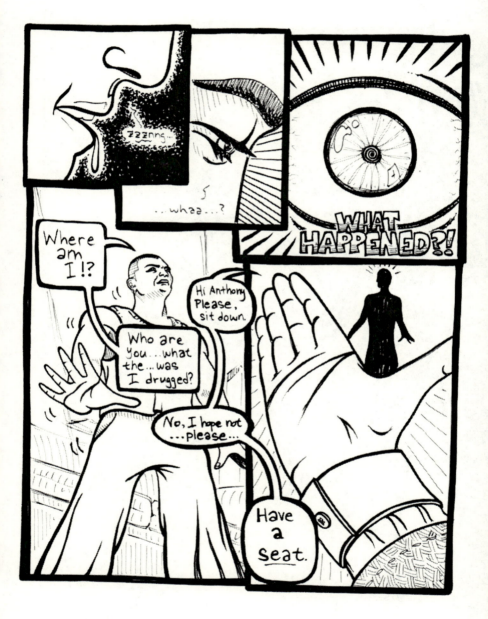

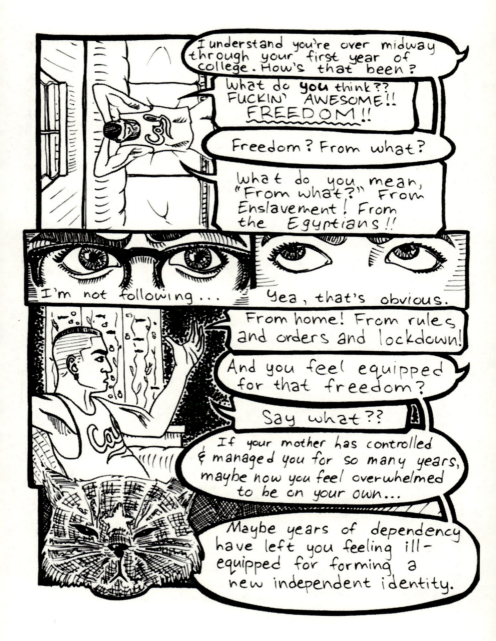

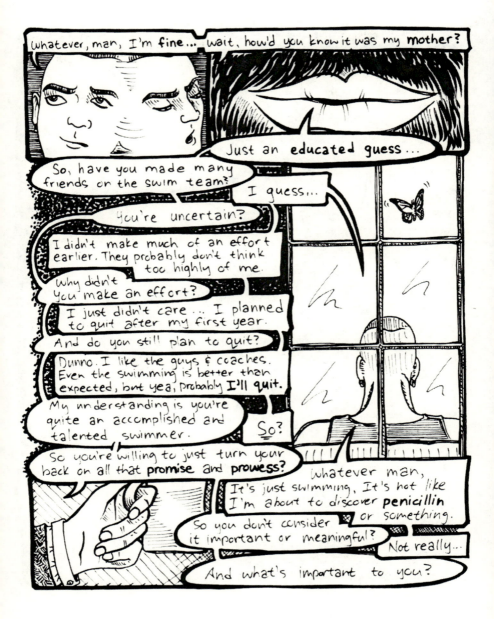

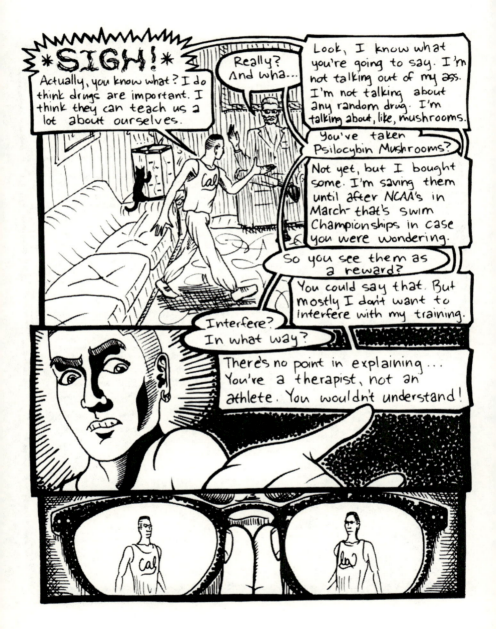

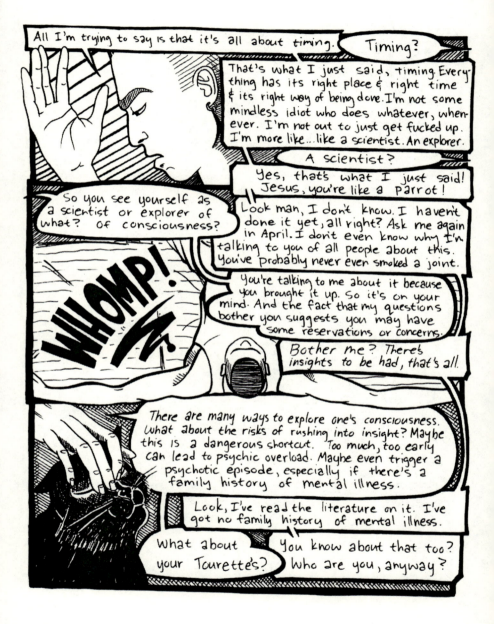

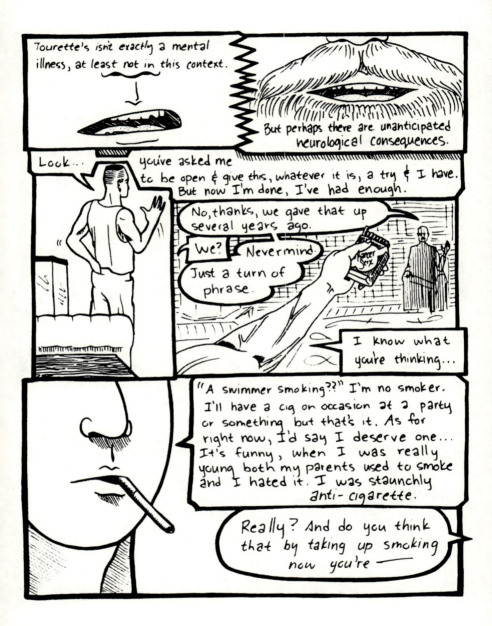

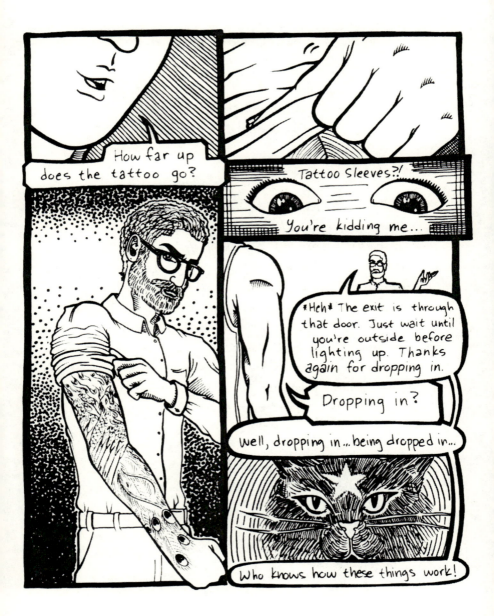

Appendix B
(from page 129)

Southern Campaign American Revolution
Pension Application of Shadrach Battles

Nov 24, 1820, Staunton, Virginia

Dear Sir *[The hon'ble Hugh Nelson Esqr, Washington]*,

I take the liberty of enclosing to you the papers of Henry Painter & Shadrach Battles, two revolutionary soldiers both of whom reside in your County & consequently have some claim to your friendly services in aiding their efforts to obtain pensions. They are both men of good character & are far advanced in life & are in the lowest grade of poverty. Battles is a man of color & was the right-hand man of Clough Shelton at the Storming of Stony Point *[in New York, 15 July 1779]* and in all the daring acts of that most intrepid officer. Independent of the enclosed papers he made his declaration in my Court holden at Charlottesville in Oct'r last when he was in such a low state of health that he was brought to court in a litter . . .

—*Arch. Stuart*

Battles, Shadrach / *age 26 / height 5'10¼" / black hair / yellow eyes / yellow complexion / planter / born in Albemarle County / residing in Louisa County, Virginia.*

[Taken from a roll of noncommissioned officers and privates of Virginia who enlisted between 1777 and 1783.]

Speak, man, the trials in war and peace of Shadrach Battles, father
across seven generations to unlikely hero Anthony Ervin,
the waterman whose exploits at the second millennial turning would
make proud his forebears.

A free black in time of bondage, Battles was listed in town records
as a mulatto person of color, but the white men of Albemarle
called him half-Indian, half-mulatto, that youth of uncertain bloodline,
that private whose amber eyes and skin perplexities bespoke,
that veteran in whose heart ran crosscurrents, muddying its waters.
The calm of Shadrach's early years ended once revolution's fever
rode the northerly wind to Virginia, stirring the slumbering god
of war to fierce life across the land, urging Loyalists and Patriots alike
to clash upon the grassy knolls, roaring oaths, dyeing the cold earth
black with steaming blood. A wanderer who labored unbound
by spouse or spawn, his home his head's place of rest, Battles enlisted
with the Continental Army, proving himself a warrior worthy
of his name. His first combat was in seventeen seventy-seven,
on September the eleventh, a day of death, terrible, tragic
for the Patriots: the Battle of Brandywine. Aided by dawn fog,
the British outflanked Washington's troops; under the noon rays,
they cut down his men and mares, wrenching the life from them, forcing
the surviving Loyalists to flee, abandoning dead and wounded alike
on rolling hills to rot under the sun. Despite the carnage,
battle-worthy Battles endured to see another moon, another battle,
this time in Germantown, a surprise attack Washington ordered
and might have won had ammunition not run dry amidst the strife.
Another loss, yet Battles would see another day, destined to prevail,
as he did the following year at the Battle of Monmouth,
an infernal encounter, almost half the men perishing of heatstroke;
or the one after at the Storming of Stony Point, wading through black
chest-high water at night under fire; or at the Siege of Savannah,
that bloodbath in the swamp, the gods sparing him once more,
returning him to Virginia after two tours of duty, uncrippled, undead.

Soldier no more, Battles wedded Dolly Moss, trading conflict
for wedlock, or trying to, for once the hounds of war, baying,
sink their fangs in a man's heart, their bloods mingle, rousing
man to trouble. So battle-worthy Battles faced lawsuits, court dates,
some of his own doing, some of his color, such are life's labors,
but embattled Battles endured, war had taught him that lesson.
Landless, a day laborer, Battles took odd jobs, often for odd pay,
like planting locust trees, accepting a whiskey quart as payment
for each surviving tree, so when a sapling sent forth its green life,
he clapped his ravaged hands and bellowed, "Another quart saved!"

A soft spot in his heart for gambling and drink—the classical vices—
he closed out his years poor in health but rich in spirits. Even when carried
into court on a stretcher—infirm, an aged man owning nothing
but a broad axe, an oven, and a handsaw, in request of pension,
a pittance for years of dancing with death in the trenches and bayous,
for securing the fame and rule of powdered sons of liberty—even
then, embattled battle-worthy Shadrach Battles could, craning his neck up,
smile and say, *I came, I saw, and I bloody still live.*

Appendix C

(from page 130)

1864 Report of Brig. Gen. Truman Seymour of the Union Army

WILLIAMSTOWN, MASS.
August 12, 1864

GENERAL: I have the honor to submit the following report of my command . . . in connection with the battles of May 5 and 6 in the Wilderness:

To this brigade I was assigned on the morning of the 5th instant. . . . The Sixth Maryland and One hundred and tenth Ohio were placed in the first line. . . . The position was on gently rolling ground, thickly covered with trees. . . . A vigorous advance was made and the enemy was soon found, but sheltered by log breastworks and extending so far beyond me that his fire came upon the prolongation of our line with the greatest severity. . . . The Sixth Maryland and One hundred and tenth Ohio suffered very severely, the Sixth Maryland losing 180 officers and men, killed and wounded [in] that superior regiment . . .

❦

Sixth Regiment of Maryland Infantry Descendants Association
["Fighting Sixth Maryland" for the Union Cause]

Company B—Muster Roll

Slaughter, Wm. H., *Corporal, mustered Aug. 14, 1862; killed in action, May 5, 1864, Wilderness, Virginia.*

[Great-great-great-grandfather of Anthony Ervin]

May 4, 1864, Wilderness of Spotsylvania, Virginia
The sun bled out behind the tree line as the infantrymen of Sixth Regiment Maryland crossed the Rapidan River at Germanna Ford. The two canvas-and-wood pontoon bridges that federal engineers had raised in the predawn saved the men from making the passage like the troops six miles downstream at Ely's Ford. Those men had waded across the swollen river holding muskets and cartridges aloft like a ragged line of robbers in surrender, the cold brown water fingering their navels and mosquitoes droning at their ears before anchoring on their faces to feed. But this regiment stayed dry and bivouacked that night just off the muddy banks. The men clutched their moonlit rifles and shuddered at the looping cry of a whip-poor-will that in another time would be welcome birdsong but here seemed a cackling and hysterical requiem of the day to come.

The Sixth Regiment Maryland set off in the morning along the Germanna Ford road. After receiving command to picket the riverbank against Confederate advance they retraced their steps, only to recommence marching three hours later.

–Goddamn shitshow out here, muttered one soldier. The generals don't know shit. They passing us around like a hot potato.

The young corporal next to him did not answer.

–I reckon we be just as good off blindfolded and spun round in circles before walkin off into rebel hands.

The corporal remained silent, his expression unchanged.

The soldier sucked in through his nose with a rattling sound and spat hard. The phlegm flew dense and palpable and landed in a quivering blob in the dust. He stubbed it down into the ground with his toeheel and eyed the young corporal again. He had deep-set narrow eyes in a round wrinkled face like some oversized progeny of a shrew and a pug.

–You're a right goddamn party to march with, ain't you, he said, and then fell back in search of kinder ears.

The teenage corporal, William Slaughter, had heard the man's words but had been thinking about what a sergeant told him by fireside two nights prior. How Grant meant to crush the rebels and end the War of Rebellion by waging a bloodletting against Lee. How he was pressing for mass killing 'cause he knew the Union had more numbers and reckoned if North and South traded lives long enough there'd be no more rebels to go round. How the two of them was disposable. But more than his words Slaughter remembered the man's eyes, haunted and far-off and whited out in smoke like the pupilless horror of some blind soothsayer. The young corporal drank from his canteen and tried to put out the thought.

One year ago to the day in this same tract of timber, the Confederates routed the Union army in a squalid slaying that was later given the genteel name Battle of Chancellorsville. In this place too did Stonewall Jackson under confusion of dark receive mortal bullet wounds from his own troops. It was an accursed place for any man. The ashen skulls and remains of those who just one year prior still wore their flesh now flanked the road, the clean-picked bones littering the woods like ungodly cairns guiding fresh meat into some impending reincarnation of carnage past. The men of the Army of the Potomac averted their eyes and said nothing. One hundred and twenty thousand strong, they advanced laboriously through that dreaded wilderness, dragging a support tail almost seventy miles long of over four thousand supply wagons and eight hundred–plus field ambulances and an entire herd of cattle. They slogged ahead in grim hope of traversing the dense forest to make battle in the open ground to the southeast where their superior manpower and firepower would favor them. That was Grant's plan. That was not to be.

The Confederates moved in and surprised them near Saunders

Field. At one p.m. skirmishing broke out. Troops poured in like ants spilling forth from a decapitated ant mound and soon the woods steamed and churned with killing. From its hostile perch the sun beat down through a haze upon those wretched men whose uniforms stuck to them in a paste of blood and sweat and urine. Abandoned knapsacks and blankets and jackets of gray and blue lay strewn about as soldiers shed themselves of all but food and water and instruments of destruction. The forest whistled with flying death and rained twigs and leaves and flecks of bark. In places bullets pattered down upon the duff like hail. Spooked out of their subterranean shelters by exploding shells, rabbits skittered in terror across the killing fields. White clouds born of black powder burst forth and drifted untroubled overhead like wraiths bearing languid witness to man's unerring folly. Those who would desert had done so earlier when news broke of the fray, and the soldiers who now remained fought with the abandon of sinners who had long since consigned themselves to hell. By late afternoon many had already been captured by their own men and held down as branding irons sizzled a *D*, for *Deserter*, into their cheeks and were then delivered whimpering back into service marked with their raw scarlet letter. There was nowhere to run.

The Sixth Maryland and the One hundred and tenth Ohio were ordered to the front line to outflank the Confederate troops of Lieutenant-General Ewell. At five p.m. the forward cry rang out and they rushed forth with great shouts. The enthusiasm was brief. Their colonel sent message to Brigadier General Seymour that his men lacked support and the rebels outnumbered and outflanked them. To press on was certain butchery. The courier returned with a message to attack. The troubled colonel assumed his message did not get through. Only after a second order came did he bow his head for forgiveness and send his men forth into that woe. It was seven p.m., God's hour. The light was gold.

William Slaughter and company charged and fired and the enemy zigzagged in retreat. But the rebels soon leapt over a line of earthworks and ensconced themselves out of sight. For the attacking men there was no shelter but for the slender trunks of second-growth trees and the occasional log. At one hundred and fifty yards the musket fire opened upon them. Hot yellow fury roared down all along the line.

The last hour of Slaughter's life was the longest he had ever known. One Ohio private died in his arms, sucking at the warm canteen water that the young corporal emptied into his mouth. Another slumped dumbly against an oak as he tried to stuff back in the viscera hanging from his midsection, his fingers prodding even as his eyes began to glass over. An older veteran with blood flowing from his ear sat up in a daze and tried to light a tobacco pipe with wet trembling hands. One private sank to his knees as a purple hole bloomed in his neck and then tottered and fell facedown into a final rest of prostration and another lurched about vomiting blood and another hugged his knees and gurgled prayers through a severed tongue and another blubbered and crawled on his elbows tracking out a crimson rug behind him and everywhere there was groaning and babbling and moaning of the maimed and wounded. And Slaughter found no glory or right in any of it.

Dusk fell. Musketry flared in the twilight and shells exploded in tornadoes of fire and the rank air filled with the swooshing of shot and the steel clanking of ramrods pounding charge into musket barrels. By nightfall the shooting was blind and aimless. Comrade shot comrade. A round burst nearby and a body cartwheeled through the air and might have been made of straw except for its heavy landing. A dead tree caught fire and the flames hissed and whipped up the dry trunk, roasting its nesting denizens. Groundfires broke out in the blackness and relieved the injured of their suffering and the smell of their charred flesh carried on the evening breeze with their screams.

A flash erupted next to Slaughter and knocked him down. When he righted himself he could hear nothing but a ringing. As he cast about for his rifle, a musket ball struck him in the chest and his blood sprayed and he reeled back into some tree branches off which he hung quietly with outstretched arms. As he bled out over the black boughs, the ringing in his ears died away and he watched in awe as silent tubes of musket fire pulsed about and flames licked upward in pockets of incandescence and a man swaddled in flames flailed as he ran like some grotesque mime. In the soundlessness it was as if he had been ferried out to some removed vantage point for one final reckoning and calm accounting of the grand obscenity perpetrated on every man and martyr there. As the young corporal felt himself slip away, he thought of his wife and infant son whom he would never meet.

Then his legs buckled and Slaughter fell in the wilderness.